Study Guide

for

Microeconomics

Ninth Edition

David Colander
Middlebury College

Prepared by

David Colander
Jenifer Gamber

D1418544

 McGraw-Hill Irwin

Study Guide for
MICROECONOMICS, Ninth Edition
David Colander

Published by McGraw-Hill/Irwin, an imprint of The McGraw-Hill Companies, Inc., 1221 Avenue of the
Americas, New York, NY 10020. Copyright © 2013, 2010, 2008 by The McGraw-Hill Companies, Inc. All rights reserved. Printed in the
United States of America.

1 2 3 4 5 6 7 8 9 0 PAT/PAT 1 0 9 8 7 6 5 4 3 2

ISBN: 978-0-07-771839-8
MHID: 0-07-771839-9

www.mhhe.com

Contents

Preface

We wrote this study guide to help you do well in your economics course. We know that even using a great book such as the Colander textbook, studying is not all fun. The reality is: most studying is hard work and a study guide won't change that. Your text and lectures will give you the foundation for doing well. So the first advice we will give you is:

1. Read the textbook.
2. Attend class.

We cannot emphasize that enough. Working through the study guide will not replace the text or lectures; this study guide is designed to help you retain the knowledge from the text and classroom by practicing the tools of economics. It is not an alternative to the book and class; it is **in addition to them**.

Having said that, we should point out that buying this guide isn't enough. You have to *use* it. Really, if it sits on your desk, or even under your pillow, it won't do you any good. Osmosis only works with plants. This study guide should be well worn by the end of the semester—dog-eared pages, scribbles beneath questions, some pages even torn out. It should look used.

WHAT CAN YOU EXPECT FROM THIS BOOK?

This study guide concentrates on the terminology and models in your text. It does not expand upon the material in the textbook; it reinforces it. It primarily serves to give you a good foundation to understanding principles of economics. Your professor has chosen this study guide for you, suggesting that your economics exams are going to focus on this kind of foundational understanding. You should be sure of this: if your professor is going to give you mainly essay exams, or complex questions about applying the foundations (such as the more difficult end-of-chapter questions in your textbook) this study guide will not be enough to ace that exam.

To get an idea of what your exams will be like, ask your professor to take a look at these questions and tell the class whether they are representative of the type of questions that will be on the exam. And if they will differ, how.

HOW SHOULD YOU USE THIS STUDY GUIDE?

As we stated above, this book works best if you have attended class and read the book. Ideally, you were awake during class and took notes, you have read the textbook chapters more than once, and have worked through some of the questions at the end of the chapter. (So, we're optimists.)

Just in case the material in the book isn't fresh in your mind, before turning to this study guide it is a good idea to refresh your memory about the material in the text. To do so:

1. Read through the margin comments in the text; they highlight the main concepts in each chapter.
2. Turn to the last few pages of the chapter and reread the chapter summary.
3. Look through the key terms, making sure they are familiar. (O.K., we're not only optimists, we're wild optimists.)

Even if you do not do the above, working through the questions in the study guide will help to tell you whether you really do know the material in the textbook chapters.

STRUCTURE OF THE STUDY GUIDE

This study guide has two main components: (1) a chapter-by-chapter review and (2) pretests based upon groups of chapters.

Chapter-by-chapter review

Each chapter has eight elements:

1. A chapter at a glance: A brief exposition and discussion of the learning objectives for the chapter.
2. Short-answer questions keyed to the learning objectives.
3. A test of matching the terms to their definitions.

4. Problems and applications.
5. Multiple choice questions.
6. Potential essay questions
7. Answers to all questions.

Each chapter presents the sections in the order that we believe is most beneficial to you. Here is how we suggest you use them:

Chapter at a Glance: These should jog your memory about the text and lecture. If you don't remember ever seeing the material before, you should go back and reread the textbook chapter. The numbers in parentheses following each learning objective refer to the page in the text that covers that objective. Remember, reading a chapter when you are thinking about a fantasy date is almost the same as not having read the chapter at all.

Short-Answer Questions: The short-answer questions will tell you if you are familiar with the learning objectives. Try to answer each within the space below each question. Don't just read the questions and assume you can write an answer. Actually writing an answer will reveal your weaknesses. If you can answer them all perfectly, great. But, quite honestly, we don't expect you to be able to answer them all perfectly. We only expect you to be able to sketch out an answer.

Of course, some other questions are important to know. For example, if there is a question about the economic decision rule and you don't remember that it excludes past costs and benefits, you need more studying. So the rule is: Know the central ideas of the chapter; be less concerned about the specific presentation of those central ideas.

After you have sketched out all your answers, check them with those at the end of the chapter and review those that you didn't get right. Since each question is based upon a specific learning objective in the text, for those you didn't get right, you may want to return to the textbook to review the material covering that learning objective.

Match the Terms and Concepts to Their Definitions: Since the definitions are listed, you should get most of these right. The best way to match these is to read the definition first, and then find the term on the left that it defines. If you are not sure of the matching term, circle that definition and

move on to the next one. At the end, return to the remaining definitions and look at the remaining terms to complete the matches. After completing this part, check your answers with those in the back of the chapter and figure out what percent you got right. If that percent is below the grade you want to get on your exam, try to see why you missed the ones you did and review those terms and concepts in the textbook.

Problems and Applications: Now it's time to take on any problems in the chapter. These problems are generally more difficult than the short-answer questions. These problems focus on numerical and graphical aspects of the chapter.

Working through problems is perhaps one of the best ways to practice your understanding of economic principles. Even if you are expecting a multiple choice exam, working through these problems will give you a good handle on using the concepts in each chapter.

If you expect a multiple choice exam with no problems, you can work through these fairly quickly, making sure you understand the concepts being tested. If you will have a test with problems and exercises, make sure you can answer each of these questions accurately.

Work out the answers to all the problems in the space provided before checking them against the answers in the back of the chapter. Where our answers differ from yours, check to find out why. The answers refer to specific pages in the textbook so you can review the text again too.

Most of the problems are objective and have only one answer. A few are interpretative and have many answers. We recognize that some questions can be answered in different ways than we did. If you cannot reconcile your answer with ours, check with your professor. Once you are at this stage—worrying about different interpretations—you're ahead of most students and, most likely, prepared for the exam.

Multiple Choice Questions: The next exercise in each chapter is the multiple choice test. It serves to test the breadth of your knowledge of the text material. Multiple choice questions are not the final arbiters of your understanding. They are, instead, a way of determining whether you have read the book and generally understood the material.

Take this test after having worked through the other questions. Give the answer that most closely corresponds to the answer presented in your text. If you can answer these questions you should be ready for the multiple choice part of your exam.

Work through all the questions in the test before grading yourself. Looking up the answer before you try to answer the questions is a poor way to study. For a multiple choice exam, the percent you answer correctly will be a good predictor of how well you will do on the test.

You can foul up on multiple choice questions in two ways—you can know too little and you can know too much. The answer to knowing too little is obvious: Study more—that is, read the chapters more carefully (and maybe more often). The answer to knowing too much is more complicated. Our suggestions for students who know too much is not to ask themselves "What is the answer?" but instead to ask "What is the answer the person writing the question wants?" Since, with these multiple choice questions, the writer of many of the questions is the textbook author, ask yourself: "What answer would the textbook author want me to give?" Answering the questions in this way will stop you from going too deeply into them and trying to see nuances that aren't supposed to be there.

For the most part questions in this study guide are meant to be straightforward. There may be deeper levels at which other answers could be relevant, but searching for those deeper answers will generally get you in trouble and not be worth the cost.

If you are having difficulty answering a multiple choice question, make your best guess. Once you are familiar with the material, even if you don't know the answer to a question you can generally make a reasonable guess. What point do you think the writer of the question wanted to make with the question? Figuring out that point and then thinking of incorrect answers may be a way for you to eliminate wrong answers and then choose among the remaining options.

Notice that the answers at the end of the chapter are not just the lettered answers. We have provided an explanation for each answer — why the right one is right and why some of the other choices are wrong. If you miss a question, read that rationale carefully. If you are not convinced, or do not follow the reasoning, go to the page in the text referred to in the answer and reread the

material. If you are still not convinced, see the caveat on the next page.

Potential Essay Questions: These questions provide yet another opportunity to test your understanding of what you have learned. Answering these questions will be especially helpful if you expect these types of questions on the exams. We have only sketched the beginning of an answer to these. This beginning should give you a good sense of the direction to go in your answer, but be aware that on an exam a more complete answer will be required.

Questions on Appendixes: In the chapters we have included a number of questions on the text appendixes. To separate these questions from the others, the letter A precedes the question number. They are for students who have been assigned the appendixes. If you have not been assigned them (and you have not read them on your own out of your great interest in economics) you can skip these.

Answers to All Questions: The answers to all questions appear at the end of each chapter. They begin on a new page so that you can tear out the answers and more easily check your answers against ours. We cannot emphasize enough that the best way to study is to answer the questions yourself first, and then check out our answers. Just looking at the questions and our answers may tell you what the answers are but will not give you the chance to see where your knowledge of the material is weak.

Pretests

Most class exams cover more than one chapter. To prepare you for such an exam, we provide multiple choice pretests for groups of chapters. These pretests consist of 15-40 multiple choice questions from the selected group of chapters. These questions are identical to earlier questions so if you have done the work, you should do well on these. We suggest you complete the entire exam before grading yourself.

We also suggest taking these under test conditions. Specifically,

Use a set time period to complete the exam.
Sit at a hard chair at a desk with good lighting.

Each answer will tell you the chapter on which the question is based, so if you did not cover one of the chapters in the text for your class, don't worry if you get that question wrong. If you get a number of questions wrong from the chapters your class has covered, worry.

There is another way to use these pretests that we hesitate to mention, but we're realists so we will. That way is to forget doing the chapter-by-chapter work and simply take the pretests. Go back and review the material you get wrong.

However you use the pretests, if it turns out that you consistently miss questions from the same chapter, return to your notes from the lecture and reread your textbook chapters.

A FINAL WORD OF ADVICE

That's about it. If you use it, this study guide can help you do better on the exam by giving you the opportunity to use the terms and models of economics. However, we reiterate one last time: The best way to do well in a course is to attend every class and read every chapter in the text as well as work through the chapters in this study guide. Start early and work consistently. Do not do all your studying the night before the exam.

THANKS AND A CAVEAT

We and our friends went through this book more times than we want to remember. All the authors proofed the entire book, as did our good friends, Pam Bodenhorn and Elizabeth DeVault. We also had some superb students who worked on the study guide, editing and proofing the questions. They include Emily Duh, Samantha Gluck, Olivia Lau, Anne Powers, Taran Veerman, Andrew Vollmer, and Elena Zhang. (Our sincere thanks go to them for doing so.) Despite our best efforts, there is always a chance that there's a correct answer other than the one the book tells you is the correct answer, or even that the answer the book gives is wrong. If you find a mistake, and it is a small problem about a number or an obvious mistake, assume the error is typographical. If that is not the case, and you still think another answer is the correct one, write up an alternative rationale and e-mail Professor Colander the question and the alternative rationale. Professor Colander's e-mail is:

colander@middlebury.edu.

When he gets it he will send you a note either thanking you immensely for finding another example of his fallibility, or explaining why we disagree with you. If you're the first one to have pointed out an error he will also send you a copy of one of his latests books—just what you always wanted, right?

David Colander
Jenifer Gamber

ECONOMICS AND ECONOMIC REASONING

1

● CHAPTER AT A GLANCE

1a. Economics is the study of how human beings coordinate their wants and desires, given the decision-making mechanisms, social customs, and political realities of the society. (4)

1b. Three central coordination problems any economy must solve are: (5)
- What, and how much, to produce.
- How to produce it.
- For whom to produce it.

Most economic coordination problems involve scarcity.

2. Microeconomics considers economic reasoning from the viewpoint of individuals and builds up; macroeconomics considers economic reasoning from the aggregate and builds down. (5-6)

Microeconomics (micro) → concerned with some particular segment of the economy. Macroeconomics (macro) → concerned with the entire economy.

3. If the marginal benefits of doing something exceed the marginal costs, do it. If the marginal costs of doing something exceed the marginal benefits, don't do it. This is known as the economic decision rule. (7-8)

You really need to think in terms of the marginal, or "extra" benefits (MB) and marginal, or "extra" costs (MC) of a course of action. Also, ignore sunk costs.

Economic decision rule:
If MB>MC→Do more of it because "it's worth it."

If MB<MC→Do less of it because "it's not worth it."

NOTE: The symbol "→" means "implies" or "logically follows."

4. Opportunity cost is the basis of cost/benefit reasoning; it is the benefit forgone, or the cost

of the next-best alternative to the activity you've chosen. That cost should be less than the benefit of what you've chosen. (9)

Opportunity cost → "What must be given up in order to get something else."

5. Economic reality is controlled by economic forces, social forces, and political forces. (10-11)

What happens in a society can be seen as the reaction and interaction of these 3 forces.

- *Economic forces: Market forces.*

- *Social and cultural forces: Social and cultural forces can prevent economic forces from becoming market forces.*

- *Political and legal forces: Political and legal forces affect decisions too.*

6. Economic insights are based on generalizations about the workings of an abstract economy. These are called theories. (12-13)

Precepts are based on theorems combined with knowledge of the real world and value judgments.

7a. <u>Positive economics</u> is the study of what is, and how the economy works. (17)

Deals with "what is" (objective analysis).

7b. <u>Normative economics</u> is the study of what the goals of the economy should be. (17)

Deals with "what ought to be" (subjective).

7c. The <u>art of economics</u> is the application of the knowledge learned in positive economics to the achievement of the goals determined in normative economics. (18)

The art of economics is sometimes referred to as "policy economics."

● SHORT-ANSWER QUESTIONS

1. How does microeconomics differ from macro-economics? Give an example of a macroeconomic issue and a microeconomic issue.

2. What are the three central problems that every economy must solve?

3. What is scarcity? What are two elements that comprise scarcity? How do they affect relative scarcity?

4. State the economic decision rule.

5. Define opportunity cost.

6. What is the importance of opportunity cost to economic reasoning?

7. What is an economic force? What are the forces that can keep an economic force from becoming a market force?

8. Define positive economics, normative economics, and the art of economics. How do they relate to one another?

MATCHING THE TERMS
Match the terms to their definitions

____	**1.** art of economics	**a.**	Additional benefit above what you've already derived.
____	**2.** economic decision rule	**b.**	Additional cost above what you've already incurred.
____	**3.** economic force	**c.**	If benefits exceed costs, do it. If costs exceed benefits, don't.
____	**4.** economic model	**d.**	The study of individual choice, and how that choice is influenced by economic forces.
____	**5.** economic policy	**e.**	Necessary reactions to scarcity.
____	**6.** economic principle	**f.**	The benefit forgone, or the cost, of the next-best alternative to the activity you've chosen.
____	**7.** economics	**g.**	The study of what is, and how the economy works.
____	**8.** efficiency	**h.**	The insight that a market economy, through the price mechanism, will allocate resources efficiently.
____	**9.** experimental economics		
____	**10.** invisible hand	**i.**	The study of the economy as a whole.
____	**11.** invisible hand theorem	**j.**	The study of how human beings coordinate their wants.
____	**12.** macroeconomics	**k.**	Goods available are too few to satisfy individuals' desires.
____	**13.** marginal benefit	**l.**	The application of the knowledge learned in positive economics to the achievement of the goals determined in normative economics.
____	**14.** marginal cost	**m.**	An economic force that is given relatively free rein by society to work through the market.
____	**15.** market force		
____	**16.** microeconomics	**n.**	The price mechanism.
____	**17.** natural experiment	**o.**	A framework that places the generalized insights of theory in a more specific contextual setting.
____	**18.** normative economics	**p.**	A commonly-held economic insight stated as a law or general assumption.
____	**19.** opportunity cost	**q.**	Achieving a goal as cheaply as possible.
____	**20.** positive economics	**r.**	Action taken by government to influence economic actions.
____	**21.** precept	**s.**	Study of what the goals of the economy should be.
____	**22.** scarcity	**t.**	Cost that has already been incurred and cannot be recovered.
____	**23.** sunk cost	**u.**	A naturally occuring event that approximates a controlled experiment.
____	**24.** theorem	**v.**	A branch of economics that studies the economy through controlled laboratory experiments.
		w.	Rules that conclude that a particular course of action is preferable.
		x.	Propositions that are logically true based on the assumptions in a model.

PROBLEMS AND APPLICATIONS

1. State what happens to scarcity for each good in the following situations:

   a. New storage technology allows college dining services to keep peaches from rotting for a longer time. (Good: peaches).

   b. More students desire to live in single-sex dormitories. No new single-sex dormitories are established. (Good: single-sex dormitory rooms).

2. State as best you can:

   a. The opportunity cost of going out on a date tonight that was scheduled last Wednesday.

   b. The opportunity cost of breaking the date for tonight that you made last Wednesday.

   c. The opportunity cost of working through this study guide.

3. Assume you have purchased a $15,000 car. The salesperson has offered you a maintenance contract covering all major repairs for the next 3 years, with some exclusions, for $750.

   a. What is the sunk cost of purchasing the maintenance contract? Should this sunk cost be considered when deciding to purchase a maintenance contract?

   b. What is the opportunity cost of purchasing that maintenance contract?

   c. What information would you need to make a decision based on the economic decision rule?

   d. Based upon that information how would you make your decision?

4. State whether the following is a theorem or precept:

   a. The price mechanism tends to allocate resources efficiently.

   b. Because people find the selling of babies repugnant, government should ban their sale because the invisible hand will not be efficient.

5. State for each of the following whether it is an example of political forces, social forces, or economic forces at work:

   a. Warm weather arrives and more people take Sunday afternoon drives. As a result, the price of gasoline rises.

   b. In some states, liquor cannot be sold before noon on Sunday.

   c. Minors cannot purchase cigarettes.

● MULTIPLE CHOICE

Circle the one best answer for each of the following questions:

1. Economic reasoning:
   a. provides a framework with which to approach questions.
   b. provides correct answers to just about every question.
   c. is only used by economists.
   d. should only be applied to economic business matters.

2. Scarcity could be reduced if:
   a. individuals work less and want fewer consumption goods.
   b. individuals work more and want fewer consumption goods.
   c. world population grows and world production remains the same.
   d. innovation comes to a halt.

3. In the textbook, the author focuses on coordination rather than scarcity as the central point of the definition of economics because:
   a. economics is not really about scarcity.
   b. scarcity involves coercion, and the author doesn't like coercion.
   c. the author wants to emphasize that the quantity of goods and services depends upon human action and the ability to coordinate that human action.
   d. the concept "scarcity" does not fit within the institutional structure of the economy.

4. In the U.S. economy, who is in charge of organizing and coordinating overall economic activities?
   a. Government.
   b. Corporations.
   c. No one.
   d. Consumers.

5. You bought stock A for $10 and stock B for $50. The price of each is currently $20. Assuming no tax issues, which should you sell if you need money?
   a. Stock A.
   b. Stock B.
   c. There is not enough information to tell which to sell.
   d. You should sell an equal amount of both.

6. In deciding whether to go to lectures in the final weeks the semester, you should:
   a. include tuition as part of the cost of that decision.
   b. not include tuition as part of the cost of that decision.
   c. include a portion of tuition as part of the cost of that decision.
   d. only include tuition if you paid it rather than your parents.

7. In making economic decisions you should consider:
   a. marginal costs and marginal benefits.
   b. marginal costs and average benefits.
   c. average costs and average benefits.
   d. total costs and total benefits, including past costs and benefits.

8. According to the economic decision rule, if MB>MC, one should:
   a. do less.
   b. do more.
   c. do nothing
   d. exit the market.

9. In arriving at a decision, a good economist would say that:
   a. one should consider only total costs and total benefits.
   b. one should consider only marginal costs and marginal benefits.
   c. after one has considered marginal costs and benefits, one should integrate the social and moral implications and reconsider those costs and benefits.
   d. after considering the marginal costs and benefits, one should make the decision on social and moral grounds.

10. In making decisions economists primarily use:
    a. monetary costs.
    b. opportunity costs.
    c. benefit costs.
    d. dollar costs.

11. The opportunity cost of reading Chapter 1 of a 38-chapter text:
    a. is about 1/38 of the price you paid for the book because the chapter is about 1/38 of the book.

    b. is zero since you have already paid for the book.

    c. has nothing to do with the price you paid for the book.

    d. is 1/38 the price of the book plus 1/38 the price of tuition for the course.

12. Rationing devices that our society uses include:
    a. the invisible hand only.
    b. the invisible hand and social forces only.
    c. the invisible hand and political forces only.
    d. the invisible hand, social forces, and political forces.

13. If at Female College there are significantly more females than males (and there are not a significant number of gays or off-campus dating opportunities), economic forces:
    a. will likely push for females to pay for dinners on dates.
    b. will likely push for males to pay for dinners on dates.
    c. will likely push for neither to pay for dinners on dates.
    d. are irrelevant to this issue. Everyone knows that the males always should pay.

14. Individuals are prohibited from practicing medicine without a license. The legal prohibition is a direct example of:
    a. the invisible hand.
    b. social forces.
    c. political forces.
    d. market forces.

15. Which of the following is most likely an example of a microeconomic topic?
    a. The effect of a flood in the Midwest on the price of bottled water.
    b. How a government policy will affect inflation.
    c. The relationship between unemployment and inflation.
    d. Why an economy goes into a recession.

16. Which of the following is most strongly an example of a macroeconomic topic?
    a. The effect of a frost on the Florida orange crop.
    b. Wages of cross-country truckers.

    c. How the unemployment and inflation rates are related.
    d. How income is distributed in the United States.

17. What best states the difference between theorems and precepts?
    a. Theorems are based on models while precepts add knowledge of real-world institutions and judgment.
    b. Theorems are based on models while precepts are not.
    c. Theorems lead to economic principles while precepts lead to economic insights.
    d. Theorems are not based on real-world observations while precepts are.

18. The statement, "The distribution of income should be left to the market," is:
    a. a positive statement.
    b. a normative statement.
    c. an art-of-economics statement.
    d. an objective statement.

19. "Given certain conditions, the market achieves efficient results" is an example of:
    a. a positive statement.
    b. a normative statement.
    c. an art-of-economics statement.
    d. a subjective statement.

● POTENTIAL ESSAY QUESTIONS

You may also see essay questions similar to the "Problems & Applications" exercises.

1. Respond to the following statement: "Theories are of no use to me because they are not very practical. All I need are the facts because they speak for themselves."

2. The United States is one of the wealthiest nations on earth, yet our fundamental economic problem is scarcity. How can this be?

3. Does economics help teach us how to approach problems, or does it give us a set of answers to problems?

ANSWERS

SHORT-ANSWER QUESTIONS

1. Microeconomics is the study of how individual choice is influenced by economic forces. Microeconomics focuses on a particular segment of the economy, like how a specific market price and quantity sold is determined. Macroeconomics is the study of the economy as a whole. It considers the problems of inflation, unemployment, business cycles, and growth. (5)

2. The three central problems that every economy must solve are (1) what and how much to produce, (2) how to produce it, and (3) for whom to produce it. (5)

3. Scarcity occurs when there are not enough goods available to satisfy individuals' desires. Scarcity has two elements: our wants and our means of fulfilling those wants. Since each of these two elements can change, relative scarcity can also change. If we can reduce our wants, relative scarcity will be reduced. Likewise if we can increase our efforts to produce more goods or if technological changes allow people to produce more using the same resources, relative scarcity will be reduced. (5)

4. If the marginal benefits of doing something exceed the marginal costs, do it. If the marginal costs of doing something exceed the marginal benefits, don't do it. (8)

5. Opportunity cost is the benefit forgone by undertaking an activity. That is, it is the benefit forgone of the next best alternative to the activity you have chosen. Otherwise stated, it is what must be given up in order to get something else. (9-10)

6. Opportunity cost is the basis of cost/benefit economic reasoning. It takes into account benefits of all other options, and converts these alternative benefits into costs of the decision you're now making. In economic reasoning, opportunity cost will be less than the benefit of what you have chosen. (9-10)

7. An economic force is the necessary reaction to scarcity. All scarce goods must be rationed in some way. If an economic force is allowed to work through the market, that economic force becomes a market force. Social and political forces can keep economic forces from becoming market forces. (11-12)

8. Positive economics is the study of what is and how the economy works. Normative economics is the study of what the goals of the economy should be. The art of economics is the application of the knowledge learned in positive economics to the achievement of the goals determined in normative economics. (17-18)

ANSWERS

MATCHING

1-l; 2-c; 3-e; 4-o; 5-r; 6-p; 7-j; 8-q; 9-v; 10-n; 11-h; 12-i; 13-a; 14-b; 15-m; 16-d; 17-u; 18-s; 19-f; 20-g; 21-w; 22-k; 23-t; 24-x.

ANSWERS

PROBLEMS AND APPLICATIONS

1. a. Scarcity will fall because fewer peaches will rot. (5)
   b. Scarcity of single-sex dorm rooms will rise since the number of students desiring single-sex dorm rooms has risen, but the number available has not. (5)

2. a. The opportunity cost of going out on a date tonight that was scheduled last Wednesday is the benefit forgone of the best alternative. If my best alternative was to study for an economics exam, it would be the increase in my exam grade that I would have otherwise gotten had I studied. Many answers are possible. (9-10)
   b. The opportunity cost of breaking the date for tonight that I made last Wednesday is the benefit forgone of going out on that date. It would be all the fun I would have had on that date. Other answers are possible. (9-10)

c. The opportunity cost of working through this study guide is the benefit forgone of the next-best alternative to studying. It could be the increase in the grade I would have received by studying for another exam, or the money I could have earned if I were working at the library. Many answers are possible. (9-10)

3. a. The sunk cost of purchasing the maintenance contract is the $15,000 cost of the car because it is a cost that has already been incurred and cannot be recovered. Sunk costs should always be ignored when making a current decision because only marginal costs are relevant to the current decision. (7)

b. The opportunity cost of purchasing the maintenance contract is the benefit I could receive by spending that $750 on something else, such as a moon roof. (9-10)

c. I would need to know the benefit of the maintenance contract to assess whether the cost of $750 is worthwhile. (7-8)

d. For me the benefit of the maintenance contract is the expected cost of future repairs that would be covered and the peace of mind of knowing that future repairs are covered by the contract. The cost is the opportunity cost of using the $750 in another way. Notice that the cost of a decision includes opportunity costs only; it does not include sunk costs because they are not relevant. If the benefit exceeds the cost, do it. If the cost exceeds the benefit, do not do it. (7-8)

4. a. This is a theorem since it is the logical conclusion of a model. (12-13)

b. This is a precept since it adds knowledge of social mores to the invisible hand theorem.(12-13)

5. a. This is an example of an economic force. (11)

b. This is an example of a political force. Some states have laws, called blue laws, against selling liquor on Sundays altogether or selling it before noon. (10-12)

c. This is an example of a political force. This is a federal law. (10-12)

ANSWERS

MULTIPLE CHOICE

1. a As discussed on pages 6-7, the textbook author clearly believes that economic reasoning applies to just about everything. This eliminates c and d. He also carefully points out that it is not the only reasoning that can be used; hence b does not fit. So the correct answer must be a.

2. b On page 5 of the textbook, the author states that the problem of scarcity depends upon our wants and our means of fulfilling those wants. An implication of this is that scarcity could be reduced if individuals worked more and/or wanted less.

3. c On page 6 of the textbook the author emphasizes the human action reason for focusing on coordination. He explicitly points out that scarcity is important, but that the concept of coordination is broader.

4. c As discussed on page 11, the invisible hand of the market coordinates the activities and is a composite of many individuals rather than just any one individual. If you were tempted to say b, corporations, your instincts are right, but the "overall" eliminated that as a possible answer.

5. c As discussed on pages 7-8 of the textbook, in making economic decisions you consider that only costs from this point on are relevant; historical costs are sunk costs and therefore have no relevance. Since the prices of the stocks are currently the same, it doesn't matter which you sell.

6. b As discussed on pages 7-8, in economic decisions, you only look at costs from this point on; sunk costs are sunk costs, so tuition can be forgotten. Economic decisions focus on forward-looking marginal costs and marginal benefits.

7. a The economic decision rule is "If marginal benefits exceed marginal costs, do it." As

is discussed on pages 7-8 of the text, the relevant benefits and relevant costs to be considered are *marginal* (additional) costs and *marginal* benefits. The answer d is definitely ruled out by the qualifying phrase referring to past benefits and costs. Thus, only a is correct.

8. b   The economic decision rule is "If marginal benefits exceed marginal costs, do it." See page 8 of the text.

9. c   As the textbook points out on pages 7 and 10-11, economists use a framework of costs and benefits initially, but then later they add the social and moral implications to their conclusions. Adding these can change the estimates of costs and benefits, and in doing so can change the result of economic analysis, so there is an integration between the two. (This was a hard question that required careful reading of the text to answer correctly.)

10. b   As discussed on page 9 of the text, opportunity costs include measures of nonmonetary costs. The other answers either do not include all the costs that an economist would consider, or are simply two words put together. The opportunity costs include the benefit forgone by undertaking an activity and should always be included in measuring marginal costs.

11. c   As discussed on pages 7-8, the correct answer is that it has nothing to do with the price you paid since that is a sunk cost that has already been paid, so a and d are wrong. The opportunity cost is not zero, however, since there are costs of reading the book. The primary opportunity cost of reading the book is the value of the time you're spending on it, which is determined by what you could be doing with that time otherwise.

12. d   As discussed on page 11 of the text, all of these are rationing devices. The invisible hand works through the market and thus is focused on in economics. However, the others also play a role in determining what people want, either through legal means or through social control.

13. a   As discussed on page 11 of the text, if there are significantly more of one gender than another, dates with that group must be rationed out among the other group. Economic forces will be pushing for the group in excess quantity supplied (in this case women) to pay. Economic forces may be pushing in that direction even though historical forces may push in the opposite direction. Thus, even if males pay because of social forces, economic forces will be pushing for females to pay.

14. c   As discussed on pages 11-12, laws are political forces.

15. a   As discussed on pages 5-6, macroeconomics is concerned with inflation, unemployment, business cycles and growth. Microeconomics is the study of individuals and individual markets.

16. c   As discussed on pages 5-6, macroeconomics is concerned with inflation, unemployment, business cycles, and growth. Microeconomics is the study of individuals and individual markets. The distribution of income is a micro topic because it is concerned with the distribution of income among individuals.

17. a   See the definitions of both terms in the text, pages 12-13. Since models are informed by real-world observations, d is not correct.

18. b   As discussed on page 17, this could be either a normative or an art-of-economics statement, depending on whether there is an explicit "given the way the real-world economy operates." This qualifier is not there, so "normative" is the preferable answer. After all, normative economics deals with what *should* be.

19. a   As discussed on page 17, this is a positive statement. It is a statement about *what is,* not about what should be.

━━━ ⬤ **ANSWERS** ━━━

POTENTIAL ESSAY QUESTIONS

The following are annotated answers. They indicate the general idea behind the answer.

1. Theories are practical because they are generalizations based on real-world observations or facts. They enable us to predict and to explain real-world economic behavior. Because they are generalizations, they enable us to avoid unnecessary details or facts. The drawback, however, is that because they are generalizations, at times there will be exceptions to the prediction we would generally expect to observe.

    Facts, on the other hand, do not always speak for themselves. One can often be overwhelmed by a large set of data or facts. Not until one systematically arranges, interprets, and generalizes upon facts, tying them together, and distilling out a theory (general statement) related to those facts, do they take on any real meaning. In short, theory and facts are inseparable in the scientific process because theory gives meaning to facts and facts check the validity of theory.

2. The United States is still faced with scarcity because we are unable to have as much as we would like to have. Our resources (as vast as they are) are still scarce relative to the amount of goods and services we would like to have (indeed, our wants appear to be unlimited).

3. Economics is a methodology, or an approach to how we think about the world. It does not come to us equipped with a whole set of solutions to complex real-world problems. However, it may help shed some light on the complexities of real-world issues and thus help us to find solutions.

THE PRODUCTION POSSIBILITY MODEL, TRADE, AND GLOBALIZATION

2

CHAPTER AT A GLANCE

1. The production possibilities curve shows the trade-off between two things. (25-27)

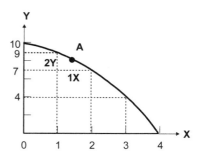

The slope tells you the opportunity cost of good X in terms of good Y. In this particular graph you have to give up 2 Y to get 1 X when you're around point A.

2. In order to get more of something, generally one must give up ever-increasing quantities of something else. (26-27)

The production possibility curve shown in #1 demonstrates this principle.

3. The production possibility curve is bowed outward, meaning that in order to get more and more of something, we must give up ever-increasing quantities of something else. (26-27)

The outward bow of the production possibility curve reflects that when more and more of a good is produced, we must use resources whose comparative advantage is in the production of the other good.

4. Countries can consume more if they specialize in those goods for which they have a comparative advantage and then trade. (30-34)

Country A can produce 30Y or 10X, or any combination thereof, while Country B can produce 20Y or 30X or any combination thereof. Since country A has a comparative advantage in Y, it should produce 30Y and Country B should produce 30X. If they divide the goods equally, each can consume 15 units of each good, or point C in the graph below. Each can consume beyond its individual production possibilities.

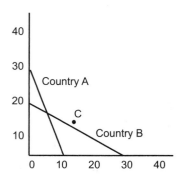

5. Globalization is a response to the forces of the law of one price. (34-38)

The law of one price states that wages of workers in one country will not differ significantly from the wages of equal workers in countries with similar institutions.

Remember: all jobs cannot be outsourced. Every country has, by definition, a compara-tive advantage in the production of some good if the other country has a comparative advantage in the production of another good.

See also, Appendix A: "Graphish: The Language of Graphs."

SHORT-ANSWER QUESTIONS

1. Design a grade production possibility curve for studying economics and English, and show how it demonstrates the concept of opportunity cost.

2. State the principle that is the basis of a production possibility curve that is bowed out.

3. What does the production possibility curve look like if opportunity cost is constant?

4. What happens to the production possibility curve when people specialize and trade? Why do specialization and trade make individuals better off?

5. What is the positive effect of globalization for firms? What is the negative effect?

6. State the law of one price. How is it related to globalization and U.S. companies moving production to foreign countries?

MATCHING THE TERMS
Match the terms to their definitions

___ 1. comparative advantage

___ 2. efficiency

___ 3. globalization

___ 4. inefficiency

___ 5. laissez-faire

___ 6. law of one price

___ 7. production possibility curve

___ 8. production possibility table

___ 9. productive efficiency

a. A curve measuring the maximum combination of outputs that can be obtained from a given number of inputs.

b. Achieving as much output as possible from a given amount of inputs.

c. An economic policy of leaving coordination of individuals' actions to the market.

d. Table that lists a choice's opportunity cost by summarizing alternative outputs that can be achieved with your inputs.

e. The advantage that attaches to a resource when that resource is better suited to the production of one good than to the production of another good.

f. Wages of (equal) workers in one country will not differ significantly from wages in another institutionally similar country.

g. Getting less output from inputs that, if devoted to some other activity, would produce more output.

h. Achieving a goal with as few inputs as possible.

i. The increasing integration of economies, cultures, and institutions across the world.

● PROBLEMS AND APPLICATIONS

1. Suppose a restaurant has the following production possibility table:

Resources devoted to pizza in % of total	Output of pizza in pies per week	Resources devoted to spaghetti in % of total	Output of spaghetti in bowls per week
100	50	0	0
80	40	20	10
60	30	40	17
40	20	60	22
20	10	80	25
0	0	100	27

a. Plot the restaurant's production possibility curve. Put output of pizza in pies on the horizontal axis.

b. What happens to the trade-off between making spaghetti and pizzas as the number of bowls of spaghetti made increases?

c. What would happen to the production possibility curve if the restaurant found a way to toss and cook pizzas faster?

d. What would happen to the production possibility curve if the restaurant bought new stoves and ovens that cooked both pizzas and spaghetti faster?

2. Suppose Ecoland has the following production possibility table:

% resources devoted to production of guns	Number of guns	% resources devoted to production of butter	Pounds of butter
100	50	0	0
80	40	20	5
60	30	40	10
40	20	60	15
20	10	80	20
0	0	100	25

a. Plot the production possibility curve for the production of guns and butter. Put the number of guns on the horizontal axis.

b. What is the per unit opportunity cost of increasing the production of guns from 20 to 30? From 40 to 50?

c. What happens to the opportunity cost of producing guns as the production of guns increases?

d. What is the per unit opportunity cost of increasing the production of butter from 10 to 15? From 20 to 25?

e. What happens to the opportunity cost of producing butter as the production of butter increases?

f. Given this production possibility curve, is producing 26 guns and 13 pounds of butter possible?

g. Is producing 34 guns and 7 pounds of butter possible? Is it efficient?

3. Using the following production possibility tables and using production possibility curves, show how the United States and Japan would be better off specializing in the production of either food or machinery and then trading rather than producing both food and machinery themselves and not trading.

United States Production per year		Japan Production per year	
Food (tons)	Machinery (1000 units)	Food (tons)	Machinery (1000 units)
10	0	12.5	0
8	5	10.0	1
6	10	7.5	2
4	15	5.0	3
2	20	2.5	4
0	25	0.0	5

4. Assume that France can produce wine for 25 euros per bottle and can produce butter for 5 euros per pound. Assume that Italy can produce wine for 16 euros per bottle and butter for 10 euros per pound.

a. In terms of pounds of butter, what is the opportunity cost of producing wine in each country?

b. Who has the comparative advantage in producing butter?

c. To obtain the greatest combined production possibilities, which country should specialize in wine and which should specialize in butter?

d. What is likely to happen to each country's consumption possibilities if each specializes in the good for which it has a comparative advantage and then trades?

● MULTIPLE CHOICE

Circle the one best answer for each of the following questions:

1. If the opportunity cost of good X in terms of good Y is 2Y, so you'll have to give up 2Y to get one X, the production possibility curve would look like:

a. a.
b. b.
c. c.
d. a, b and c.

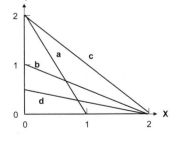

2. If the opportunity cost of good X in terms of good Y is 2Y, so you'll have to give up 2Y to get one X, the production possibility curve would look like:

    a. a.
    b. b.
    c. c.
    d. d.

    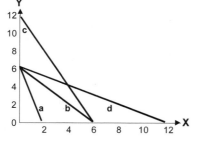

3. If the opportunity cost of good X in terms of good Y is 2Y, so you'll have to give up 2Y to get one X, the production possibility curve could look like:

    a. A only.
    b. B only.
    c. C only.
    d. A, B, or C.

    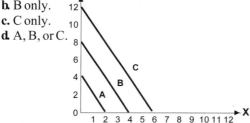

4. If the opportunity cost is constant for all combinations, the production possibility curve will look like:

    a. a.
    b. b.
    c. c.
    d. d.

    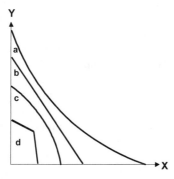

5. If the principle that in order to get more of something one must give up ever-increasing quantities of something else applies at all points, using the graph for Question #4, the production possibility curve looks like:

    a. a.
    b. b.
    c. c.
    d. d.

6. Given the accompanying production possibility curve, when you're moving from point C to point B the opportunity cost of butter in terms of guns is:

    a. 1/3.
    b. 1.
    c. 2.
    d. 3/2.

    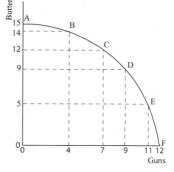

7. In the graph for question 6, in the range of points between A and B there is:

    a. a high opportunity cost of guns in terms of butter.
    b. a low opportunity cost of guns in terms of butter.
    c. no opportunity cost of guns in terms of butter.
    d. a high monetary cost of guns in terms of butter.

8. In the accompanying production possibility diagram, point A would be:

    a. an efficient point.
    b. a superefficient point.
    c. an inefficient point.
    d. a non-attainable point.

9. The efficiency of producing computers is increasing each year. In the graphs on the top of the next page, which of the four arrows would demonstrate the appropriate shifting of the production possibility curve?

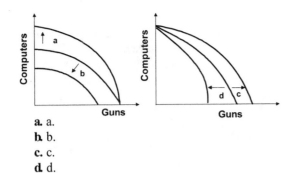

a. a.

b. b.

c. c.

d d.

10. Say that methods of production are tied to particular income distributions, so that choosing one method will help some people but hurt others and that the society's income distribution is one of its goals. Say also that method A produces significantly more total output than method B. In this case:

a. method A is more efficient than method B.

b. method B is more efficient than method A.

c. if method A produces more and gives more to the poor people, method A is more efficient.

d one can't say whether A or B is more efficient.

11. If the United States and Japan have production possibility curves as shown in the diagram below, at what point would their consumption possibilities most likely be after trade?

a. A.

b. B.

c. C.

d D.

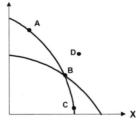

12. If countries A and B have production possibility curves A and B respectively, country A has a comparative advantage in the production of:

a. no good.

b. both goods.

c. good X only.

d. good Y only.

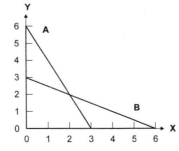

13. Suppose country A can produce either 100 cars or 50 tractors, or any combination thereof, while country B can produce either 200 cars or 50 tractors, or any combination thereof, and both countries consume both goods. Which of the following combination of goods can be produced only if the countries specialize and trade:

a. 300 cars, 0 tractors.

b. 0 cars, 100 tractors.

c. 200 cars, 50 tractors.

d. 300 cars, 100 tractors.

14. When trade is allowed between two countries, the slope of the combined production possibility curve is determined by the country with the:

a. highest output.

b. lowest output.

c. highest opportunity cost.

d. lowest opportunity cost.

15. According to the law of one price:

a. wages will eventually be the same for every industry.

b. wages will eventually be the same in every country.

c. wage differences cannot continue unless they reflect differences in productivity.

d wage differences can continue as long as product prices can differ among countries.

16. Assuming productivity differentials diminish, the law of one price will likely result in:

a. a decline in nominal U.S. wages.

b. a rise in nominal U.S. wages.

c. a decline in the value of the U.S. dollar.

d a rise in the value of the U.S. dollar.

17. Because of international competition and the ease with which technology is transferable among many nations with similar institutional structures, we can expect the wages for workers with similar skills to:

a. increase in developing countries faster than they increase in developed nations.

b. decrease in developing countries while they increase in developed nations.

c. increase in developing countries while they decrease in developed nations.

d decrease in both developed and developing countries.

A1. In the graph below, point A represents:

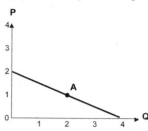

  a. a price of 1 and a quantity of 2.
  b. a price of 2 and a quantity of 2.
  c. a price of 2 and a quantity of 1.
  d. a price of 1 and a quantity of 1.

A2. The slope of the line in the graph below is:
  a. 1/2.
  b. 2.
  c. minus 1/2.
  d. minus 2.

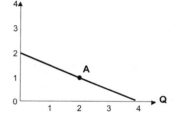

A3. At the maximum and minimum points of a nonlinear curve, the value of the slope is equal to
  a. 1.
  b. zero.
  c. minus 1.
  d. indeterminate.

A4. Which of the four lines in the graphs below has the largest slope?

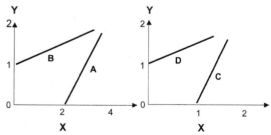

  a. A.
  b. B.
  c. C.
  d. A and C.

A5. Which of the following equations represents the line depicted in the graph to question A2?
  a. $P = 2 - .5Q$.
  b. $P = 2 - 2Q$.
  c. $Q = 4 - 2P$.
  d. $Q = 2 - .5P$.

A6. Suppose the demand curve is represented by $P = -2Q + 8$. Which of the following equations represents a *shift to the right* in that demand curve, with no change in slope?
  a. $P = -Q + 8$.
  b. $P = -2Q + 10$.
  c. $P = -2Q + 6$.
  d. $P = -4Q + 8$.

● POTENTIAL ESSAY QUESTIONS

You may also see essay questions similar to the "Problems & Applications" exercises.

1. What did Adam Smith mean when he said, "It is not from the benevolence of the butcher, the brewer, or the baker, that we expect our dinner, but from their regard to their own interest" (*Wealth of Nations*, Book 1, Chapter 2)? How does this quotation relate to specialization?

2. Your study partner tells you that because wages are higher in the United States than in many other countries, eventually all U.S. production will move abroad. How do you respond?

ANSWERS

SHORT-ANSWER QUESTIONS

1. The production possibility curve below shows the highest combination of grades you can get with 20 hours of studying economics and English. The grade received in economics is on the vertical axis and the grade received in English is on the horizontal axis. The graph tells us the opportunity cost of spending any combination of 20 hours on economics and English. For example, the opportunity cost of increasing your grade in economics by 6 points is decreasing your English grade by 4 points (a 2/3-point reduction in English grade for each one-point improvement in economics grade). (24-30)

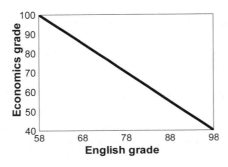

2. The principle that underlies a production possibility curve that is bowed out states that in order to get more of something, one must give up ever-increasing quantities of something else. (24-30)

3. Such a production possibility curve would be a straight line connecting the maximum number of units of each product that could be produced if all inputs were devoted to one or the other good. (24-30)

4. By concentrating on those activities for which one has a comparative advantage and trading those goods for goods for which others have a comparative advantage, individuals can end up with a combination of goods to consume that is greater than without trade. (30-34)

5. The rewards for winning in a global market are bigger because the market is larger. The negative effect is that the firm faces more competitors, some of which may have lower costs. (34-36)

6. The law of one price is that wages of workers in one country will not differ significantly from the wages of equal workers in another institutionally similar country. Globalization means that firms will seek low-cost areas for production throughout the world. Outsourcing is the result of differing wages among countries. As the high-wage country outsources some jobs to lower-wage countries, wages will tend to equalize. So, the fact that companies move production to foreign countries is the result of the law of one price in action. (37)

ANSWERS

MATCHING

1-e; 2-h; 3-i; 4-g; 5-c; 6-f; 7-a; 8-d; 9-b.

ANSWERS

PROBLEMS AND APPLICATIONS

1. **a.** The restaurant's production possibility curve is shown below. (25-27)

  b. The trade-off between spaghetti and pizza increases because the number of pizza pies that must be given up to make an additional bowl of spaghetti increases as the number of bowls of spaghetti produced increases. (24-30)

  c. If the restaurant found a way to toss and cook pizzas faster, the production possibility curve would rotate out along the pizza axis as shown below. (28-30)

d. The production possibility curve would shift out to the right as shown in the figure below. (25-29)

2. a. The production possibility curve is a straight line as shown below. (25-28)

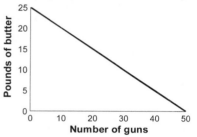

b. The opportunity cost of increasing the production of guns from 20 to 30 is 0.5 pounds of butter per gun (5/10). The opportunity cost of increasing the production of guns from 40 to 50 is also 0.5 pounds of butter per gun (5/10). (25-28)

c. The opportunity cost of producing guns stays the same as the production of guns increases. (25-28)

d. The per unit opportunity cost of increasing the production of butter from 10 to 15 is 2 guns per pound of butter. The opportunity cost of increasing the production of butter from 20 to 25 is also 2 guns per pound of butter. (25-28)

e. The opportunity cost of producing butter stays the same as the production of butter increases. (25-28)

f. Producing 26 guns and 13 lbs of butter is not attainable given this production possibility curve. We can produce 20 guns and 15 lbs of butter. To produce six more guns, Ecoland must give up 3 lbs of butter. Ecoland can produce only 26 guns and 12 lbs of butter. (25-28)

g. Ecoland can produce 34 guns and 7 pounds of butter. To see this, begin at 30

guns and 10 pounds of butter. To produce 4 more guns, 2 pounds of butter must be given up. Ecoland can produce 34 guns and 8 pounds of butter, which is more than 34 guns and 7 pounds of butter. 34 guns and 7 pounds of butter is an inefficient point of production. (25-29)

3. The production possibility of producing food and machinery for both Japan and the United States is shown in the graph below. The United States has a comparative advantage in the production of machinery. It must give up only 0.4 tons of food for each additional thousand units of machinery produced. Japan must give up 2.5 tons of food for each additional thousand units of machinery produced. If they specialize and trade, they could attain the combined production possibility curve shown below.

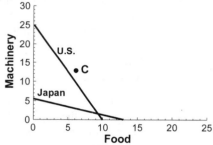

If each country specializes in their comparative advantage and equally divides that production they will each consume 6.25 units of food and 12.5 units of machinery (point C in the graph)—more than either could have consumed if they produced just for themselves. (32-34)

4. a. In France, the opportunity cost of producing wine is 5 pounds of butter. In Italy, the opportunity cost of producing wine is 1.6 pounds of butter. Calculate this by finding how much butter must be forgone for each bottle of wine in each country. (25-28)

b. France has the comparative advantage in producing butter because it can produce butter at a lower opportunity cost. (27-30)

c. To obtain the greatest combined production possibilities Italy should specialize in producing only wine and France should specialize in producing only butter. (32-34)

d. Each country's consumption possibilities increase. (30-34)

ANSWERS

MULTIPLE CHOICE

1. a   As discussed on pages 24-27, the production possibility curve tells how much of one good you must give up to get more of the other good; here you must give up 2Y to get one X, making a the correct answer.

2. c   As discussed on pages 24-27, the production possibility curve tells how much of one good you must give up to get more of another good. Opportunity cost is a ratio; it determines the slope, not the position, of the production possibility curve. Thus, the correct answer is c because the 12 to 6 trade-off reduces to a 2 to 1 trade-off.

3. d   As discussed on pages 24-27, the production possibility curve tells how much of one good you must give up to get more of the other good. Opportunity cost is a ratio; it determines the slope, not the position, of the PPC curve. Since all have the same correct slope, all three are correct, so d is the right answer.

4. b   As discussed in the "Reminder" box on page 28 of the book, if the opportunity costs are constant, the PPC is a straight line, so b must be the answer.

5. c   As discussed on pages 24-27 of the book, according to this principle, as you produce more and more of a good, you will have to give up more and more of the other good to do so. This means that the slope of the PPC must be bowed outward, so c is the correct answer. See Figure 2-2, pages 25-27 for an in-depth discussion.

6. d   As discussed on pages 24-27, the slope of the PPC measures the trade-off of one good for the other. Since moving from point C to B means giving up 3 guns for 2 pounds of butter, the correct answer is 3/2 (d).

7. b   As discussed on pages 24-27, the flatter the slope, the higher the opportunity cost of the good measured on the vertical axis; alternatively, the flatter the slope the lower the opportunity cost of the good measured on the horizontal axis. In the AB range the slope is flat so guns have a low opportunity cost in terms of butter; one need give up only one pound of butter to get four guns.

8. c   As discussed on pages 28-29 (See Figure 2-3), point A is an inefficient point because it is inside the PPC.

9. a   As discussed on pages 28-29 (See Figure 2-3), technological change that improves the efficiency of producing a good shifts the PPC out for that good, but not for the other good. So a is the correct answer.

10. d   The answer is "You can't say," as discussed on pages 28-31. The term "efficiency" involves *achieving a goal as cheaply as possible*. Without specifying one's goal, one cannot say what method is more efficient. The concept of efficiency generally presumes that the goal includes preferring more to less, so if any method is more productive, it will be method A. But because there are distributional effects that involve making additional judgments, the correct answer is d. Some students may have been tempted to choose c because their goals involve more equity, but that is their particular judgment, and not all people may agree. Thus c would be incorrect, leaving d as the correct answer.

11. d   As discussed on pages 30-34 and Figure 2-7 on page 33, with trade, both countries can attain consumption possibilities outside their production possibility curves. The only point not already attainable by either country is D.

12. d   Country A must give up 2Y to produce an additional X while Country B must give up only 1/2 Y to produce an additional X. Therefore, Country A has a comparative advantage in good Y and Country B has a comparative advantage in good X. See pages 30-34.

13. c   The greatest gains are when each country specializes in the good for which it has the lowest opportunity cost. If Country A specializes in tractors, producing 50 tractors, and Country B specializes in cars and produces 200 cars, production of 200

cars and 50 tractors is possible. The combination of 300 cars and 100 tractors is unattainable even with specialization and trade. The other combinations are possible without trade. See pages 30-34, especially Figure 2-7.

14. d   This is the principle of lowest cost rules. It is by producing where costs are lowest that countries can achieve gains from trade. See page 36.

15. c   According to the law of one price, wages of workers in one country will not differ substantially from wages of <u>equal</u> workers in another country with similar institutions. That is, there will be pressure for equally productive workers to receive similar wages. See page 37 for a discussion of the law of one price.

16. c   The text suggests that it is unlikely that nominal wages will decline in the United States. It is more likely that the exchange value of the dollar will decline to offset wage differentials between the United States and other countries. See pages 36-37.

17. a   According to the law of one price, wages of (equal) workers in one country will not differ significantly from the wages of workers in another institutionally similar country. It is unlikely that wages will fall, but if the law of one price holds, then wages in developing countries will rise faster than wages in developed nations rise. See page 37.

A1. a   As discussed in Appendix A, pages 42 and 43, point A represents the corresponding numbers on the horizontal and vertical number lines.

A2. c   As discussed on page 44 of Appendix A, the slope of a line is defined as rise over run. Since the rise is −2 and the run is 4, the slope of the above line is minus 1/2.

A3. b   As discussed on page 45 of Appendix A, at the maximum and minimum points of a nonlinear curve the slope is zero.

A4. c   As discussed in Appendix A, pages 44 and 45, the slope is defined as rise over run. Line C has the largest rise for a given run so c is the answer. Even though, visually, line A seems to have the same slope as line C, it has a different coordinate system. Line A has a slope of 1 and line B has a slope of 1/4. Always be careful about checking coordinate systems when visually interpreting a graph.

A5. a   To construct the equation, use the form $y = mx + b$ where m is the slope and b is the y-axis intercept. The y-axis intercept is 2 and the slope is rise/run $= -2/4 = -.5$. Plugging in these values we get $y = -.5x + 2$. Since P is on the y-axis and Q is on the x axis, this can also be written as $P = 2 - .5Q$. See page 46.

A6. b   A change in the intercept represents a shift in the curve. A higher intercept is a shift to the right. See page 46.

━━━━━━ ANSWERS ━━━━━━

POTENTIAL ESSAY QUESTIONS

The following are annotated answers. They indicate the general idea behind the answer.

1. Adam Smith was saying that it is not out of the kindness of producers that we are able to purchase what we want to consume, but the benefit that they will receive from selling their products. If each producer specializes in producing that good for which he receives the greatest benefit (produce at lowest cost) then the consumer will be able to consume the most goods at the lowest cost.

2. I would remind my study partner that the U.S. does have a comparative advantage in creativity and innovation in industries such as advertising and marketing. In addition, I would remind my partner that the very definition of comparative advantage means that if one country has a comparative advantage in one good, the other country has a comparative advantage in another good.

ECONOMIC INSTITUTIONS

3

CHAPTER AT A GLANCE

1. A <u>market economy</u> is an economic system based on private property and the market. It gives private property rights to individuals, and relies on market forces to coordinate economic activity. (52)

   A market economy's solutions to the central economic problems are:
   - *What to produce: what businesses believe people want and what is profitable.*
   - *How to produce: businesses decide how to produce efficiently, guided by their desire to make a profit.*
   - *For whom to produce: distribution according to individuals' ability and/or inherited wealth.*

2. <u>Capitalism</u> is an economic system based on the market in which the ownership of the means of production resides with a small group of individuals called capitalists. (53)

   <u>Socialism</u> is, in theory, an economic system that tries to organize society in the same way that most families are organized—all people contribute what they can, and get what they need. (53)

   A command, or centrally planned socialist economy's solutions to the three central economic problems are:
   - *What to produce: what central planners believe is socially beneficial.*
   - *How to produce: central planners decide, based on what they think is good for the country.*
   - *For whom to produce: central planners distribute goods based on what they determine are individuals' needs.*

All economic systems are dynamic and evolve over time, so the meaning of terms referring to economic systems is evolving. Ours has evolved from feudalism, mercantilism, and capitalism.

3. Businesses, households, and government interact in a market economy. (55-56)

   For a bird's-eye view of the U.S. economy, see Figure 3-1 (sometimes called the "circular flow of income model"). Be able to draw and explain it.

   Note: there are 3 basic economic institutions:

   - *Businesses:*
     a. Supply goods in a goods market.
     b. Demand factors in a factor market.
     c. Pay taxes and receive benefits from government.

   - *Households:*
     a. Supply factors.
     b. Demand goods.
     c. Pay taxes and receive benefits from government.

   - *Government:*
     a. Demands goods.
     b. Demands factors.
     c. Collects taxes and provides services.

   It will be important to remember who does the demanding and the supplying in goods and factor (resource) markets.

4. The advantages and disadvantages of the three forms of business are shown in a table on page 59.

✓ *Know the advantages and disadvantages of the three forms of business:*
- *Sole Proprietorship*
- *Partnership*
- *Corporation*

Flexible-purpose, or benefit, corporations are emerging as a new type of business.

5. Although, in principle, ultimate power resides with the people and households (consumer sovereignty), in practice the representatives of the people–firms and government–are sometimes removed from the people and, in the short run, are only indirectly monitored by the people. (57-59)

Also note: Economics focuses on households' role as the suppliers of labor.

- *Do we control business and government, or do they control us?*
- *The distribution of income (rich vs. poor) determines the "for whom" question. If you're rich you get more.*
- *Social forces affect what business and government do or don't do.*

6. Six roles of government in a market economy are: (63-66)

- Provide a stable set of institutions and rules.
  The government specifies "the rules of the game."

- Promote effective and workable competition.
✓ *Know the different consequences associated with competition vs. monopoly power.*

- Correct for externalities.
  Government attempts to restrict the production and consumption of negative externalities, while promoting the production and consumption of positive externalities.

- Ensure economic stability and growth.
  Government tries to ensure: full employment, low inflation, and economic growth (which increases the standard of living).

- Provide public goods.
  A public good is a good that if supplied to one person must be supplied to all and whose consumption by one individual does not prevent its consumption by another individual.

- Adjust for undesired market results.
  Sometimes the market result is not what society wants. For example, an unequal distribution of income may be undesirable. Government can adjust for these failures, but when doing so, it may make matters even worse. These are called "government failures."

7. It is impossible to talk about U.S. institutions apart from the world economy. (66-67)

Most large corporations are global.

Countries have developed international institutions to oversee global business as well as promote economic relations among countries. These include the UN, the World Bank, the WTO, and the IMF. Regional trade organizations such as the EU and NAFTA work to reduce trade barriers among member countries.

See also, Appendix A: "The History of Economic Systems."

● SHORT-ANSWER QUESTIONS

1. What is a market economy? How does it solve the three central economic problems?

2. What is socialism? In practice, how have socialist economies addressed the three central economic problems?

3. Draw a diagram showing the three groups that comprise the U.S. economy. What is the role of each group?

4. Your friend wants to buy a coin-operated laundromat. Her brother has offered to be a partner in the operation and put up half the money to buy the business. They have come to you for advice about what form of business to create. Of course you oblige, letting them know the three possibilities and the advantages and disadvantages of each.

5. What is consumer sovereignty? Why is much of the economic decision-making done by business and government even though households have the ultimate power?

6. Briefly distinguish between the two general roles of government.

7. What are the six roles of government?

8. Should government always intervene when markets fail?

9. Why are trade agreements important in the international market?

A1. Why did feudalism evolve into mercantilism?

A2. Why did mercantilism evolve into capitalism?

A3. Explain what is meant by the statement that capitalism has evolved into welfare capitalism.

MATCHING THE TERMS
Match the terms to their definitions

____ **1.** business	**a.** A business with two or more owners.
____ **2.** capitalism	**b.** Principle that the consumer's wishes rule what's produced.
____ **3.** consumer sovereignty	**c.** Corporation with substantial operations on both production and sales in more than one country.
____ **4.** corporation	**d.** A business that has only one owner.
____ **5.** demerit good or activity	**e.** Private producing units in our society.
____ **6.** entrepreneurship	**f.** What's left over from total revenue after all appropriate costs have been subtracted.
____ **7.** externality	**g.** The ability to organize and get something done.
____ **8.** global corporation	**h.** A business that is treated as a person, and is legally owned by its shareholders who are not liable for the actions of the corporate "person."
____ **9.** government failure	
____ **10.** households	**i.** An economic system based on individuals' goodwill toward others, not on their own self-interest, in which society decides what, how, and for whom to produce.
____ **11.** institutions	
____ **12.** macroeconomic externalities	**j.** An economic system based on private property and the market, in which individuals decide how, what, and for whom to produce.
____ **13.** market economy	**k.** A good that if supplied to one person must be supplied to all and whose consumption by one individual does not prevent its consumption by another individual.
____ **14.** market failure	
____ **15.** merit good or activity	**l.** A good or activity that government believes is good for you even though you may not choose to engage in the activity or consume the good.
____ **16.** partnership	
____ **17.** private good	**m.** A situation where the government intervenes and makes things worse.
____ **18.** private property right	**n.** A good or service that society believes is bad for people even though they choose to use the good or engage in the activity.
____ **19.** profit	
____ **20.** public good	**o.** The effect of a decision on a third party not taken into account by the decision maker.
____ **21.** socialism	**p.** The formal and informal rules that constrain human economic behavior.
____ **22.** sole proprietorship	
	q. A good that, when consumed by one individual, cannot be consumed by another individual.
	r. An economic system based on the market in which the ownership of the means of production resides with a small group of individuals called capitalists.
	s. Externalities that affect the levels of unemployment, inflation, or growth in the economy as a whole.
	t. Groups of individuals living together and making joint decisions.
	u. Situations in which the market does not lead to a desired result.
	v. The control a private individual or firm has over an asset.

● PROBLEMS AND APPLICATIONS

1. Fill in the blanks with the appropriate economic institution (households, businesses, or government).

    a. In the goods market, _____ and _____ buy goods and services from _____.

    b. In the goods market, _____ sell goods and services to _____ and _____.

    c. In the factor market, _____ and _____ buy (or employ) the resources owned by _____.

    d. In the factor market, _____ supply labor and other factors of production to _____ and _____.

    e. _____ redistributes income.

    f. _____ provides services to the public with tax revenue.

2. For each of the following, state for which of the three forms of business it is an advantage.

    a. Minimum bureaucratic hassle.

    b. Ability to share work and risks.

    c. Direct control by owner.

    d. Relatively easy (but not the easiest) to form.

    e. Limited individual liability.

    f. Greatest ability to get funds.

3. For each of the following, state for which form of business it is a disadvantage. (Some may have two answers.)

    a. Unlimited personal liability.

    b. Possible double taxation of income.

    c. Limited ability to get funds.

    d. Legal hassle to organize.

4. State some of the benefits global corporations offer countries. What is one problem that global corporations pose for governments?

● MULTIPLE CHOICE

Circle the one best answer for each of the following questions:

1. For a market to exist, you have to have:
    a. a capitalist economy.
    b. private property rights.
    c. no government intervention.
    d. externalities.

2. In theory, socialism is an economic system:
    a. that tries to organize society in the same ways as most families are organized, striving to see that individuals get what they need.
    b. based on central planning and government ownership of the means of production.
    c. based on private property rights.
    d. based on markets.

3. In practice, a command or socialist economy is an economic system:
   a. that tries to organize society in the same ways as most families organize, striving to see that individuals get what they need.
   b. based on central planning and government ownership of the means of production.
   c. based on private property rights.
   d. based on markets.

4. In practice, in command or socialist economies, the "what to produce" decision is most often made by:
   a. consumers.
   b. the market.
   c. government.
   d. firms.

5. In a market economy, the "what to produce" decision in practice is most often made directly by:
   a. consumers.
   b. the market.
   c. government.
   d. firms.

6. In the factor market:
   a. businesses supply goods and services to households and government.
   b. government provides income support to households unable to supply factors of production to businesses.
   c. households supply labor and other factors of production to businesses.
   d. households purchase goods and services from businesses.

7. The ability to organize and get something done generally goes under the term:
   a. the corporate approach.
   b. entrepreneurship.
   c. efficiency.
   d. consumer sovereignty.

8. In terms of numbers, the largest percentage of businesses are:
   a. partnerships.
   b. sole proprietorships.
   c. corporations.
   d. nonprofit companies.

9. The largest percentage of business receipts are by:
   a. partnerships.
   b. sole proprietorships.
   c. corporations.
   d. nonprofit companies.

10. A sole proprietorship has the advantage of:
    a. raising funds by selling stocks or bonds.
    b. limited personal liability.
    c. minimum bureaucratic hassle.
    d. sharing work and risks.

11. The largest percentage of state and local expenditures is on:
    a. education.
    b. health and medical care.
    c. highways.
    d. income security.

12. The largest percentage of federal government expenditures is on:
    a. education.
    b. health and medical care.
    c. infrastructure.
    d. income security.

13. All of the following are examples of government's role as referee *except*:
    a. setting limitations on when someone can be fired.
    b. collecting Social Security taxes from workers' paychecks.
    c. setting minimum safety regulations for the workplace.
    d. disallowing two competitors to meet to fix prices of their products.

14. When government attempts to adjust for the effect of decisions on third parties not taken into account by the decision makers, the government is attempting to:
    a. provide for a stable set of institutions and rules.
    b. promote effective and workable competition.
    c. provide public goods and services.
    d. correct for externalities.

15. The pressure for one firm to try to control the market is pressure to:
    a. take comparative advantage.
    b. fail the market.
    c. monopolize.
    d. externalize.

16. A good whose consumption by one individual does not prevent its consumption by another individual has a characteristic of:
    a. a public good.
    b. a private good.
    c. a macroeconomic good.
    d. a demerit good.

17. Global corporations:
    a. offer enormous benefits to countries but rarely any problems.
    b. are easy for governments to control.
    c. reduce competition in countries.
    d. have substantial operations on both the production and the sales sides in more than one country.

A1. In feudalism the most important force was:
    a. the price mechanism.
    b. cultural force.
    c. government.
    d. anarchy.

A2. In mercantilism, the guiding force is:
    a. the price mechanism.
    b. government.
    c. cultural force.
    d. anarchy.

A3. Mercantilism evolved into capitalism because:
    a. government investments did not pan out.
    b. the Industrial Revolution undermined the craft guilds' mercantilist method of production.
    c. the guilds wanted more freedom.
    d. serfs wanted more freedom.

A4. Marx saw the strongest tension between:
    a. rich capitalists and poor capitalists.
    b. capitalists and government.
    c. capitalists and the proletariat.
    d. government and the proletariat.

A5. State socialism is an economic system in which:
    a. business sees to it that people work for their own good until the people can be relied upon to do that on their own.
    b. business sees to it that people work for the common good until they can be relied upon to do that on their own.
    c. government sees to it that people work for their own good until they can be relied upon to do so on their own.
    d. government sees to it that people work for the common good until they can be relied upon to do so on their own.

● POTENTIAL ESSAY QUESTIONS

You may also see essay questions similar to the "Problems & Applications" exercises.

1. Contrast the market economy and the command economy in addressing the three fundamental economic problems.

2. Uglies is a brand of boxer shorts sold on the Internet. Their claim to fame is that the front of the shorts doesn't match the back. Their marketing ploy is the boxer-short-of-the-month club. Suppose you were the one who came up with the idea for Uglies and wanted to start the business. What form of business would you select and why? (Thinking about where the funds to start the business will come from, who will make the shorts, and how the shorts will be sold will help you answer this question.)

3. How are global economic issues different from national economic issues? How have governments attempted to grapple with global economic issues? What is a major drawback associated with these attempts?

━━━━━ ANSWERS ━━━━━

SHORT-ANSWER QUESTIONS

1. A market economy is an economic system based on private property and the market. It gives private property rights to individuals and relies on market forces to coordinate economic activity. In a market economy, businesses produce what they believe people want and what they think can make a profit supplying. Businesses decide how to produce efficiently, guided by their desire to make a profit. Goods are distributed according to individuals' ability and/or inherited wealth. (52)

2. In theory, socialism is an economic system that tries to organize society in the same way as most families are organized—all people contribute what they can and get what they need. In practice, socialism is an economic system based on government ownership of the means of production, with economic activity governed by central planning. So, central planners (not market forces) decide *what* is produced, *how* it is produced, and *for whom* it is produced. (53-55)

3. As seen in the diagram below, the three groups that comprise the U.S. economy are households, businesses, and government. Households supply factors of production to businesses in exchange for money; businesses produce goods and services and sell them to households and government in exchange for money. The government taxes businesses and households, buys goods and services from businesses and labor services from households, and provides goods and services to each of them. (55-56)

4. I would advise each of them to think hard about their situation. There are three main possibilities: sole proprietorship, partnership and a corporation. Each form of business has its disadvantages and advantages. If your friend wants to minimize bureaucratic hassle and be her own boss, the best form of business would be a sole proprietorship. However, she would be personally liable for all losses and might have difficulty obtaining additional funds should that be necessary. If her brother has some skills to offer the new business and is willing to share in the cost of purchasing the company, she might want to form a partnership with him. Beware though: Both partners are liable for any losses regardless of whose fault it is. I would ask her if she trusts her brother's decision-making abilities.

As a partnership they still might have problems getting additional funds. What about becoming a corporation? Her liability would be limited to her initial investment, her ability to get funds is greater, and she can shed personal income and gain added expenses to limit taxation. However, a corporation is a legal hassle to organize, may involve possible double taxation of income, and if she plans to hire many employees she may face difficulty monitoring the business once she becomes less involved. I would tell her she needs to weigh the costs and benefits of each option and choose the one that best suits her needs. (58-59)

5. Consumer sovereignty is the notion that the consumer's wishes rule what's produced. It means that if businesses wish to make a profit, they will need to produce what households want. That is not to say that businesses don't affect the desires of consumers through advertising. However, in practice, business and government do much of the economic decision-making even though households retain the ultimate power. This is because people have delegated much of that power to institutions and representatives—firms and the government—that are sometimes removed from the people. In the short run, households only indirectly control government and business. (57-60)

6. Two general roles of government are as actor and as referee. As an actor, government collects taxes and spends money. As a referee, government sets the rules governing relations between households and businesses. (61-62)

7. Six roles of government are (1) provide a stable set of institutions and rules, (2) promote effective and workable competition, (3) correct for externalities, (4) provide public goods, (5) ensure economic stability and growth, and (6) adjust for undesirable market results. (63-65)

8. The fact that a market has failed does not mean that government intervention will improve the situation; it may make things worse. (65-66)

9. Ongoing trade requires rules and methods of trade. The international market has no central government to set rules and methods for trade. Governments enter into voluntary trade agreements to fulfill some of these roles. (66-67)

A1. Feudalism evolved into mercantilism as the development of money allowed trade to grow, undermining the traditional base of feudalism. Politics rather than social forces came to control the central economic decisions. (72-73)

A2. Mercantilism evolved into capitalism because the Industrial Revolution shifted the economic power base away from craftsmen toward industrialists and toward an understanding that markets could coordinate the economy without the active involvement of the government. (73-74)

A3. Capitalism has evolved into welfare capitalism. That is, the human abuses marked by early capitalist developments led to a criticism of the market economic system. Political forces have changed government's role in the market, making government a key player in determining distribution and in making the what, how, and for whom decisions. This characterizes the U.S. economy today. (74-75)

━━━━━━━ **ANSWERS** ━━━━━━━

MATCHING

1-e; 2-r; 3-b; 4-h; 5-n; 6-g; 7-o; 8-c; 9-m; 10-t; 11-p; 12-s; 13-j; 14-u; 15-l; 16-a; 17-q; 18-v; 19-f; 20-k; 21-i; 22-d.

━━━━━━━ **ANSWERS** ━━━━━━━

PROBLEMS AND APPLICATIONS

1. a. In the goods market, **households** and **government** buy goods and services from **businesses**. (55-56)
   b. In the goods market, **businesses** sell goods and services to **households** and **government**. (55-56)
   c. In the factor market, **businesses** and **government** buy (or employ) the resources owned by **households**. (55-56)
   d. In the factor market, **households** supply labor and other factors of production to **businesses** and **government**. (55-56)
   e. **Government** redistributes income. (55-56)
   f. **Government** provides services to the public with tax revenue. (55-56)

2. a. Sole proprietorship. No special bureaucratic forms are required to start one. (59)
   b. Partnership. The owners have each other to work with and risks are shared. (59)
   c. Sole proprietorship. This is a firm of one person who controls the business. (59)
   d. Partnership. This is easy to form relative to the easiest (sole proprietorship) and the hardest (corporation). (59)
   e. Corporation. The individual liability is limited by individual investment. (59)
   f. Corporation. Because it can issue stock and has limited liability, it has more access to financial capital. (59)

3. a. Sole proprietorship and partnership. (59)
   b. Corporation. (59)
   c. Sole proprietorship and partnership. (59)
   d. Corporation. (59)

4. Global corporations can benefit countries by creating jobs, by bringing new ideas and new technologies to a country, and by providing competition to domestic companies, keeping them on their toes. But, global corporations, because they exist in many countries and there is no world government, may be difficult to regulate or to control. If they don't like one government's taxes, regulation, or other policies, they can shift operations to another country with more favorable policies. (66-67)

■■■■■ ANSWERS ■■■■■

MULTIPLE CHOICE

1. b   As discussed on page 52, markets require private property rights because these give people the framework within which they can trade, and markets rely on trading. Markets also require government, but government and private property rights are not the same thing, which rules out a and c. And d is a throwaway answer.

2. a   As discussed on page 53, a is the correct answer. If the question had said "In practice," b would have been an acceptable answer.

3. b   As discussed on page 54, b is the correct answer. If the question had said "In theory, a socialist economy..." a would have been an acceptable answer.

4. c   As discussed on page 54, in command economies, central planners decide what to produce based upon what they believe society needs.

5. d   Under a market economy, firms decide what to produce based on what they think will sell. See pages 55-56.

6. c.   In Figure 3-1 households supply labor and other factors of production while businesses demand these inputs used in the production process. See pages 55-56.

7. b   Entrepreneurship is the ability to organize and get something done. See page 57.

8. b   Most businesses are sole proprietorships. See Figure 3-2 on page 58.

9. c   Corporations account for most business receipts (revenues). See Figure 3-2 on page 58.

10. c   Corporations have the advantages of options a and b. Partnerships have the advantage of option d. See page 59.

11. a   The largest state and local government spending is on education. See Figure 3-3 on page 61.

12. d   The largest component of federal government spending is income security. See Figure 3-4 on page 62.

13. b   Collecting Social Security taxes to fund the Social Security system is government as an actor. Government as referee refers to laws regulating interaction between households and businesses. See pages 61-62.

14. d   Economists call the effect of a decision on a third party not taken into account by the decision maker an externality. Government sometimes attempts to adjust for these effects. See pages 63-64.

15. c   To monopolize is to try to be the only producer and control the market. See page 63.

16. a   A public good is a good that if supplied to one person must be supplied to all and whose consumption by one individual does not prevent its consumption by another individual. See page 64.

17. d   Option d is the definition of global corporations. They often create problems. Governments often find it difficult to control them and they increase competition, not decrease it. See pages 66-67.

A1. b   As discussed on page 71, in feudalism tradition reigned.

A2. b   As discussed on pages 72-73, in mercantilism government directed the economy.

A3. b   Mercantilism evolved into capitalism because of the changes brought about by the Industrial Revolution. See page 73.

A4. c   To the degree that government was controlled by capitalists, d would be a correct answer, but it is not as good an answer as c, which represents the primary conflict. Remember, you are choosing the answer that best reflects the discussion in the text. See page 74.

A5. d The author defines state socialism as option d. Socialists saw state socialism as a transition stage to pure socialism. See page 75.

ANSWERS

POTENTIAL ESSAY QUESTIONS

The following are annotated answers. They indicate the general idea behind the answer.

1. Both economic systems have to address the three central economic problems. (1) What to produce? In a market economy, firms produce what they believe people want and what will make them a profit. In socialism, or a command economy, central planners decide what is produced. (2) How to produce? In a market economy, firms decide how to produce efficiently, guided by their desire to make a profit. In socialism, central planners decide how to produce. (3) For whom to produce? In a market economy, distribution is decided according to ability and inherited wealth. In socialism, distribution is according to individuals' needs (as determined by central planners).

2. The answer to this question will vary from person to person and will depend on personal finances, how much risk one is able and willing to undertake, how much responsibility one wants to take on, and whether or not you want to share any profits. Given limited financial resources, I'd find a partner I can trust who has the funds needed to launch a website, hire a firm to carry out transactions, and build inventory. With a partnership, I can share the work and the risks of the venture. Since the liability associated with selling boxer shorts is not too great, unlimited liability with a partnership is not a problem. I would not choose a corporation because establishing one is a legal hassle requiring even more money. I would not choose a sole proprietorship because I don't have the funds to start the company on my own.

3. Global economic issues differ from national economic issues because national economies have governments to referee disputes among players in the economy; global economies do not; no international government exists. Governments, however, have developed a variety of international institutions to promote negotiations and coordinate economic relations among countries. These include the UN, the World Bank, the World Court and the International Monetary Fund. Countries also have developed global and regional organizations whose jobs are to coordinate trade among countries and reduce trade barriers. Some are the WTO, the EU, and NAFTA. In addition to these formal institutions, there are informal meetings of various countries like the Group of Eight.

   A major drawback associated with governmental attempts to deal with global economic issues is that because government membership in international organizations is voluntary, the power of international organizations is limited. An individual government may simply choose to ignore an international ruling with little impunity.

SUPPLY AND DEMAND

CHAPTER AT A GLANCE

1. The <u>law of demand</u> states that the quantity of a good demanded is <u>inversely related</u> to the good's price. When price goes up, quantity demanded goes down. When price goes down, quantity demanded goes up. (78)

   Law of Demand (Inverse Relationship):
   arrows move in $\uparrow P \rightarrow \downarrow Q_d$
   opposite directions $\downarrow P \rightarrow \uparrow Q_d$

   Law of Demand expressed as a <u>downward-sloping curve</u>:

   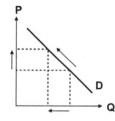

   To derive a demand curve from a demand table, plot each point on the demand table on a graph and connect the points.

   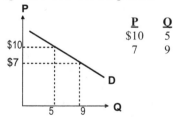

P	**Q**
$10	5
7	9

2a. The law of demand is based on opportunity cost and individuals' ability to substitute. If the price of a good rises, the opportunity cost of purchasing that good will also rise and consumers will substitute a good with a lower opportunity cost. (78)

   As the P of beef ↑, we buy less beef and more chicken.

2b. The law of supply, like the law of demand, is based on opportunity cost and the individual firm's ability to substitute. Suppliers will substitute toward goods for which they receive higher relative prices. (84-85)

If the P of wheat ↑, farmers grow more wheat and less corn.

3. Changes in quantity demanded are shown by movements along a demand curve. Shifts in demand are shown by a shift of the entire demand curve. (79) *(Note: "Δ" means "change.")*

   $\uparrow P \rightarrow \downarrow Q_d$ *is a movement along a curve (e.g. from point A to point B).*

   ΔD is caused only by Δs in the shift factors of D (<u>not</u> a Δ in the P of the good itself!)
   Δ <u>in shift factors of D</u> → ΔD → <u>shift of a D curve</u>

   ✓ *Know what can cause an increase and decrease in demand:*

4. The <u>law of supply</u> states that the quantity of a good supplied is <u>directly related</u> to the good's price. When price goes up, quantity supplied goes up. When price goes down, quantity supplied goes down. (84-88)

   Law of Supply expressed as an <u>upward-sloping curve</u>:

5. Just as with demand, it is important to distinguish between a change in supply (due to a change in shift factors and reflected as a shift of the entire supply curve) and a change in the quantity supplied (due to a change in price and reflected as a movement along a supply curve). (85-87)
   Don't get this confused on the exam!

$\uparrow P \rightarrow \uparrow Q_s$: *movement along a curve (e.g. from point A to point B).*

ΔS *is caused only by Δs in the shift factors of S (not a Δ in the P of the good itself!)*

Δ *in shift factors of S $\rightarrow \Delta S \rightarrow$ shift of a S curve*

✓ *Know what can cause an increase and decrease in supply:*

6. Equilibrium is where quantity supplied equals quantity demanded: (88-91)

   • If quantity demanded is greater than quantity supplied (excess demand), prices tend to rise.
   • If quantity supplied is greater than quantity demanded (excess supply), prices tend to fall.
   • When quantity demanded equals quantity supplied, prices have no tendency to change.

Shortage	**Surplus**	**Equilibrium**
$(Q_d > Q_s)$	$(Q_s > Q_d)$	$(Q_s = Q_d)$
P is below equilibrium	P is above equilibrium	P is at equilibrium

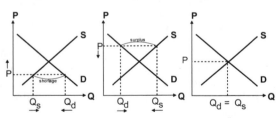

7. Demand and supply curves enable us to determine the equilibrium price and quantity. In addition, changes (shifts) in demand and supply curves enable us to predict the effect on the equilibrium price and quantity in a market. (92-93)

Anything other than price that affects demand or supply will shift the curves.

✓ *Know how a change in demand or supply affects the equilibrium price and quantity!*

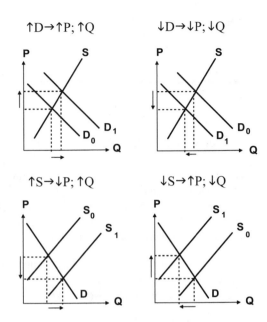

8. Simple supply and demand analysis holds other things constant. Sometimes supply and demand are interconnected, making it impossible to hold other things constant. When there is interdependence between supply and demand, a movement along one curve can cause the other curve to shift. This is especially prevalent when one analyzes goods that constitute a large percentage of the entire economy. Thus, supply and demand analysis used alone is not enough to determine where the equilibrium will be. (94)

When the "other things are constant" assumption is not realistic, feedback or ripple effects can become relevant. The degree of interdependence differs among various sets of issues. That is why there is a separate micro and macro analysis–microeconomics and macroeconomics.

The fallacy of composition is the false assumption that what is true for a part will also be true for the whole. This means that what is true in microeconomics may not be true in macroeconomics.

● SHORT-ANSWER QUESTIONS

1. What is the law of demand?

2. Draw a demand curve from the following demand table.

   Demand Table

Q	**P**
50	1
40	2
30	3
20	4

3. Demonstrate graphically a shift in demand and on another graph demonstrate movement along the demand curve.

4. State the law of supply.

5. What does the law of supply say that most individuals would do with the quantity of labor they supply employers if their wage increased? Explain the importance of substitution in this decision.

6. Draw a supply curve from the following supply table.

   Supply Table

Q	**P**
20	1
30	2
40	3
50	4

7. Demonstrate graphically the effect of a new technology that reduces the cost of producing Adele CDs on the supply of Adele CDs.

8. Demonstrate graphically the effect of a rise in the price of Adele CDs on the quantity supplied.

9. What are three things to note about supply and demand that help to explain how they interact to bring about equilibrium in a market?

10. Demonstrate graphically what happens to the equilibrium price and quantity of M&Ms if they suddenly become more popular.

11. Demonstrate graphically what happens to the equilibrium price and quantity of oranges if a frost destroys 50 percent of the orange crop.

12. What is the fallacy of composition and how is it related to why economists separate micro from macro economics?

MATCHING THE TERMS
Match the terms to their definitions

____ 1. demand

____ 2. demand curve

____ 3. equilibrium

____ 4. equilibrium price

____ 5. equilibrium quantity

____ 6. excess demand

____ 7. excess supply

____ 8. fallacy of composition

____ 9. law of demand

____ 10. law of supply

____ 11. market demand curve

____ 12. market supply curve

____ 13. movement along a demand curve

____ 14. movement along a supply curve

____ 15. quantity demanded

____ 16. quantity supplied

____ 17. shift in demand

____ 18. shift in supply

____ 19. supply

____ 20. supply curve

a. A specific amount that will be demanded per unit of time at a specific price, other things constant.

b. Curve that tells how much of a good will be bought at various prices.

c. The effect of a change in a shift factor on the supply curve.

d. Curve that tells how much will be offered for sale at various prices.

e. The graphic representation of the effect of a change in price on the quantity supplied.

f. Quantity demanded rises as price falls, other things constant.

g. Quantity supplied rises as price rises, other things constant.

h. A schedule of quantities of a good that will be bought per unit of time at various prices, other things constant.

i. Quantity supplied is greater than quantity demanded.

j. A concept in which opposing dynamic forces cancel each other out.

k. The effect of a change in a shift factor on the demand curve.

l. The price toward which the invisible hand (economic forces) drives the market.

m. The horizontal sum of all individual demand curves.

n. Amount bought and sold at the equilibrium price.

o. Quantity demanded is greater than quantity supplied.

p. The graphic representation of the effect of a change in price on the quantity demanded.

q. A specific amount that will be offered for sale per unit of time at a specific price.

r. A schedule of quantities a seller is willing to sell per unit of time at various prices, other things constant.

s. The false assumption that what is true for a part will also be true for the whole.

t. The horizontal sum of all individual supply curves.

● PROBLEMS AND APPLICATIONS

1. Draw two linear curves on the same graph from the following table, one relating P with Q_1 and the other relating P with Q_2.

P	Q_1	Q_2
$30	60	100
35	70	90
40	80	80
45	90	70

a. Label the curve that is most likely a demand curve. Explain your choice.

b. Label the curve that is most likely a supply curve. Explain your choice.

c. What is the equilibrium price and quantity? Choose points above and below that price and explain why each is not the equilibrium price.

2. Correct the following statements, if needed, so that the terms "demand," "quantity demanded," "supply," and "quantity supplied" are used correctly.

a. As the price of pizza increases, consumers demand less pizza.

b. Whenever the price of bicycles increases, the supply of bicycles increases.

c. The price of electricity is cheaper in the northwestern part of the United States and therefore the demand for electricity is greater in the northwest.

d. An increase in the incomes of car buyers will increase the quantity demanded for cars.

e. An increase in the quantity demanded of lobsters means consumers are willing and able to buy more lobsters at any given price.

f. A decrease in the supply of frog legs means suppliers will provide fewer frog legs at any given price.

3. You are given the following individual demand tables for compact discs:

Price	Juan	Philippe	Ramone
$7	3	20	50
$10	2	10	40
$13	1	7	32
$16	0	5	26
$19	0	3	20
$22	0	0	14

a. Determine the market demand table.

b. Graph the individual and market demand curves.

c. If the current market price is $13, what is the total market quantity demanded? What happens to total market quantity demanded if the price rises to $19 a disc?

d. Say that a new popular Usher compact disc hits the market that increases demand for compact discs by 25%. Show with a demand table what happens to the individual and market demand curves. Demonstrate graphically what happens to market demand.

4. The following table depicts the market supply and demand for oranges in the United States (in thousands of bushels):

Price per bushel	Quantity supplied	Quantity demanded
$15	7000	2000
$14	5500	3000
$13	4000	4000
$12	2500	5000
$11	1000	6000

a. Graph the market supply and demand for oranges.

b. What is the equilibrium price and quantity of oranges in the market? Why?

c. Suppose the price is $14. Would we observe a surplus (excess supply) or a shortage (excess demand)? If so, by how much? What could be expected to happen to the price over time? Why?

d. Suppose the price is $12. Would we observe a surplus or a shortage? If so, by how much? What could be expected to happen to the price over time? Why?

5. Draw a hypothetical demand and supply curve for Netflix movies streamed through the Internet. Show how demand or supply is affected by the following:

a. A technological breakthrough lowers the cost of streaming.

b. Consumers' income rises.

c. Movie producers charge Netflix higher prices to stream their movies.

d. The price of streaming videos using iTunes rises.

e. Possible suppliers expect streaming videos to become more popular.

6. Use supply and demand curves to help you determine the impact that each of the following events has on the market for surfboards in Southern California.

   a. Southern California experiences unusually high temperatures, sending an unusually large number of people to its beaches.

b. Large sharks are reported feeding near the beaches of Southern California.

c. Due to the large profits earned by surfboard producers there is a significant increase in the number of producers of surfboards.

d. There is a significant increase in the price of epoxy paint used to coat surfboards.

7. Use supply and demand curves to help you determine the impact that each of the following events has on the market for beef.

   a. New genetic engineering technology enables ranchers to raise healthier, heavier cattle, significantly reducing costs.

   b. The CBS program "60 Minutes" reports on the unsanitary conditions in poultry processing plants that may increase the chances of consumers getting sick by eating chicken.

c. In addition to developing new genetic engineering technology, highly credible new research results report that abundant consumption of fatty red meats actually prolongs average life expectancy.

d. Consumers expect the price of beef to fall in the near future.

● MULTIPLE CHOICE

Circle the one best answer for each of the following questions:

1. The law of demand states:
    a. quantity demanded increases as price falls, other things constant.
    b. more of a good will be demanded the higher its price, other things constant.
    c. people always want more.
    d. you can't always get what you want at the price you want.

2. There are many more substitutes for good A than for good B.
    a. The demand curve for good B will likely shift out further.
    b. The demand curve for good B will likely be flatter.
    c. You can't say anything about the likely relative flatness of the demand curves.
    d. The demand curve for good A will likely be flatter.

3. If the weather gets very hot, what will most likely happen?
    a. The supply of air conditioners will increase.
    b. Quantity of air conditioners demanded will increase.
    c. Demand for air conditioners will increase.
    d. The quality of air conditioners demanded will increase.

4. If the price of air conditioners falls, there will be:
    a. an increase in demand for air conditioners.
    b. an increase in the quantity of air conditioners demanded.
    c. an increase in the quantity of air conditioners supplied.
    d. a shift out of the supply curve for air conditioners.

5. An increase in demand:
    a. is reflected as a rightward (outward) shift of the demand curve.
    b. is caused by a decrease in price.
    c. means demanders are buying less at any price
    d. shifts the demand curve to the left (inward).

6. The demand curve will likely shift outward to the right if:
    a. society's income falls.
    b. the price of a substitute good falls.
    c. the price of the good is expected to rise in the near future.
    d. the good goes out of style.

7. The difference between the quantity demanded and demand is:
    a. the quantity demanded is associated with a whole set of prices, whereas demand is associated with a particular price.
    b. the quantity demanded is associated with a particular price, whereas demand is associated with a whole set of prices.
    c. the quantity demanded is the whole demand curve, whereas demand is a particular point along a demand curve.
    d. a change in the quantity demanded is reflected graphically as a shift of the demand curve, whereas a change in demand is reflected as movement along a given demand curve.

8. The movement in the graph below from point A to point B represents:

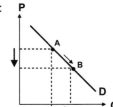

    a. an increase in demand.
    b. an increase in the quantity demanded.
    c. an increase in the quantity supplied.
    d. an increase in supply.

9. If there is a flood, what will most likely happen in the market for bottled water?
   a. Demand will increase.
   b. Demand will fall.
   c. Supply will increase.
   d. Supply will decrease.

10. Using the standard axes, the demand curve associated with the following demand table is:

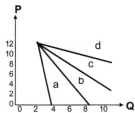

Demand Table

P	Q
7	5
9	4
11	3

   a. a
   b. b
   c. c
   d. d

11. To derive a market demand curve from two individual demand curves:
   a. one adds the two demand curves horizontally.
   b. one adds the two demand curves vertically.
   c. one subtracts one demand curve from the other demand curve.
   d. one adds the demand curves both horizontally and vertically.

12. The market demand curve will always:
   a. be unrelated to the individual demand curves and slope.
   b. be steeper than the individual demand curves that make it up.
   c. have the same slope as the individual demand curves that make it up.
   d. be flatter than the individual demand curves that make it up.

13. The law of supply states that:
   a. quantity supplied increases as price increases, other things constant.
   b. quantity supplied decreases as price increases, other things constant.
   c. more of a good will be supplied the higher its price, other things changing proportionately.
   d. less of a good will be supplied the higher its price, other things changing proportionately.

14. In the graph below, the arrow refers to:

   a. a shift in demand.
   b. a shift in supply.
   c. a change in the quantity demanded.
   d. a change in the quantity supplied.

15. If there is an improvement in technology one would expect:
   a. a movement along the supply curve.
   b. a shift upward (or to the left) of the supply curve.
   c. a shift downward (or to the right) of the supply curve.
   d. a movement down along the supply curve.

16. You're the supplier of a good and suddenly a number of your long-lost friends call you to buy your product. Your good is most likely:
   a. in excess supply.
   b. in excess demand.
   c. in equilibrium.
   d. in both excess supply and demand.

17. At which point on the graph below will you expect the strongest downward pressure on prices?

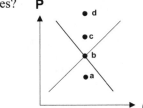

   a. a.
   b. b.
   c. c.
   d. d.

18. If at some price the quantity supplied exceeds the quantity demanded, then:
   a. a surplus (excess supply) exists and the price will fall over time as sellers competitively bid down the price.
   b. a shortage (excess demand) exists and the price will rise over time as buyers competitively bid up the price.
   c. the price is below equilibrium.
   d. equilibrium will be reestablished as the demand curve shifts to the left.

19. If the price of a good:
    a. rises, it is a response to a surplus (excess supply).
    b. falls, it is a response to a shortage (excess demand).
    c. is below equilibrium, then a shortage will be observed.
    d. is below equilibrium, then a surplus will be observed.

20. If the demand for a good increases, you will expect price to:
    a. fall and quantity to rise.
    b. rise and quantity to rise.
    c. fall and quantity to fall.
    d. rise and quantity to fall.

21. If the supply of a good decreases, you will expect price to:
    a. fall and quantity to rise.
    b. rise and quantity to rise.
    c. fall and quantity to fall.
    d. rise and quantity to fall.

22. Consider the market for bikinis. If bikinis suddenly become more fashionable, you will expect:
    a. a temporary shortage of bikinis that will be eliminated over time as the market price of bikinis rises and a greater quantity is bought and sold.
    b. a temporary shortage of bikinis that will be eliminated over time as the market price of bikinis rises and a smaller quantity is bought and sold.
    c. a temporary surplus of bikinis that will be eliminated over time as the market price of bikinis falls and a smaller quantity is bought and sold.
    d. a temporary surplus of bikinis that will be eliminated over time as the market price of bikinis rises and a greater quantity is bought and sold.

23. Compared to last year, fewer oranges are being purchased and the selling price has decreased. This could have been caused by:
    a. an increase in demand.
    b. an increase in supply.
    c. a decrease in demand.
    d. a decrease in supply.

24. If demand and supply both increase, this will cause:
    a. an increase in the equilibrium quantity, but an uncertain effect on the equilibrium price.
    b. an increase in the equilibrium price, but an uncertain effect on the equilibrium quantity.
    c. an increase in the equilibrium price and quantity.
    d. a decrease in the equilibrium price and quantity.

25. An increase in demand for a good will cause:
    a. excess demand (a shortage) until price changes.
    b. movement down along the demand curve as price changes.
    c. movement down along the supply curve as price changes.
    d. a higher price and a smaller quantity traded in the market.

26. The fallacy of composition is:
    a. the false assumption that what is false for a part will also be false for the whole.
    b. the false assumption that what is true for a part will also be true for the whole.
    c. the false assumption that what is false for a whole will also be false for the part.
    d. the false assumption that what is true for a whole will also be true for the part.

● POTENTIAL ESSAY QUESTIONS

You may also see essay questions similar to the "Problems & Applications" exercises.

1. Many university campuses sell parking permits to their students allowing them to park on campus in designated areas. Although most students complain about the relatively high cost of these parking permits, what annoys many students even more is that after having paid for their permits, vacant parking spaces in the designated lots are very difficult to find during much of the day. Many end up having to park off campus anyway, where permits are not required. Assuming the university is unable to build new parking facilities on campus due to insufficient funds, what recommendation might you make to remedy the problem of students with permits being unable to find places to park on campus?

2. Discuss how changes in demand or supply impact a market equilibrium.

ANSWERS

SHORT-ANSWER QUESTIONS

1. The law of demand states that the quantity of a good demanded is inversely related to the good's price, other things constant. (78)

2. To derive a demand curve from a demand table, plot each point of the demand table on a graph and connect the points. This is shown on the graph below. (81-82)

3. A shift in demand is shown by a shift of the entire demand curve resulting from a change in a shift factor of demand as shown in the graph below on the left (which illustrates an increase in demand because it is a rightward shift). A movement along a demand curve is shown on the right as a movement from point A to point B due to a price decrease. (79 and Figure 4-2 on page 80)

4. The law of supply states that the quantity supplied rises as price rises, other things constant. Or alternatively: quantity supplied falls as price falls. (84)

5. The law of supply states that quantity supplied rises as price rises; quantity supplied falls as price falls. According to this law, most individuals would choose to supply a greater quantity of labor hours if their wage increased. They will substitute work for leisure. (Figure 4-5 on page 85)

6. To derive a supply curve from a supply table, you plot each point on the supply table on a graph and connect the points. This is shown on the graph in the next column. (87)

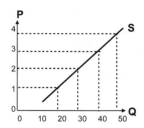

7. A new technology that reduces the cost of producing Adele CDs will shift the entire supply curve to the right from S_0 to S_1, as shown in the graph below. (86-87)

8. A rise in the price of Adele CDs from P_0 to P_1 results in a movement up along a supply curve and the quantity of Adele CDs supplied will rise from Q_0 to Q_1 as shown in the graph below. (86-87)

    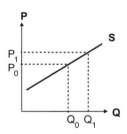

9. The first thing to note is that when quantity demanded is greater than quantity supplied, prices tend to rise and when quantity supplied is greater than quantity demanded, prices tend to fall. Each case is demonstrated in the graph below. Price tends away from P_1 and P_2 and toward P_0.

    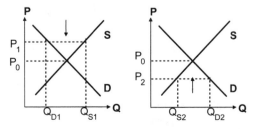

    The second thing to note is that the larger the difference between quantity supplied and quantity demanded, the greater the pressure on prices to rise (if there is excess demand; a shortage) or fall (if there is excess supply; a surplus). This is demonstrated in the graph below. At P_2, the pressure for prices to fall toward P_0 is greater than the pressure at P_1 because excess supply (surplus) is greater at P_2 compared to excess supply at P_1.

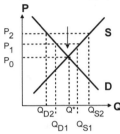

The third thing to note is that when quantity demanded equals quantity supplied, the market is in equilibrium. This is shown graphically at the point of intersection between the demand and supply curves. (89-91)

10. Increasing popularity of M&Ms means that at every price, more M&Ms are demanded. The demand curve shifts out to the right from D_0 to D_1, and both equilibrium price and quantity rise to P_1 and Q_1 respectively. (92-93)

11. A frost damaging oranges means that at every price, suppliers will supply fewer oranges. The supply curve shifts in to the left from S_0 to S_1, and equilibrium price rises to P_1, and quantity traded falls to Q_1. (92-93)

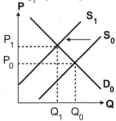

12. The fallacy of composition is the false assumption that what is true for a part will also be true for the whole. In micro, economists isolate an individual person's or firm's behavior and consider its effects, while the many side effects are kept in the background. In macro, those

side effects become too large and can no longer be held constant. These side effects are what account for the interdependence of supply and demand. Macro, thus, is not simply a summation of all micro results; it would be a fallacy of composition to take the sum of each individual's (micro) actions and say that this will be the aggregate (macro) result. (94)

━━━━━ ANSWERS ━━━━━

MATCHING

1-h; 2-b; 3-j; 4-l; 5-n; 6-o; 7-i; 8-s; 9-f; 10-g; 11-m; 12-t; 13-p; 14-e; 15-a; 16-q; 17-k 18-c; 19-r; 20-d.

━━━━━ ANSWERS ━━━━━

PROBLEMS AND APPLICATIONS

1. The linear curves are shown on the right. See Figure 4-8 on page 91.

   a. As shown in the graph, the downward sloping curve is a demand curve. We deduce this from the law of demand: Quantity demanded rises (falls) as the price decreases (increases). (78)

   b. As shown in the graph, the upward sloping curve is a supply curve. We deduce this from the law of supply: Quantity supplied rises (falls) as the price rises (falls). (84-85)

   c. The equilibrium price and quantity are where the demand and supply curves intersect. This is at $P = \$40$, $Q = 80$. At a price above $40, such as $45, quantity supplied exceeds quantity demanded and there is pressure for price to fall. At a price below $40, such as $35, quantity demanded exceeds quantity supplied and there is pressure for price to rise. (89)

2. a. As the price of pizza increases, the *quantity demanded* of pizza decreases. (79)

Note that a change in the price of an item will cause a change in the quantity demanded; not a change in demand! A change in something else other than the price may cause a change in demand– such as a change in one of the shift factors of demand discussed in the textbook.

b. Whenever the price of bicycles increases, the *quantity of bicycles supplied* also increases. (84-85)

Note that a change in the price will cause a change in the quantity supplied; not supply! A change in something else other than the price–such as a change in one of the shift factors of supply discussed in the textbook–may cause a change in supply.

c. The price of electricity is cheaper in the NW part of the U. S. and therefore the *quantity demanded* of electricity is greater in the NW. (79)

d. An increase in incomes of car buyers will increase the *demand* for cars. (79)

Notice that a change in a shift factor of demand, such as income, will change demand; not the quantity demanded!

e. An increase in the *demand* for lobsters means consumers are willing and able to buy more lobsters at any given price (whatever the current price is). (79)

In order for there to be an increase in the quantity demanded there would have to be a decrease in the price. Moreover, recall that an increase in demand is reflected as a rightward shift of the demand curve. Upon viewing a graph where the demand curve has shifted to the right you will see that more will be purchased at any given price.

f. This is a correct use of the term "supply." Notice that a decrease in supply is reflected graphically as a leftward shift of the curve and less will be provided in the market at any given price. (84-85)

3. a. The market demand table is the summation of individual quantities demanded at each price as follows (82-83):

P	Q
$7	73
10	52
13	40
16	31
19	23
22	14

b. The individual and market demand curves are shown to the right of the demand table. (82-83)

c. At $13 a disc, total market quantity demanded is 40 discs. Total market quantity demanded falls to 23 when the price of discs rises to $19 per disc. (82-83)

d. Quantity demanded at each price rises by 25% for each individual and for the market as a whole. The new demand table is shown below. Graphically, both the individual and market demand curves shift to the right. The graph below shows the rightward shift in market demand. (82-83)

Price	Juan	Philippe	Ramone	Market
$7	3.75	25	62.50	91.25
$10	2.50	12.5	50	65
$13	1.25	8.75	40	50
$16	0	6.25	32.5	38.75
$19	0	3.75	25	28.75
$21	0	0	17.5	17.5

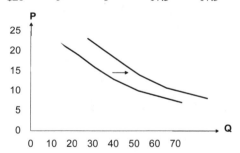

4. a. See the graph below. (See Figure 4-8 on page 91.)

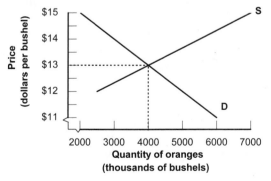

b. The equilibrium price is $13, the equilibrium quantity is 4000. This is an equilibrium because the quantity supplied equals the quantity demanded at this price. That is, there is neither a surplus (excess supply) nor a shortage (excess demand) and hence no tendency for the price to change. (89-90)

c. Because the quantity supplied exceeds the quantity demanded when the price is $14 per bushel, we would observe a surplus of 2500 bushels (in thousands of bushels). We can expect the price of oranges per bushel to fall as sellers scramble to rid themselves of their excess supplies. (89-90)

d. Because the quantity demanded exceeds the quantity supplied at $12 per bushel, we would observe a shortage of 2500 bushels (in thousands of bushels). We can expect the price of oranges per bushel to rise as some buyers competitively bid up the price just to get some oranges. (89-90)

5. A hypothetical market for Netflix streamed video shows an upward sloping supply curve, a downward sloping demand curve and an equilibrium price and quantity where the two curves intersect.

   a. A technological breakthrough that lowers the cost of streaming will shift the supply of streamed Netflix movies to the right as shown in the graph below. (86-87)

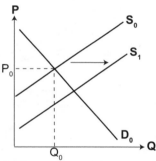

   b. A rise in consumers' income will shift the demand for streamed Netflix movies to the right as shown in the graph below. (80-81)

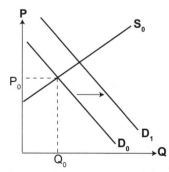

   c. Higher usage fees imposed by movie producers to Netflix will shift the supply of

streamed movies to the left as shown in the graph below. (86-87)

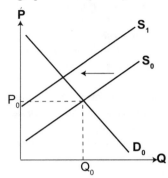

   d. If the price of iTune movies rises, the demand for cyber cafes will shift to the right as shown in the graph for the answer to part *b*. (86-87)

   e. If possible suppliers expect streamed movies to become more popular, the supply of streamed Netflix movies will shift to the right as shown in the graph for the answer to part *a*. (86-87)

6. a. This will increase the demand for surf-boards shifting the demand curve to the right. At the original price a temporary shortage would be observed putting upward pressure on price. We end up with a higher equilibrium price and a greater equilibrium quantity as illustrated in the graph below. (*When dealing with a change in D or S curves, just remember to go from the initial point of intersection to the new point of intersection. The initial point of intersection will give you the initial equilibrium P and Q and the new point of intersection the new equilibrium P and Q. Then recall that if the price went up in the market, it was a response to a temporary shortage (excess demand). If the equilibrium price went down, then it was a response to a temporary surplus (excess supply). (92-93)*

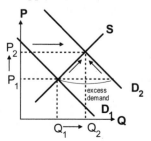

b. This would cause a decrease in the demand for surfboards shifting the demand curve to the left. At the original price a temporary surplus would be observed putting downward pressure on price. We end up with a lower equilibrium price and a lower equilibrium quantity, as illustrated in the graph below. (92-93)

c. This would cause an increase in the supply of surfboards, shifting the supply curve to the right. At the original price a temporary surplus would be observed, putting downward pressure on price. We end up with a lower equilibrium price and a higher equilibrium quantity, as illustrated in the graph below. (92-93)

d. This would cause a decrease in the supply of surfboards, shifting the supply curve to the left. At the original price a temporary shortage would be observed, putting upward pressure on price. We end up with a higher equilibrium price and a lower equilibrium quantity, as illustrated in the graph below. (92-93)

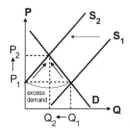

7. **a.** An increase in production technology will increase the supply of beef. The temporary surplus (excess supply) of beef at the original price will cause the market price to fall. Eventually we get a lower equilibrium price of beef and a greater amount bought and sold in the market. (92-93)

b. Chicken and beef are substitute goods—they can be used instead of each other. Therefore, this "60 Minutes" report will likely increase the demand for beef. The temporary shortage (excess demand) at the original price will cause the price to be competitively bid up. Eventually we observe a higher equilibrium price and a greater equilibrium quantity. (92-93)

c. The new development would increase the supply of beef while the reports of the health benefits of beef would increase the demand for beef. Quantity of beef sold would definitely rise. The impact on equilibrium price, however, depends upon the relative sizes of the shifts. (92-93)

d. Because people will postpone their purchases of beef until the price decreases, the demand for beef will fall today. A decrease in demand is reflected as a leftward shift of the demand curve. The temporary excess supply (surplus) that is created at the original price puts downward pressure on the market price of beef. Eventually we get a lower equilibrium price and quantity. (92-93)

━━━━━━━ **ANSWERS** ━━━━━━━

MULTIPLE CHOICE

1. **a** As discussed on page 78, the correct answer is a. A possible answer is d, which is a restatement of the law of demand, but since the actual law was among the choices, and is more precise, a is the correct answer.

2. **d** An equal rise in price will cause individuals to switch more to other goods when there are more substitutes. See page 78.

3. **c** As discussed on pages 79-80, it is important to distinguish between a change in the quantity demanded and a change in demand. Weather is a shift factor of demand, so demand, not quantity demanded, will increase. Supply will not increase; the quantity supplied will, however. Who knows what will happen to the quality demanded? We don't.

4. b   As discussed on pages 78-80, when the price falls there is a movement along the demand curve which is expressed by saying the quantity demanded increased. Moreover, as the price falls, the quantity supplied falls.

5. a   As discussed on pages 79-81, an increase in demand is expressed as an outward (or rightward) shift of the demand curve. It is caused by something other than the price. It means people will buy more at any price or pay a higher price for a given quantity demanded.

6. c   All of these are shift factors of demand. However, only c will increase demand and shift the demand curve to the right. See pages 80-81.

7. b   As is discussed on pages 79-80, b is the only correct response.

8. b   The curve slopes downward, so we can surmise that it is a demand curve; and the two points are on the demand curve, so the movement represents an increase in the quantity demanded, not an increase in demand. Moreover, as price falls, the quantity demanded rises. A shift in demand would be a shift of the entire curve. See the figures on page 80.

9. a   A flood will likely bring about a significant increase in the demand for bottled water since a flood makes most other water undrinkable. A flood would be a shift factor of demand for bottled water. See pages 79-80.

10. b   This demand curve is the only demand curve that goes through all the points in the table. See pages 81-82.

11. a   As discussed in the text on pages 82-83 (Figure 4-4), market demand curves are determined by adding individuals' demand curves horizontally. That is, you add the quantities demanded at each price.

12. d   Since the market demand curve is derived by adding the individual demand curves horizontally, it will always be flatter. See pages 82-83 and Figure 4-4.

13. a   As discussed on page 84, the law of supply is stated in a. The others either have the movement in the wrong direction or are not holding all other things constant.

14. b   It is a shift in supply because the curve is upward sloping; and it's a shift of the entire curve, so it is not a movement along. See pages 85-86 and Figure 4-6.

15. c   As discussed on pages 86-87, technology is a shift factor of supply so it must be a shift of the supply curve. Since it is an improvement, it must be a shift rightward (or downward). See also Figure 4-6 on page 86.

16. b   When there is excess demand, demanders start searching for new suppliers, as discussed on page 89.

17. d   The greater the extent to which the quantity supplied exceeds the quantity demanded, the greater the surplus (excess supply) and the greater the pressure for the price to fall. See page 90.

18. a   As discussed on page 89, there is a surplus (excess supply) when the price is above equilibrium. A surplus will motivate sellers to reduce price to rid themselves of their excess supplies. As the price falls, the quantity demand rises and the quantity supplied falls; demand and supply curves do *not* shift.

19. c   As discussed on page 89, whenever price is below equilibrium, a shortage is observed, and price rises.

20. b   Since this statement says demand increases, then the demand curve shifts rightward. There is no change in the supply curve. Assuming an upward sloping supply curve, that means that price will rise and quantity will rise. See pages 92-93.

21. d   Since this statement says supply decreases, then the supply curve shifts

leftward. There is no change in the demand curve. Assuming a downward sloping demand curve, that means that price will rise and quantity will fall. See pages 92-93.

22. a The demand for bikinis would rise, shifting the demand curve to the right. The supply curve does not change. This creates a temporary shortage that is eliminated over time as the market moves to its new equilibrium at a higher price and a greater quantity traded. See pages 92-93.

23. c Only a decrease in demand will result in a decrease in quantity and a decrease in price. See pages 92-93.

24. a An increase in demand has a tendency to increase price and increase the quantity. An increase in supply has a tendency to *decrease* the price and increase the quantity. So, on balance, we are certain of an increase in the equilibrium quantity, but we are uncertain about the impact on the price in the market. See pages 92-93.

25. a An increase in demand causes the quantity demanded to exceed the quantity supplied, creating excess demand (a shortage). This increases the price causing movement *up* along the demand and supply curves resulting in a *greater* quantity traded in the market. See pages 92-93.

26. b The fallacy of composition is the false assumption that what is true for a part will also be true for the whole. See page 93.

═══════ **ANSWERS** ═══════

POTENTIAL ESSAY QUESTIONS

The following are annotated answers. They indicate the general idea behind the answer.

1. The shortage of parking spaces implies that permit prices are below equilibrium. The price of a permit should be increased. At least with the purchase of a permit you could be reasonably certain that a space would be available.

2. Suppose there is an increase in demand. The demand curve shifts out to the right, creating a temporary shortage (excess demand) at the original price. As a result, buyers competitively bid up the price. As the price rises, the quantity demanded falls (movement up along the demand curve toward the new point of intersection) and the quantity supplied rises (movement up along the supply curve toward the new point of intersection). Eventually, the price rises enough until the quantity demanded is once again equal to the quantity supplied. Because there is neither a shortage nor a surplus at this new point of intersection, the new market equilibrium price and quantity is obtained. The market equilibrium price and quantity will both increase as a result of an increase in demand. *You should be able to illustrate this graphically as well.*

USING SUPPLY AND DEMAND

5

CHAPTER AT A GLANCE

1. Changes (shifts) in demand and supply are what cause changes in the price and the quantity traded in real-world markets. (100-103)

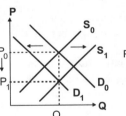

2. Price ceilings cause shortages; price floors cause surpluses. (103-107)

    A price ceiling is a legal price set by government below equilibrium. An example is rent controls. A price floor is a legal price set by government above equilibrium. An example is the minimum wage.

3. Excise taxes and tariffs raise price and reduce quantity. Quantity restrictions also decrease supply (shift the supply curve up, to the left) raising the price and reducing the quantity. 107-109)

Any excise tax imposed on suppliers shifts the supply curve up by the amount of the tax. Quantity restrictions also decrease supply.

With tax t, price rises to P_2 and the government collects revenue shown by the shaded region. A quantity restriction of Q_2 has the same effect on price and quantity.

4. In a third-party payer system, the consumer and the one who pays the cost differ. In third-party payer systems quantity demanded, price, and total spending are greater than when the consumer pays. (109-111)

The graph below shows the effects of a third-party payer market. In a free market, given the supply and demand curve shown, equilibrium price is P_1 and equilibrium quantity is Q_1. If the co-payment, however, is P_0, the consumer purchases quantity Q_2. The supplier will only sell that quantity at price P_2, so the third party pays the difference $(P_2 - P_0)$. Under a third-party payer system, total expenditures are larger—shown by the larger shaded square—than a free market—shown by the smaller and darker shaded square.

See also, "Appendix A: Algebraic Representation of Supply, Demand, and Equilibrium."

● SHORT-ANSWER QUESTIONS

1. Demonstrate graphically what happens in the following situation: Income in the U.S. rose in the 1990s and more and more people began to buy luxury items such as caviar. However, about that same time, the dissolution of the Soviet Union threw suppliers of caviar from the Caspian Sea into a mire of bureaucracy, reducing their ability to export caviar. Market: Caviar sold in the United States.

2. What is a price ceiling? Demonstrate graphically the effect of a price ceiling on a market.

3. What is a price floor? Demonstrate graphically the effect of a price floor on a market.

4. Why are rent controls likely to worsen an existing shortage of housing?

5. Demonstrate graphically what happens to equilibrium price and quantity when a tariff is imposed on imports.

6. What is a third-party payer system? Name one example.

MATCHING THE TERMS
Match the terms to their definitions

___ 1.	excise tax	a.	The law that sets lowest wage a firm can legally pay an employee.
___ 2.	minimum wage law		
___ 3.	price ceiling	b.	Tax on an imported good.
___ 4.	price floor	c.	Tax that is levied on a specific good.
___ 5.	rent control	d.	The person who decides how much of the good to buy differs from the person paying for the good.
___ 6.	tariff		
___ 7.	third-party payer market	e.	A government-imposed limit on how high a price can be charged.
		f.	Price ceiling on rents set by government.
		g.	A government-imposed limit on how low a price can be charged.

PROBLEMS AND APPLICATIONS

1. Suppose you are told that the price of Cadillacs has increased from last year, as has the number bought and sold. Is this an exception to the law of demand, or has there been a change in demand or supply that could account for this?

2. The following table depicts the market supply and demand for milk in the United States.

Price in dollars per gal.	Quantity of gal. supplied in 1,000s	Quantity of gal. demanded in 1,000s
$1.50	600	800
$1.75	620	720
$2.00	640	640
$2.25	660	560
$2.50	680	480

    a. Graph the market supply and demand for milk.

    b. What is the equilibrium market price and quantity in the market?

    c. Show the effect of a government-imposed price floor of $2.25 on the quantity supplied and quantity demanded.

    d. Show the effect of a government-imposed price ceiling of $1.75 on the quantity supplied and quantity demanded.

    e. What would happen to equilibrium price and quantity if the government imposes a $1 per gallon tax on the sellers and as a result, at every price supply decreases by 100,000 gallons? What price would the sellers receive?

3. Suppose the U.S. government imposes stricter entry barriers on Japanese cars imported into the United States. This could be accomplished by the U.S. government either raising tariffs or imposing a quantity restriction (such as a quota).

    a. What impact would this have on the market for Japanese cars in the United States?

    b. What impact would this likely have on the market for American-made cars in the United States?

    c. What do you think could motivate the U.S. government to pursue these stricter entry barriers on Japanese cars coming into the U.S.?

    d. Would Japanese car manufacturers prefer a tariff or a quota? Why?

4. Describe what likely happens to market price and quantity for the particular goods in each of the following cases:

    a. A technological breakthrough lowers the costs of producing tractors in India while there is an increase in incomes of all citizens in India. Market: Tractors.

    b. The United States imposes a ban on the sale of oil by companies that do business with Libya and Iran. At the same time, very surprisingly, a large reserve of drillable oil is discovered in Barrington, Rhode Island. Market: Oil.

    c. In the summer of 2004, many people watched the Summer Olympics on television instead of going to the movies. At the same time, thinking that summer is the peak season for movies, Hollywood released a record number of movies. Market: Movie tickets.

    d. After a promotional visit by Michael Jordan to France, a craze for Nike Air shoes develops, while workers in Nike's manufacturing plants in China go on strike, decreasing the production of these shoes. Market: Nike shoes.

A1. The supply and demand equations for strawberries are given by $Q_s = -10 + 5P$ and $Q_d = 20 - 5P$ respectively, where P is price in dollars per quart, Q_s is millions of quarts of strawberries supplied, and Q_d is millions of quarts of strawberries demanded.

    a. What is the equilibrium market price and quantity for strawberries in the market?

    b. Suppose a new preservative is introduced that prevents more strawberries from rotting on their way from the farm to the store. As a result, the supply of strawberries increases by 20 million quarts at every price. What effect does this have on market price and quantity sold?

    c. Given the original supply, now suppose it has been found that the spray used on cherry trees has ill effects on those who eat the cherries. As a result, the demand for strawberries increases by 10 million quarts at every price. What effect does this have on market price for strawberries and quantity of strawberries sold?

A2. The supply and demand equations for roses are given by $Q_s = -10 + 3P$ and $Q_d = 20 - 2P$ respectively, where P is dollars per dozen roses and Q is dozens of roses in hundred thousands.

    a. What is the equilibrium market price and quantity of roses sold?

    b. Suppose the government decides to make it more affordable for individuals to give roses to their significant others, and sets a price ceiling for roses at $4 a dozen. What is the likely result?

c. Suppose the government decides to tax the suppliers of roses $1 per dozen roses sold. What is the equilibrium price and quantity in the market? How much do buyers pay for each dozen they buy for their significant others? How much do suppliers receive for each dozen they sell?

d. Suppose the government decides instead to impose a $1 tax on buyers for each dozen roses purchased. (Government has determined buying roses for love to be a demerit good.) What is the equilibrium price and quantity in the market? How much do the buyers pay and how much do the sellers receive?

● MULTIPLE CHOICE

Circle the one best answer for each of the following questions:

1. If a frost in Florida damages oranges, what will likely happen to the market for Florida oranges?
a. Demand will increase.
b. Demand will fall.
c. Supply will increase.
d. Supply will decrease.

2. Assume that the cost of shipping automobiles from the United States to Japan decreases. What will most likely happen to the selling price and quantity of cars made in the U.S. and sold in Japan?
a. The price will rise, and quantity will fall.
b. Both price and quantity will rise.
c. The price will fall, and quantity will rise.
d. The price will fall. What happens to quantity is not clear.

3. Assuming standard supply and demand curves, what will likely happen to the price and quantity of cricket bats in Trinidad as interest in cricket dwindles following the dismal performance of the national cricket team, while at the same time taxes are repealed on producing cricket bats?
a. The price will decrease, but what happens to quantity is not clear.
b. The price will decrease, and quantity will increase.
c. The price will increase, but what happens to quantity is not clear.
d. It is not clear what happens to either price or quantity.

4. A higher equilibrium price with no change in market equilibrium quantity could be caused by:
a. supply shifting in and no change in demand.
b. supply and demand both increasing.
c. a decrease in supply and an increase in demand.
d. demand and supply both shifting in.

5. Referring to the graph below, if there is a price ceiling imposed on this market of P_2, consumers will pay:

a. P_1 and buy quantity Q_1.
b. P_2 and buy quantity Q_2.
c. P_0 and buy quantity Q_0.
d. P_2 and buy quantity Q_0.

6. Referring to the graph below, if there is a price floor imposed on this market of P_2, consumers will pay:

a. P_1 and buy quantity Q_1.
b. P_2 and buy quantity Q_2.
c. P_0 and buy quantity Q_0.
d. P_2 and buy quantity Q_0.

7. Effective rent controls:
   a. are examples of price floors.
   b. cause the quantity of rental occupied housing demanded to exceed the quantity supplied.
   c. create a greater amount of higher quality housing to be made available to renters.
   d. create a surplus of rental occupied housing.

8. An increase in the minimum wage can be expected to:
   a. cause unemployment for some workers.
   b. cause a shortage of workers.
   c. increase employment.
   d. help businesses by reducing their costs of production.

9. A tariff:
   a. is a tax imposed on an imported good.
   b. is a quantitative restriction on the amount that one country can export to another.
   c. imposed on a good will shift the supply of that good outward to the right.
   d. will reduce the price paid by the consumer of the good.

10. Quantity restrictions on supply imposed below equilibrium quantity on a market:
    a. increase price and reduce quantity traded.
    b. increase price and increase quantity traded.
    c. decrease price and reduce quantity traded.
    d. decrease price and increase quantity traded.

11. Referring to the graph below, suppose initial supply is represented by S_0. A tax T on suppliers will raise the price that:

a. suppliers receive net of the tax to P_0.
b. suppliers receive net of the tax to P_1.
c. consumers pay to P_2.
d. consumers pay to P_3.

12. In a third-party payer system:
    a. the person who chooses the product pays the entire cost.
    b. the quantity demanded would be lower than it otherwise would be.
    c. the quantity demanded will be higher than it otherwise would be.
    d. consumers are hurt.

13. In the graph below that demonstrates a third-party payer market, suppose the consumer is required to make a co-payment of P_0. Which of the following areas represents the cost of the program to the third party?

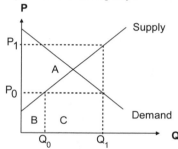

a. Rectangle A.
b. Rectangle B.
c. Rectangle C.
d. The sum of rectangles A, B, and C.

14. Third-party payer markets result in:
    a. a lower equilibrium price received by the supplier.
    b. a smaller quantity supplied.
    c. a smaller quantity demanded.
    d. increased total spending.

A1. The supply and demand equations for Nantucket Nectar's Kiwi-berry juice are given by $Q_s = -4 + 5P$ and $Q_d = 18 - 6P$ respectively, where price is dollars per quart and quantity is thousands of quarts. The equilibrium market price and quantity is:
    a. $P = \$2$, $Q = 6$ thousand quarts.
    b. $P = \$3$, $Q = 5$ thousand quarts.
    c. $P = \$14$, $Q = 66$ thousand quarts.
    d. $P = \$22$, $Q = 106$ thousand quarts.

A2. The supply and demand equations for sidewalk snow removal in a small town in Montana are given by $Q_s = -50 + 5P$ and $Q_d = 100 - 5P$ respectively, where price is in dollars per removal and quantity is numbers of removals per week. It snows so much that demand for sidewalk snow removals increases by 30 removals per week. The new equilibrium market price and quantity is:

a. $P = \$15$, $Q = 6$ sidewalk snow removals.
b. $P = \$15$, $Q = 5$ sidewalk snow removals.
c. $P = \$18$, $Q = 66$ sidewalk snow removals.
d. $P = \$18$, $Q = 40$ sidewalk snow removals.

A3. The supply and demand equations for Arizona Ice Tea in Arizona are given by $Q_s = -10 + 6P$ and $Q_d = 40 - 8P$; P is the price of each bottle in dollars; and quantity is in hundreds of thousands of bottles per month. Suppose the state government imposes a $1 per bottle tax on the suppliers. The market price the suppliers receive and the equilibrium quantity in the market are:

a. $3 per bottle and 800 thousand bottles per month.
b. $3 per bottle and 1,600 thousand bottles per month.
c. $4 per bottle and 800 thousand bottles per month.
d. $4 per bottle and 1,600 thousand bottles per month.

● POTENTIAL ESSAY QUESTIONS

You may also see essay questions similar to the "Problems & Applications" exercises.

1. Who wins and who loses with a minimum wage? Explain your answer. How might it help those who had been unemployed without the minimum wage?

2. Explain why a third-party payer system results in a greater quantity demanded and increases total spending.

ANSWERS

SHORT-ANSWER QUESTIONS

1. The demand curve for Russian caviar shifts out; supply shifts in; the price rises substantially. What happens to quantity depends upon the relative sizes of the shifts. (100-103)

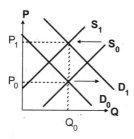

2. A price ceiling is a government-imposed limit on how high a price can be charged. An effective price ceiling below market equilibrium price will cause $Q_D > Q_S$ (a shortage) as shown in the graph below. (103-105)

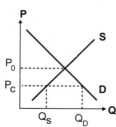

3. A price floor is a government-imposed limit on how low a price can be charged. An effective price floor above market equilibrium price will cause $Q_S > Q_D$ (a surplus) as shown in the graph below. (106-107)

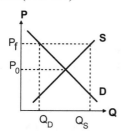

4. Rent controls are price ceilings and result in shortages in rental housing. As time passes and as the population rises, the demand for rental housing rises. On the supply side, other ventures become more lucrative relative to renting out housing. Owners have less incentive to repair existing buildings, let alone build new ones, reducing the supply of rental housing over time. As a result, the shortage becomes more acute over time (104-105)

5. A tariff is an excise tax paid by foreign producers on an imported good. As a tariff of t is imposed, the supply curve shifts upward to S_1 by the amount of the tariff. The equilibrium price goes up and quantity goes down. (107-108)

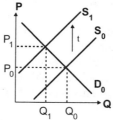

6. In a third-party payer system the person who decides how much of a good to buy differs from the person who pays for the good. One example is the health care system in the United States today. (109-111)

ANSWERS

MATCHING

1-c; 2-a; 3-e; 4-g; 5-f; 6-b; 7-d.

ANSWERS

PROBLEMS AND APPLICATIONS

1. This is not an exception to the law of demand (there are very few exceptions). Instead, an increase in demand could account for a higher price and a greater amount bought and sold, as is illustrated in the figure below. (102-103)

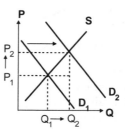

2. **a.** The market supply and demand for milk is graphed below. (100-103)

   b. The equilibrium market price is $2 and equilibrium quantity in the market is 640 thousand gallons of milk because the quantity supplied equals the quantity demanded. This is point *A* on the graph above. (100-103)

   c. A government-imposed price floor of $2.25 is shown in the figure below. Since it is a price above market price, quantity supplied (660) exceeds quantity demanded (560) by 100 thousand gallons. (106-107)

   d. A government-imposed price ceiling of $1.75 is below market price. Quantity supplied (620 thousand gallons) will be less than quantity demanded (720 thousand gallons) by 100 thousand gallons, as shown below. (103-104)

   e. Because of the tax, the quantity supplied at every price level will decline by 100 thousand gallons. The supply and demand table will change as follows:

Price in dollars per gal.	Quantity of gal. supplied 1,000s	Quantity of gal. demanded 1,000s
$1.50	500	800
$1.75	520	720
$2.00	540	640
$2.25	560	560
$2.50	580	480

The market equilibrium price would be $2.25 and the equilibrium quantity would be 560 thousand gallons. Since the sellers will have to pay $1 tax on every gallon they sell, they will receive $1.25 per gallon of milk. (107-109)

3. **a.** A higher tariff or a stricter quota imposed on Japanese cars would decrease the supply of Japanese cars in the United States. The upward (leftward) shift of the supply curve, such as from S_1 to S_2 shown in the figure below, creates a temporary shortage (excess demand) at the original price that puts upward pressure on the prices of Japanese cars. The result over time will be higher prices for Japanese cars, as well as a decrease in the amount bought and sold in the U.S. market, as shown below. (107-109)

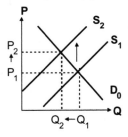

   b. Because Japanese and American-made cars are substitutes for each other, some people will switch from buying the now relatively more expensive Japanese cars (law of demand in action) to buying more American-made cars. (Notice that "relative" prices are what are relevant.) This increases the demand for American-made cars, increasing their prices as well as the amount bought and sold. This is illustrated in the figure following. (107-109)

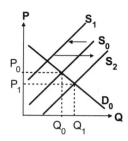

c. These trade barriers may be advocated by American car manufacturers. They could obviously benefit from the higher prices and greater sales. American automotive workers could also benefit from the greater job security that comes with more cars being produced and sold. These "special interest groups" may put political pressure on government, and the government may succumb to that pressure. (107-109)

d. The Japanese would prefer a quota over a tariff. This is because a tariff would require them to pay taxes to the U.S. government, while a quota would not. (107-108)

4. a. The supply curve will shift out from S_0 to S_1 as the new technology makes it cheaper to produce tractors. Increased incomes will shift the demand for tractors out from D_0 to D_1. Equilibrium price may go up, remain the same, or go down, depending on the relative shifts in the two curves. Equilibrium quantity, however, will definitely increase. (100-103)

b. The ban on the companies doing business with Libya and Iran will shift the supply curve in from S_0 to S_1. The discovery of oil will, however, shift it back out to possibly S_2. Depending on the relative shifts, equilibrium price and quantity will change. In the case shown in the diagram, the shift resulting from the discovery of the new oil source dominates the shift resulting from the ban, and the equilibrium price falls and quantity goes up. (100-103)

c. With more people watching the Olympics, the demand for movies shifts in from D_0 to D_1. At the same time the increased supply of movies will shift the supply curve out from S_0 to S_1. Equilibrium price will fall, while the change in equilibrium quantity will depend on the relative shifts in the curves. (100-103)

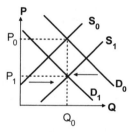

d. With more people demanding Nike Air shoes, the demand curve will shift out from D_0 to D_1. The worker strike will, however, reduce supply and shift it in from S_0 to S_1. The resulting equilibrium price will be higher, while the change in quantity depends on the relative shifts in the curves. (100-103)

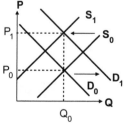

A1. a. Equating Q_s to Q_d and then solving for equilibrium price gives us $3 per quart. Substituting $3 into the demand and supply equations, we find that equilibrium quantity is 5 million quarts. (116)

b. Since supply increases by 20 million quarts, the new supply equation is $Q_s = 10 + 5P$. Equating this with the demand equation, we find the new equilibrium price to be $1 per quart. Substituting into either the new supply equation or the demand equation we find that equilibrium quantity is 15 million quarts. (116-118)

c. With demand increasing, the new demand equation is $Q_d = 30 - 5P$. Setting Q_s equal to Q_d and solving for price we find equilibrium price to be $4 per quart. Substituting this into either the new demand or the supply equation we find equilibrium quantity to be 10 million quarts. (116-118)

A2. a. Equating Q_s and Q_d, then solving gives equilibrium price $6 and quantity 8 hundred thousand dozen. (116)

b. If price ceiling is set at $4, $Q_s = 2$, and $Q_d = 12$, resulting in a shortage of ten hundred thousand dozen. (116-118)

c. If a $1 tax is imposed on suppliers, the new supply equation will be $Q_s = -10 + 3(P-1) = -13 + 3P$. Equating this with Q_d gives equilibrium price $6.60 and quantity 6.8 hundred thousand. Buyers pay $6.60 for each dozen they buy, and the sellers receive $1 less than that, or $5.60, for each dozen they sell. (116-118)

d. As a result of the tax, the new demand equation will be $Q_d = 20 - 2(P+1) = 18 - 2P$. Equating this with Q_s gives equilibrium price $5.60 and quantity 6.8 hundred thousand. Buyers pay $6.60 (P + 1) for each dozen they buy, and the sellers receive $5.60 for each dozen they sell. (116-118)

ANSWERS

MULTIPLE CHOICE

1. d A frost will reduce the quantity of oranges available for sale at every price. Supply will decrease. See pages 100-101.

2. c The supply curve will shift out, market price will fall and the quantity will rise. See pages 100-101.

3. a Demand for cricket bats will fall, shifting the demand curve in, while the tax repeal will shift the supply curve out. Price will fall, and quantity may change depending on the relative shifts of the supply and demand curves. See pages 100-101.

4. c When the demand curve shifts out, while the supply curve shifts in, the price rises and the quantity can remain the same. See pages 100-101.

5. a As discussed on pages 104-105, a price ceiling above equilibrium price will not affect the market price or quantity. Equilibrium price and quantity, in this case will be determined by the intersection of the supply and demand curves—at price P_1 and quantity Q_1.

6. d At a price of P_2 the quantity demanded by consumers is Q_0. The quantity supplied by sellers would be Q_2 at price P_2. A surplus of $Q_2 - Q_0$ would put downward pressure on price. However, government does not allow a lower price. So, the equilibrium price and quantity of P_1 and Q_1 would not prevail when government intervenes with a price floor. See pages 106-107.

7. b Rent controls are price ceilings and therefore cause the quantity demanded to exceed the quantity supplied. Indeed, the quantity demanded rises while the quantity supplied falls, creating a shortage. See pages 104-105.

8. a Because the minimum wage is a price floor it increases the quantity supplied and decreases the quantity demanded (*decreasing* employment) and creating a *surplus* of workers (causing some unemployment). The higher minimum wage would *increase* costs of production to businesses. See pages 106-107.

9. a The correct answer is a by definition. Also, a tariff will decrease supply, shifting the supply curve inward to the left. This causes the price consumers must pay to rise. See pages 107-108.

10. a Quantity restrictions reduce supply and create a higher price and lower quantity traded in a market. See pages 108-109.

11. c A tax shifts the supply curve up by the amount of the tax. The price consumers pay is determined by the price where the demand curve and the after-tax supply curve intersect. The after-tax price suppliers receive falls to P_0, the new equilibrium price less the tax (P_2-T). See pages 107-108.

12. c In a third-party payer system the person who chooses the product pays some but not all of the cost. As a result of a lower effective price to the consumer, the quantity demanded will be higher than otherwise. See pages 109-110.

13. a At a price of P_0, the consumer demands quantity Q_1. The supplier requires a price of P_1 for that quantity. Therefore, total expenditures are P_1 times Q_1 or areas A, B, and C. Of these, consumers pay areas B and C. The third party pays area A. See pages 109-110.

14. d In third-party payer markets the quantity demanded, price, and total spending are greater than when the consumer pays. See pages 109-110.

A1. a Equating the supply and demand equations gives equilibrium P = $2. Substituting this into either the supply or demand equation tells us that Q = 6 thousand quarts. See page 116.

A2. d The new demand becomes $Q_d = 130-5P$. Equating the supply and demand equations gives equilibrium P = $18. Substituting this into either the supply or demand equation tells us that Q = 40 sidewalk snow removals. See pages 117-118.

A3. a A $1 per bottle tax on suppliers makes the supply equation $Q_s = -10 + 6(P-1) = -16 + 6P$. Equating this with the demand equation gives equilibrium P = $4 and Q = 8 hundred thousand. The supplier receives $3 ($4 - $1). See pages 117-118.

━━━━━━ ANSWERS ━━━━━━

POTENTIAL ESSAY QUESTIONS

The following are annotated answers. They indicate the general idea behind the answer.

1. A minimum wage is a wage set by government that sets a floor in wages paid to employees. The effect is to reduce the quantity of employees firms demand and increase the quantity of people seeking work. Those who were previously employed but now are not are hurt. Firms are hurt because their costs rise. Because the limited supply must be rationed in some way, a person who had a job when price rationed jobs might not with non-price rationing.

2. Because part of the costs of obtaining a good or service in a third-party payer system is paid by someone other than the consumer, the effective price to the consumer is lower and the quantity demanded is greater. At this higher quantity demanded the price charged by sellers is greater. The result is greater consumption at a higher price and therefore greater total spending on the good or service. See Figure 5-6 on page 110 for a graphic illustration of this.

Pretest
Chapters 1 - 5

I

Take this test in test conditions, giving yourself a limited amount of time to complete the questions. Ideally, check with your professor to see how much time he or she allows for an average multiple choice question and multiply this by 22. This is the time limit you should set for yourself for this pretest. If you do not know how much time your teacher would allow, we suggest 1 minute per question, or about 22 minutes.

1. You bought stock A for $10 and stock B for $50. The price of each is currently $20. Assuming no tax issues, which should you sell if you need money?
    a. Stock A.
    b. Stock B.
    c. There is not enough information to tell which to sell.
    d. You should sell an equal amount of both.

2. The opportunity cost of reading Chapter 1 of a 38-chapter text:
    a. is about 1/38 of the price you paid for the book because the chapter is about 1/38 of the book.
    b. is zero since you have already paid for the book.
    c. has nothing to do with the price you paid for the book.
    d. is 1/38 the price of the book plus 1/38 the price of tuition for the course.

3. If at Female College there are significantly more females than males (and there are not a significant number of gays or off-campus dating opportunities), economic forces:
    a. will likely push for females to pay for dinners on dates.
    b. will likely push for males to pay for dinners on dates.
    c. will likely push for neither to pay for dinners on dates.
    d. are irrelevant to this issue. Everyone knows that the males always should pay.

4. The statement, "The distribution of income should be left to the market," is:
    a. a positive statement.
    b. a normative statement.
    c. an art-of-economics statement.
    d. an objective statement.

5. If the opportunity cost of good X in terms of good Y is 2Y, so you'll have to give up 2Y to get one X, the production possibility curve could look like:
    a. A only.
    b. B only.
    c. C only.
    d. A, B, or C.

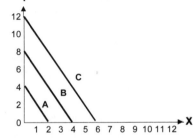

6. Given the accompanying production possibility curve, when you're moving from point C to point B the opportunity cost of butter in terms of guns is:
    a. 1/3.
    b. 1.
    c. 2.
    d. 3/2.

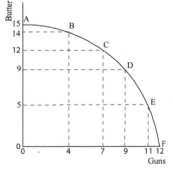

7. If countries A and B have production possibility curves A and B respectively, country A has a comparative advantage in the production of:
    a. no good.
    b. both goods.
    c. good X only.
    d. good Y only.

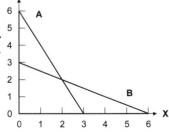

8. In theory, socialism is an economic system:
   a. that tries to organize society in the same ways as most families are organized, striving to see that individuals get what they need.
   b. based on central planning and government ownership of the means of production.
   c. based on private property rights.
   d. based on markets.

9. In practice, in command or socialist economies, the "what to produce" decision is most often made by:
   a. consumers.
   b. the market.
   c. government.
   d. firms.

10. In a market economy, the "what to produce" decision in practice is most often made directly by:
    a. consumers.
    b. the market.
    c. government.
    d. firms.

11. The largest percentage of business receipts are by:
    a. partnerships.
    b. sole proprietorships.
    c. corporations.
    d. nonprofit companies.

12. The largest percentage of state and local expenditures is on:
    a. education.
    b. health and medical care.
    c. highways.
    d. income security.

13. When government attempts to adjust for the effect of decisions on third parties not taken into account by the decision makers, the government is attempting to:
    a. provide for a stable set of institutions and rules.
    b. promote effective and workable competition.
    c. provide public goods and services.
    d. correct for externalities.

14. There are many more substitutes for good A than for good B.
    a. The demand curve for good B will likely shift out further.
    b. The demand curve for good B will likely be flatter.
    c. You can't say anything about the likely relative flatness of the demand curves.
    d. The demand curve for good A will likely be flatter.

15. If the price of air conditioners falls, there will be:
    a. an increase in demand for air conditioners.
    b. an increase in the quantity of air conditioners demanded.
    c. an increase in the quantity of air conditioners supplied.
    d. a shift out of the supply curve for air conditioners.

16. The law of supply states that:
    a. quantity supplied increases as price increases, other things constant.
    b. quantity supplied decreases as price increases, other things constant.
    c. more of a good will be supplied the higher its price, other things changing proportionately.
    d. less of a good will be supplied the higher its price, other things changing proportionately.

17. If at some price the quantity supplied exceeds the quantity demanded, then:
    a. a surplus (excess supply) exists and the price will fall over time as sellers competitively bid down the price.
    b. a shortage (excess demand) exists and the price will rise over time as buyers competitively bid up the price.
    c. the price is below equilibrium.
    d. equilibrium will be reestablished as the demand curve shifts to the left.

18. An increase in demand for a good will cause:
    a. excess demand (a shortage) until price changes.
    b. movement down along the demand curve as price changes.
    c. movement down along the supply curve as price changes.
    d. a higher price and a smaller quantity traded in the market.

19. A higher equilibrium price with no change in market equilibrium quantity could be caused by:
    a. supply shifting in and no change in demand.
    b. supply and demand both increasing.
    c. a decrease in supply and an increase in demand.
    d. demand and supply both shifting in.

20. Effective rent controls:
    a. are examples of price floors.
    b. cause the quantity of rental occupied housing demanded to exceed the quantity supplied.
    c. create a greater amount of higher quality housing to be made available to renters.
    d. create a surplus of rental occupied housing.

21. Referring to the graph below, suppose initial supply is represented by S_0. A tax T on suppliers will raise the price that:

    a. suppliers receive net of the tax to P_1.
    b. suppliers receive net of the tax to P_2.
    c. consumers pay to P_2.
    d. consumers pay to P_3.

22. Third-party payer markets result in:
    a. a lower equilibrium price received by the supplier.
    b. a smaller quantity supplied.
    c. a smaller quantity demanded.
    d. increased total spending.

━━━━━━ ANSWERS ━━━━━━

1.	c	(1:5)	**12.**	a	(3:11)
2.	c	(1:11)	**13.**	d	(3:14)
3.	a	(1:13)	**14.**	d	(4:2)
4.	b	(1:18)	**15.**	b	(4:4)
5.	d	(2:3)	**16.**	a	(4:13)
6.	d	(2:6)	**17.**	a	(4:18)
7.	d	(2:12)	**18.**	a	(4:25)
8.	a	(3:2)	**19.**	c	(5:4)
9.	c	(3:4)	**20.**	b	(5:7)
10.	d	(3:5)	**21.**	c	(5:11)
11.	c	(3:9)	**22.**	d	(5:14)

Key: The figures in parentheses refer to multiple choice question and chapter numbers. For example (1:2) is multiple choice question 2 from chapter 1.

DESCRIBING SUPPLY AND DEMAND: ELASTICITIES

CHAPTER AT A GLANCE

1. Elasticity is the percentage change in quantity divided by percentage change in some variable that affects demand or supply. The most commonly used elasticity concept is price elasticity of demand. (123)

   The price elasticity of <u>demand</u> measures <u>buyer</u> responsiveness to a price change. It equals the percentage change in <u>quantity demanded</u> divided by the percentage change in price.

   The price elasticity of <u>supply</u> measures <u>seller</u> responsiveness to a price change. It equals the percentage change in <u>quantity supplied</u> divided by the percentage change in price.

2. To calculate price elasticity of a price range, calculate the percentage change at the midpoint of the range. (124-126)

   $$Price\ Elasticity = \frac{percentage\ change\ in\ quantity}{percentage\ change\ in\ price}$$

   Percentage change in quantity = $\dfrac{Q_2 - Q_1}{1/2\,(Q_1 + Q_2)}$

   Percentage change in price = $\dfrac{P_2 - P_1}{1/2\,(P_1 + P_2)}$

   ✓ *Elasticity is not the same as slope!*

3. Five elasticity terms listed from most to least elastic are: perfectly elastic (E = infinity); elastic ($E > 1$); unit elastic ($E = 1$); inelastic ($E < 1$); and perfectly inelastic ($E = 0$). (123-128)

   Consider the price elasticity of demand for a good.

- *A <u>perfectly elastic</u> demand curve is a horizontal line.*
- *An <u>elastic</u> demand for a good means buyers are relatively responsive to a price change (the percentage change in the quantity demanded is greater than the percentage change in the price).*
- *When the demand for an item is <u>unit elastic</u>, buyers are neither relatively responsive nor unresponsive—(the percentage change in the quantity demanded equals the percentage change in the price).*
- *An <u>in</u>elastic demand for a good means buyers are relatively <u>un</u>responsive to a price change (the percentage change in the quantity demanded is less than the percentage change in the price).*
- *A <u>perfectly inelastic</u> demand curve is a vertical line, indicating there is no change in the quantity demanded given a change in the price.*

4. The more substitutes, the more elastic the demand and the more elastic the supply. (129-131)

   The number of substitutes a good has is affected by several factors. Four of the most important determinants of substitutability that give rise to a <u>greater</u> elasticity of demand for a good are:

- *The time period being considered: the longer the time interval, the larger the elasticity.*
- *The degree to which the good is a luxury: luxuries have greater elasticities.*
- *The market definition: the more specifically the good is defined the greater the elasticity. (e.g. there are more substitutes for Swiss cheese than for dairy products in general.)*
- *The importance of the good in one's budget: the greater the price relative to one's budget, the greater the elasticity.*

As for the elasticity of supply: the greater the amount of time under consideration, the greater the elasticity of supply (this is because the greater the amount of time, the greater the ability of sellers to respond to the price change).

5. With elastic demands, a rise in price decreases total revenue. With inelastic demands, a rise in price increases total revenue. (131-133)

    Therefore, firms have a strong incentive to separate people according to their price elasticity of demand. People with a more inelastic demand are charged a higher price. Economists call this price discrimination.

✓   *Know the relationship between the price elasticity of demand and total revenue:*

    Elastic: $\uparrow P \rightarrow \downarrow TR$; $\downarrow P \rightarrow \uparrow TR$
    Unit Elastic: $\uparrow P$ or $\downarrow P \rightarrow$ no change in TR
    Inelastic: $\uparrow P \rightarrow \uparrow TR$; $\downarrow P \rightarrow \downarrow TR$

    So $\downarrow P$ when demand is elastic and $\uparrow P$ when demand is inelastic to increase TR.

6. Income elasticity of demand shows the responsiveness of demand to changes in income. Cross-price elasticity shows the responsiveness of demand to changes in prices of other goods. (134-136)

    Income elasticity of demand equals the percentage change in demand divided by the percentage change in income.
    <u>Normal goods</u> have income elasticities greater than zero while <u>inferior goods</u> have negative income elasticities. Moreover, <u>luxuries</u> have an income elasticity greater than 1 while <u>necessities</u> have an income elasticity less than 1 (but still positive).

    Cross-price elasticity of demand equals the percentage change in demand divided by the percentage change in the price of another good. Substitutes have positive cross-price elasticities; complements have negative cross-price elasticities.

7. Figure 6-6 in the textbook reviews the effect of shifts in demand and supply with various elasticities. (137-138)

    Knowledge of elasticity enables us to determine to what extent the equilibrium quantity and the equilibrium price will change given a change in demand and supply. For example, if demand is highly inelastic and supply shifts in to the left, the price rises significantly while the quantity hardly decreases at all.

● SHORT-ANSWER QUESTIONS

1. Define the concepts *price elasticity of demand* and *price elasticity of supply*.

2. If the price of a good changes by 30 percent and quantity demanded for that same good remains unchanged, what is the price elasticity of demand for that good?

3. If price elasticity of supply is 4 and price changes by 10 percent, by what percent will the quantity supplied change?

4. Define the terms *elastic*, *inelastic*, and *unit elastic* as applied to points on supply and demand curves.

5. What are the four main determinants of the price elasticity of demand?

6. In each of the following cases, state what will be the effect of a rise in price on total revenue:

    a. Demand is inelastic.

    b. Demand is elastic.

    c. Demand is unit elastic.

7. Define income elasticity of demand. How do the income elasticities of demand differ among normal goods, necessities, luxuries, and inferior goods?

8. Define cross-price elasticity of demand.

9. What is a complementary good? What is the general value of the cross-price elasticity of demand for a complementary good? What is a substitute good? What is the general value of the cross-price elasticity of demand for a substitute good?

10. Explain how using the concept *elasticity* makes supply and demand analysis more useful.

MATCHING THE TERMS
Match the terms to their definitions

___	1.	complements	a. A measure of the percent change in the quantity demanded divided by the percent change in the price of that good.
___	2.	cross-price elasticity of demand	b. Goods whose consumption decreases when income increases.
___	3.	elastic	c. Goods that can be used in place of one another.
___	4.	income elasticity of demand	d. Goods that are used in conjunction with other goods.
___	5.	inelastic	e. Goods whose consumption increases with an increase in income.
___	6.	inferior goods	f. Quantity responds enormously to changes in price. E = infinity.
___	7.	luxury	g. % change in quantity is greater than % change in price. $E > 1$.
___	8.	necessity	h. % change in quantity is less than % change in price. $E < 1$.
___	9.	normal goods	i. A good that has an income elasticity between 0 and 1.
___	10.	perfectly elastic	j. The percentage change in quantity is equal to the percentage change in price. $E = 1$.
___	11.	perfectly inelastic	k. Quantity does not respond to changes in price. $E = 0$.
___	12.	price elasticity of demand	l. The percentage change in demand divided by percentage change in income.
___	13.	price elasticity of supply	m. The percentage change in demand of one good divided by the percentage change in the price of a related good.
___	14.	substitutes	n. A good that has an income elasticity greater than one.
___	15.	unit elastic	o. A measure of the percent change in the quantity supplied divided by the percent change in the price of that good.

PROBLEMS AND APPLICATIONS

1. Assume the price elasticity of demand for a good is 0.5 (after we take the absolute value—drop the negative sign). If there is a 10% decrease in the price, what would happen to the percentage change in the quantity demanded? What if the price were to rise by 15%?

2. Calculate the price elasticity for each of the following. State whether price elasticity of demand is elastic, unit elastic, or inelastic. Will revenue rise, decline, or stay the same with the given change in price?

   a. The price of pens rises 5%; the quantity demanded falls 10%.

   b. The price of a ticket to a Boston Red Sox baseball game rises from $10 to $12 a game. The quantity of tickets sold falls from 160,000 tickets to 144,000.

   c. The price of an economics textbook declines from $50 to $47.50. Quantity demanded rises from 1,000 to 1,075.

   d. The price of water beds rises from $500 to $600. Quantity demanded falls from 100,000 to 80,000.

3. Suppose that in deciding what price to set for the video *Shrek II*, Disney decided to either charge $12.95 or $15.95. It estimated the demand to be quite elastic. What price did it most likely charge and why?

4. Calculate the price elasticity of the following products. State whether elasticity of supply is elastic, unit elastic, or inelastic.

   a. Cocoa Puffs: The price of a 14-oz. box of Cocoa Puffs rises 4 percent while quantity supplied rises 15 percent.

   b. Toyota Prius: The price of the Prius rises from $25,000 to $30,000. Its quantity supplied rises from 5,000,000 to 5,300,000 per year.

   c. Jansport backpacks: The price of Jansport backpacks falls from $30 a pack to $25 a pack. The quantity supplied falls from 150,000 to 125,000 per week.

5. Calculate the income elasticity of demand for the following goods. State whether each is a luxury, a necessity, or an inferior good.

    a. As average income per student rises from $10,000 to $12,000 a year, demand for ice cream cones increases from 30,000 cones to 37,500 cones per year.

    b. As income decreases from 120,000 to 100,000 Mexican pesos per year, demand for margarine increases from 50 to 60 pounds per year.

    c. As income decreases from $20,000 to $18,000 per year, demand for summer cottages in Vermont decreases from 80 to 75.

6. Determine the cross-price elasticity of demand for the following examples. Are they substitutes or complements? How do you know?

    a. The price of a pizza rises from $9 to $12, and the quantity demanded of Big Macs increases from 3 million to 4 million burgers per year.

    b. The price of hot dogs falls from $4 a pound to $2 a pound, and the quantity demanded of mustard increases from 15 tons to 20 tons per year.

7. What will likely happen to equilibrium price and quantity in the following cases?

    a. Demand is highly inelastic. The supply curve shifts out.

    b. Supply is highly inelastic. The demand curve shifts out.

    c. Supply is highly elastic. The demand curve shifts in.

● MULTIPLE CHOICE

Circle the one best answer for each of the following questions:

1. The definition of price elasticity of demand is:
    a. the change in quantity demanded divided by the change in price.
    b. the percentage change in quantity demanded divided by the percentage change in price.
    c. the percentage change in price divided by the percentage change in quantity demanded.
    d. the percentage change in the quantity supplied divided by the percentage change in price.

2. When the price of a good was raised from $10 to $11, the quantity demanded fell from 100 to 99. The price elasticity of demand is approximately:
    a. .1.
    b. 1.
    c. 10.
    d. 100.

3. If a firm can sell 1,200 units at a price of $14 per unit and 2,000 units at a price of $10 per unit, we can conclude:
   a. the price elasticity of demand for that good is 1.5.
   b. that the demand for this good is inelastic.
   c. that a price reduction would decrease the firm's total revenue.
   d. there must be very few substitutes for this good.

4. As the manager of a hotel, you want to increase the number of occupancies by 12%. It has been determined that the price elasticity of demand for rooms in your hotel is 2. This information implies:
   a. the demand for rooms in your hotel is inelastic.
   b. if you lower your rates by 6% then you will increase the number of occupancies by 12%.
   c. if you were able to raise your rates your total revenue would rise.
   d. there must be few substitutes for your hotel services.

5. A rise in price has just increased total revenue, other things constant. One would surmise that the demand for the firm's product is:
   a. inelastic.
   b. elastic.
   c. unit elastic.
   d. none of the above.

6. As a manager, you have determined that the demand for your good is quite elastic. Therefore:
   a. increasing the price of your good will increase revenues.
   b. decreasing the price of your good will increase revenues.
   c. increasing the price of your good will have no impact on the quantity demanded.
   d. any change in your price will not impact revenues.

7. In reference to the graph below, which of the following is true? P

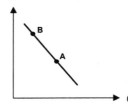

a. Point B is more elastic than point A.
b. Point A is more elastic than point B.
c. Points A and B have equal elasticity.
d. One cannot say anything about the elasticities without more information.

8. The elasticity of the curve below is:

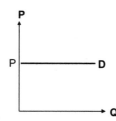

a. perfectly elastic.
b. perfectly inelastic.
c. unit elastic.
d. partially inelastic.

9. When price changes from 4 to 5, output supplied changes from 50 to 60. The elasticity of supply is approximately:
   a. .5.
   b. .8.
   c. 1.25.
   d. .25.

10. In the graph below, point A on the supply curve, S, is:

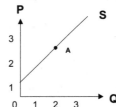

a. elastic.
b. inelastic.
c. unit elastic.
d. unknown because one cannot say from the graph.

11. The supply curve in the graph below is:

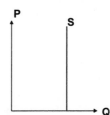

a. perfectly inelastic.
b. perfectly elastic.
c. unit elastic.
d. showing that its elasticity changes at various points.

12. In the graph below, point A on the supply curve, S, is:

   a. elastic.
   b. inelastic.
   c. unit elastic.
   d. unknown because one cannot say from the graph.

13. In the long run, the elasticity of demand is generally:
   a. greater than in the short run.
   b. smaller than in the short run.
   c. the same as in the short run.
   d. unrelated to the elasticity in the short run.

14. The more specifically or narrowly a good is defined:
   a. the more substitutes it has and therefore the more elastic its demand curve.
   b. the more substitutes it has and therefore the more inelastic its demand curve.
   c. the fewer substitutes it has and therefore the more inelastic its demand curve.
   d. the more unit elastic its demand curve.

15. The more a good is a necessity:
   a. the more elastic its demand curve.
   b. the more inelastic its demand curve.
   c. the more unit elastic its demand curve.
   d. the flatter the demand curve.

16. A good whose consumption decreases when income increases is generally called:
   a. a normal good.
   b. an inferior good.
   c. a substitute good.
   d. a complementary good.

17. Two goods are substitutes when they:
   a. are goods that are used in conjunction with each other.
   b. have negative income elasticities.
   c. have positive income elasticities.
   d. have positive cross-price elasticities.

18. Price discrimination is most likely to occur in markets:
   a. when all individuals have equal elasticities.
   b. when some individuals have highly inelastic demands and some have highly elastic demands.
   c. in which the elasticity of demand is 1.
   d. in which the elasticity of demand is 0.

19. A significant price rise with virtually no change in quantity would most likely be caused by a highly:
   a. elastic demand and supply shifts to the right.
   b. inelastic supply and a shift in demand to the right.
   c. inelastic demand and supply shifts out.
   d. elastic supply and demand shifts in.

20. A significant quantity rise with virtually no change in price would most likely be caused by a highly:
   a. elastic demand and supply shifts to the right.
   b. inelastic supply and demand shifts to the right.
   c. inelastic demand and supply shifts to the right.
   d. elastic supply and demand shifts to the left.

21. A significant price decline with virtually no change in quantity would most likely be caused by a highly:
   a. elastic demand and supply shifts to the right.
   b. inelastic supply and demand shifts to the right.
   c. inelastic demand and supply shifts out.
   d. elastic supply and demand shifts in.

● POTENTIAL ESSAY QUESTIONS

You may also see essay questions similar to the "Problems & Applications" exercises.

1. What can cause some products to exhibit elastic demand while others have inelastic demand?

2. Why are some businesses interested in trying to determine which consumers have an elastic demand and which have an inelastic demand for the product being sold?

ANSWERS

SHORT-ANSWER QUESTIONS

1. *Price elasticity of demand* is the percentage change in quantity demanded divided by the percentage change in price. *Price elasticity of supply* is the percentage change in quantity supplied divided by the percentage change in price. (122)

2. Price elasticity of demand is the percentage change in quantity demanded divided by the percentage change in price. Since the quantity demanded has not changed, the price elasticity of demand is zero. In other words, demand is perfectly inelastic. (123-127)

3. Price elasticity of supply is the percentage change in quantity supplied divided by the percentage change in price. Thus, if the elasticity of supply is 4 and price changes by 10%, quantity supplied will change by 40%. (122)

4. For elastic points, the percentage change in quantity is greater than the percentage change in price. For inelastic points, the percentage change in quantity is less than the percentage change in price. For unit elastic points, the percentage change in quantity is equal to the percentage change in price. (123-127)

5. The four main determinants of price elasticity of demand are (1) the time interval considered, (2) whether the good is a necessity or a luxury, (3) how specifically the good is defined, and (4) its price as a percentage of one's total expenditures. The larger the time interval, the more elastic is demand. The more a good is a luxury, the more demand is elastic. The more specifically a good is defined, the more elastic is demand. The more a good's price is a percentage of one's expenditures, the more elastic is demand. (133)

6. a. If demand is inelastic, the percent fall in quantity demanded will be *less than* the percent rise in price. So a rise in price will increase total revenue. (131-132)
   b. If demand is elastic, the percent fall in quantity demanded will be *greater than* the percent rise in price. So a rise in price will reduce total revenue. (131-132)
   c. If demand is unit elastic, the percent fall in quantity demanded will *equal* the percent rise in price. So a rise in price will not change total revenue. (131-132)

7. Income elasticity of demand is the percentage change in demand divided by the percentage change in income. Normal goods have positive income elasticities. Luxury goods have positive income elasticities greater than one, while necessities have positive income elasticities less than one. Inferior goods have negative income elasticities. (134-135)

8. Cross-price elasticity of demand is the percentage change in quantity demanded of one good divided by the percentage change in the price of another good. (135-136)

9. A complementary good is a good whose consumption goes down when the price of the other good (for which it is a complement) goes up. Complements have negative cross-price elasticities. A substitute good is a good whose consumption goes up when the price of the other good (for which it is a substitute) goes up. Substitutes have positive cross-price elasticities. (135-136)

10. Knowledge of elasticity enables us to determine *to what extent* there will be a change in the equilibrium quantity and the equilibrium price, given a change in demand and supply. (137-138)

ANSWERS

MATCHING

1-d; 2-m; 3-g; 4-l; 5-h; 6-b; 7-n; 8-i; 9-e; 10-f; 11-k; 12-a; 13-o; 14-c; 15-j.

■■■■■   ANSWERS   ■■■■■

PROBLEMS AND APPLICATIONS

1. Given that the $E_d = 0.5$, and the price falls by 10%, the quantity demanded will rise by 5%. [The trick is to multiply the E_d number (0.5), by the percentage change in the price (10) to get the percentage change in the quantity demanded (5). But remember, the law of demand tells us that the quantity demanded moves in the opposite direction from the change in the price.] If the price were to rise by 15%, the quantity demanded would fall by 7.5% (0.5 × 15=7.5). (122-123)

2. Price elasticity of demand is the percent change in quantity demanded divided by the percent change in price. Demand is elastic if the price elasticity is greater than one (always drop the negative sign—take the absolute value); a rise in price will lower total revenue. Demand is inelastic if the price elasticity is less than one; a rise in price will increase total revenue. Demand is unit elastic if the price elasticity is equal to one; a rise in price leaves total revenue unchanged. (122-128)

   a. Price elasticity of demand is 10%/5% = 2. Since 2 > 1, demand is elastic. Total revenue falls.

   b. Price elasticity of demand is [(144,000−160,000)/152,000]/[(12−10)/11] =0.58. Since 0.58 < 1, demand is inelastic. Total revenue rises.

   c. Price elasticity of demand is [(1,075−1,000)/1,037.5]/[(47.5−50)/48.75]= 1.41. Since 1.41 > 1, demand is elastic. Total revenue rises.

   d. Price elasticity of demand is [(80,000−100,000)/90,000]/[(600−500)/550] = 1.2. Since 1.2 > 1, demand is elastic. Total revenue falls.

3. It would charge the lower price, $12.95, because a lower price will increase total revenue when demand is elastic. (131-133)

4. a. Price elasticity of supply is 15%/4% = 3.75. Since 3.75 > 1, supply is elastic. (122-128)

   b. Price elasticity of supply is [(5,300,000−5,000,000)/5,150,000]/[(30,000-25,000)/27,500]=0.32. Since 0.32 < 1, supply is inelastic. (122-128)

   c. Price elasticity of supply is [(125,000−150,000)/137,500]/[25−30/27.5] = 1. Since 1 = 1, supply is unit elastic. (122-128)

5. a. The income elasticity of demand is [(37,500−30,000)/33,750]/[(12,000−10,000)/11,000]=1.22. Since 1.22>1, ice cream cones are a luxury good. (134-135)

   b. The income elasticity of demand is [(60−50)/55]/[(100,000−120,000)/110,000] = −1. Since −1 < 0, margarine is an inferior good. (134-135)

   c. The income elasticity of demand is [(75−80)/77.5]/[(18,000−20,000)/19,000]= 0.61. Since 0 < 0.61 < 1, summer cottages are a necessity. (134-135)

6. a. The cross-price elasticity of demand is [(4,000,000−3,000,000)/3,500,000]/[(12−9)/10.5] = 1. Since 1 > 0, pizzas and Big Macs are substitutes. (135-136)

   b. The cross-price elasticity of demand is [(20−15)/17.5]/[(2−4)/3] = −0.43. Since −0.43 < 0, hot dogs and mustard are complements. (135-136)

7. a. The price will fall considerably but quantity will not rise significantly, as shown below. (138)

   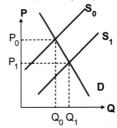

   b. The price will rise considerably but quantity will not rise significantly, as shown below. (138)

   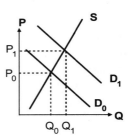

c. The quantity will fall considerably, but price will not fall significantly, as shown below. (138)

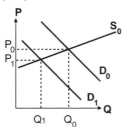

━━━━━━ ANSWERS ━━━━━━

MULTIPLE CHOICE

1. b The price elasticity of demand is the percentage change in quantity demanded divided by the percentage change in price. Option d is the definition of the price elasticity of supply. See page 122.

2. a Substituting in the basic formula for elasticity gives $0.01/0.1 = 0.1$. See pages 124-126.

3. a Using the formula for elasticity of demand (percent change in quantity divided by percent change in price = $0.5/0.33$) gives 1.5 (out of convention we always take the absolute value). Therefore, the good is elastic because its absolute value is greater than one and it likely has many substitutes. A price fall would increase the firm's total revenue. See pages 124-126, 131-132.

4. b The price elasticity of demand of 2 means that every 1% change in the price will cause a 2% change in the quantity demanded. To obtain a 12% increase in the quantity demanded means the price must fall by 6%. See the formula for elasticity of demand on pages 124-126, 131-132.

5. a The revenue gain from the increase in price had to exceed the loss from the reduction in quantity, so the demand must be inelastic. See pages 131-132.

6. b When a good is price-elastic then a price decrease will result in a proportionately larger increase in the quantity demanded and revenues will rise. See pages 131-132.

7. a The elasticity changes along a straight line demand curve from highly elastic in upper portions of the demand curve to highly inelastic in the lower portions of the curve. See pages 131-132.

8. a A horizontal demand curve is perfectly elastic because the percentage change in quantity is infinite. See Figure 6-2 on pages 126-127.

9. b Elasticity of supply is the percent change in quantity divided by the percent change in price: $18\%/22\% = 0.8$. See pages 124-125.

10. a You can either calculate the elasticity (percent change in quantity divided by the percent change in price) or you can use the trick in the "Added Dimension" box (any straight line supply curve that intersects the vertical axis is elastic) on pages 124-129.

11. a For a vertical supply curve, the percent change in quantity becomes zero, so the elasticity becomes zero, making supply perfectly inelastic. See pages 124-129.

12. c Use the trick in the "Added Dimension" box (any straight line supply curve going through the origin will be unit elastic) on page 129.

13. a The greater the time period under consideration, the greater the possibility for substitution and, therefore, the greater the elasticity of demand. See page 130.

14. a The more specifically or narrowly a good is defined, the more substitutes it tends to have and the greater its elasticity of demand. See page 130.

15. b Necessities tend to have few substitutes and the fewer the substitutes, the more inelastic the demand curve. See pages 134-135.

16. b   People buy fewer inferior goods when income rises. See pages 134-135.

17. d   When the price of a good increases and this increases the demand for its substitute, then the cross-price elasticity of demand is positive. See pages 135-136.

18. b   Price discrimination requires separating consumers by their elasticities and charging higher prices to individuals who have inelastic demands. See pages 133-134.

19. b   Since price rose significantly while quantity remained virtually unchanged, either demand or supply is inelastic. Since price rose, either demand shifted out or supply shifted in. Only option b fits these conditions. See page 138.

20. a   Since quantity rose significantly while price remained virtually unchanged either demand or supply is elastic. Since quantity rose, either demand shifted out or supply shifted out. Only option a fits these conditions. See page 138.

21. c   Since price declined significantly while quantity remained virtually unchanged, either demand or supply is inelastic. Since price declined, either demand shifted in or supply shifted out. Only option c fits these conditions. See page 137.

━━ ANSWERS ━━

POTENTIAL ESSAY QUESTIONS

The following are annotated answers. They indicate the general idea behind the answer.

1.   As a general rule, the more substitutes a good has, the more elastic is its demand. The number of substitutes is, in turn, affected by the time interval under consideration, whether the good is considered a necessity or a luxury, the specificity with which the good is defined, and the relative prices of the good compared to one's income.

2.   In order to maximize revenues firms will try to charge a higher price for the product to those consumers that have a more inelastic demand (because an increase in the price increases total revenue) and a lower price to those that have an elastic demand (because a decrease in the price increases total revenue).

TAXATION AND GOVERNMENT INTERVENTION

CHAPTER AT A GLANCE

1. Equilibrium maximizes consumer and producer surplus. (144-146)

   <u>Consumer surplus</u> is the difference between the price buyers would have been willing to pay and the price they actually had to pay. <u>Equal to Area A</u> in the graph below.

   <u>Producer surplus</u> is the difference between the price sellers would have been willing to accept and the price they actually received as payment. <u>Equal to Area B</u> in the graph below.

   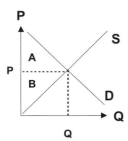

   Hint: To answer numerical problems calculating producer and consumer surplus, remember the formula for the area of a triangle is 1/2 base × height.

2. The burden of taxation to society is the loss of consumer and producer surplus caused by the tax. (146-148)

   A tax on suppliers shifts the supply curve up. A tax on consumers shifts the "after tax" demand curve down.

   Total cost to consumers and producers is more than tax revenue. Refer to the graph below. Suppose a per unit tax "t" is paid by suppliers. Consumers pay rectangle B in tax revenue and lose area C in consumer surplus. Producers pay area D in tax revenue and lose area E in producer surplus. The triangular area represented by areas C (lost consumer surplus) and E (lost producer surplus) represents a cost of taxation in excess of the revenue paid to government. It is lost consumer and producer surplus that is not

   gained by government. This loss of consumer and producer surplus from a tax is known as "deadweight loss." Graphically, deadweight loss is shown by the "welfare loss triangle"—area C + E.

3. The person who physically pays a tax is not necessarily the person who bears the burden of the tax. Who bears the burden of the tax (also known as tax incidence) depends upon who is best able to change his behavior in response to the tax, or who has the greater elasticity. (148-152)

   The more inelastic one's relative supply and demand, the larger the burden of the tax one will bear.

   The general rule about elasticities and tax burden is this: if demand is more inelastic than supply, demanders will pay a higher percentage of the tax. If supply is more inelastic than demand, suppliers will pay a higher share. More specifically:

   Fraction of tax borne by demander = price elasticity of supply divided by the sum of the price elasticity of demand and supply $= E_S / (E_D + E_S)$.

   Fraction of tax borne by supplier = price elasticity of demand divided by the sum of the price elasticity of demand and supply $= E_D / (E_D + E_S)$.

4. A price ceiling is, in essence, an implicit tax on producers and an implicit subsidy to consumers. (152-153)

Refer to the graph below. With an effective price ceiling of P_1 the quantity supplied (and the amount consumed) falls from Q_e to Q_1. The welfare loss equals area C + E. This is the same effect as a tax. However, the loss of producer surplus, area D, is now transferred to consumers. It is as if government places a tax on suppliers and then gives that tax revenue to consumers when they consume the good.

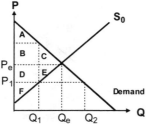

5. Rent seeking is an activity designed to transfer surplus from one group to another. If demand is inelastic, suppliers have an incentive to restrict supply to raise the price because this will raise their revenue. When the supply of a good is inelastic, consumers have an incentive to hold the price down. (153-157)

For example, the demand for food is inelastic. Farmers have an incentive to lobby government to restrict supply or to create a price floor for their commodities (sometimes called price supports) because they will be better off.

On the other hand, when the supply of a good is inelastic like that of rental-occupied housing, and demand rises, rental rates will rise significantly and consumers will scream for rent controls.

Government sometimes succumbs to political pressure for price controls (price floors and price ceilings). However, price controls create surpluses and shortages that only become more severe over time.

6. The general rule of political economy is when small groups are helped by a government action and large groups are hurt by that same action, the small group tends to lobby more effectively than the larger group. (155)

Because of the rule, policies tend to reflect the interests of small groups.

An example is the farm lobby. Farmers have been effective in getting government to hold up farm prices by restricting supply even though taxpayers are worse off.

SHORT-ANSWER QUESTIONS

1. What are consumer surplus and producer surplus? How are they related to demand and supply curves?

2. What happens to combined consumer and producer surplus when government sets a price floor above equilibrium price?

3. What is the burden of taxation to society?

4. What is the general rule about elasticities and tax burden?

5. For whom is a price ceiling an implicit tax? For whom is a price ceiling an implicit subsidy?

6. For whom is a price floor an implicit tax? For whom is a price floor an implicit subsidy?

7. What is an important similarity and an important difference between taxes and price controls (price ceilings and price floors)?

8. What is rent seeking and how is rent seeking related to elasticity?

9. What is the general rule of political economy in a democracy?

MATCHING THE TERMS
Match the terms to their definitions

____ 1. consumer surplus

____ 2. deadweight loss

____ 3. excise tax

____ 4. general rule of political economy

____ 5. price ceiling

____ 6. price floor

____ 7. producer surplus

____ 8. public choice economist

____ 9. rent-seeking activity

____ 10. welfare loss triangle

a. A tax that is levied on a specific good.

b. Economist who integrates an economic analysis of politics with the analysis of the economy.

c. A geometric representation of the welfare cost in terms of misallocated resources caused by a deviation from a supply-demand equilibrium.

d. The loss to society of consumer and producer surplus from a tax.

e. A government-set price above which price may not rise.

f. Activity designed to transfer surplus from one group to another.

g. A government-set price below which price may not fall.

h. The value the consumer gets from buying a product less its price.

i. The price the producer sells a product for less the cost of producing it.

j. Small groups that are significantly affected by a government policy will lobby more effectively than large groups that are equally affected by that same policy.

● PROBLEMS AND APPLICATIONS

1. Refer to the graph below when answering the following questions.

a. Given supply curve S_0, what is the area representing consumer surplus at the market equilibrium price?

b. Given supply curve S_0, what is the area representing producer surplus at the market equilibrium price?

c. Now suppose a per unit tax, t, paid by the supplier shifts the supply curve up from S_0 to S_1. Equilibrium price rises from P_e to P_1 and equilibrium quantity falls from Q_0 to Q_1. What area represents consumer surplus after the tax?

d. After the tax, what area represents what consumers pay in tax revenue to government?

e. What area represents lost consumer surplus caused by the tax and not gained by government?

f. What area represents producer surplus after the tax?

g. After the tax, what area represents what producers pay in tax revenue to government?

h. What area represents lost producer surplus caused by the tax and not gained by government?

i. What area represents deadweight loss; that is, what is the welfare loss triangle?

2. The supply and demand for foreign cars in Bangladesh is shown in the graph below. Suppose the government imposes a tax on supply of 10,000 takas per car. The new equilibrium price and quantity are shown in the graph below.

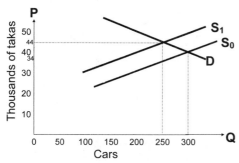

a. What would be the tax paid by consumers? Suppliers? What price do suppliers with and without the tax receive?

b. Demonstrate graphically the tax paid by each.

c. From your answer to part *b*, what can you conclude about the relative elasticities of the supply and demand curves?

3. What is the deadweight loss from the tax equal to in question #2?

4. Suppose the price elasticity of supply is 0.5 and the price elasticity of demand is 1.5. If the government imposes a tax on the good, what percentage of the tax is borne by buyers?

5. a. If government, given its targeted revenue from a tax, wants to have as large an effect on individual actions as possible, should it tax goods with an inelastic or elastic demand? Why?

b. If government wants to raise revenues from a tax and minimize welfare loss, should it tax goods with *inelastic* demand or supply, or *elastic* demand or supply? Why?

6. Refer to the graph below when answering the following questions.

a. In market equilibrium, what area represents consumer surplus? Producer surplus?

b. Suppose government imposes a price ceiling of P_1. What happens to the quantity demanded and the quantity supplied?

c. What happens to consumer and producer surplus as a result of the price ceiling?

d What is the welfare loss triangle as a result of the price ceiling?

e. How is a price ceiling equivalent to a tax on producers and a subsidy to consumers?

f. Suppose that instead of government imposing a price ceiling, it imposed a tax that reduced the quantity supplied to Q_1. What is an essential similarity between the two outcomes? What is an essential difference?

7. How could the fact that farmers lobby government to restrict the supply of agricultural production or to pursue agricultural price supports (price floors) be viewed as rent-seeking activity?

8. Why will shortages that result from price ceilings, and surpluses that result from price floors, become more acute over time?

● MULTIPLE CHOICE

Circle the one best answer for each of the following questions:

1. Refer to the graph below. The amount of consumer surplus at market equilibrium is:
   a $18.
   b $9.
   c. $72.
   d $36.

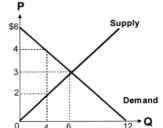

2. Refer to the graph in Question #1. The lost combined consumer and producer surplus from a price of $4 is:
   a $2.
   b $4.
   c. $12.
   d $36.

3. Assume equilibrium in the graph below. What area represents consumer surplus?
   a. A + B + C.
   b. D + C + E.
   c. E.
   d E + F.

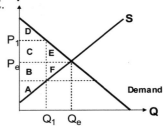

4. Refer to the graph for Question #3. Assume equilibrium. What area represents the welfare loss from a price floor of P_1?
   a B + C + E + F.
   b C + B.
   c. B.
   d E + F.

5. Refer to the graph below. If a per unit tax, t, is paid by sellers:

a. producer surplus is represented by areas A, B, and C before the tax and area A after the tax.

b. consumer surplus is represented by areas D, E and F before the tax and B after the tax.

c. the tax, t, imposes a deadweight loss represented by the welfare loss triangle–areas C and E.

d. consumers lose surplus given by area E while producers lose surplus given by area C.

6. Refer to the graph below. If a per unit tax, t, is paid by consumers, which of the following is true?

a. Tax revenue paid equals the tax, t, times the equilibrium quantity, Q_1, or areas B+D.

b. The total cost to consumers and producers is less than tax revenue to government.

c. Consumers pay areas B and D in tax revenue and also lose areas C and E in consumer surplus.

d. Consumers pay area D in tax revenue and lose area E in consumer surplus.

7. Deadweight loss from a tax is:

a. the loss of consumer surplus from a tax.

b. the loss of producer surplus from a tax.

c. the loss of consumer *and* producer surplus from a tax.

d. the amount of tax revenues collected by government.

8. The welfare loss triangle is a geometric representation of:

a. the value of lost quantity traded that would have otherwise benefited both consumers and producers.

b. the amount of tax paid by consumers and businesses.

c. the consumer surplus after a tax.

d. the producer surplus after a tax.

9. The burden of a tax is:

a. most heavily borne by those with the more inelastic demand or supply.

b. most heavily borne by those with the more elastic demand or supply.

c. usually equally split between buyers and sellers.

d. usually passed on to consumers in the form of a higher price.

10. How much of a $100 tax will consumers pay if the price elasticity of demand is 3 and the price elasticity of supply is 2?

a. $50.

b. $40.

c. $30.

d. $20.

11. How much of a $100 tax will consumers pay if the price elasticity of supply is 2 and the price elasticity of demand is 4?

a. $20.

b. $33.

c. $40.

d. $60.

12. Social Security taxes are:

a. levied by government more heavily on employees than employers, even though the burden of the tax is most heavily borne by employers.

b. most heavily borne by employers if the demand for labor tends to be more inelastic than supply.

c. most heavily borne by workers if the demand for labor tends to be more inelastic than the supply of labor.

d. most heavily borne by workers if the supply of labor tends to be more inelastic than the demand for labor.

13. An effective price ceiling:
    a. is a government-set price above market equilibrium price.
    b. is an implicit tax on producers and an implicit subsidy to consumers.
    c. will create a surplus.
    d. causes an increase in consumer and producer surplus.

14. Refer to the graph below. A price ceiling of P_1 will:

    a. create a shortage of $Q_e - Q_1$.
    b. transfer surplus D from producers to consumers.
    c. create a deadweight loss equal to areas A + B + C.
    d. increase combined producer and consumer surplus by triangles C and E.

15. Rent-seeking activity is designed to:
    a. produce additional revenue for government.
    b. minimize welfare loss.
    c. maximize welfare loss.
    d. transfer surplus from one group to another.

16. The general rule of political economy in a democracy states:
    a. small groups that are significantly affected by a government policy will lobby more effectively than will large groups who are equally affected by that policy.
    b. large groups that are significantly affected by a government policy will lobby more effectively than small groups who are equally affected by that policy.
    c. large groups will always win in majority rule situations.
    d. Congress will always be inefficient.

17. In which case will a price floor result in the greatest excess supply?
    a. When both demand and supply are highly inelastic.
    b. When both demand and supply are highly elastic.
    c. When demand is elastic and supply is inelastic.
    d. When demand is inelastic and supply is elastic.

● **POTENTIAL ESSAY QUESTIONS**

You may also see essay questions similar to the "Problems & Applications" exercises.

1. Discuss the relationship between elasticity and tax burden.

2. What are the basic similarities and differences between the effects of taxes and price controls?

■ ANSWERS ■

SHORT-ANSWER QUESTIONS

1. Consumer surplus is the difference between the price buyers are willing to pay (shown by the demand curve) and the price they actually pay. Producer surplus is the difference between what the sellers are willing to accept as payment (shown by the supply curve) and what they actually receive as payment. (144-146)

2. A price floor above equilibrium price will result in a lower quantity purchased and therefore a lower combined producer and consumer surplus. (152-153, especially Figure 7-4)

3. The burden of taxation to society is the loss of consumer and producer surplus caused by the tax. (146-147)

4. The general rule about elasticities and tax burden is this: *if demand is more inelastic than supply, consumers pay a higher percentage of the tax. If supply is more inelastic than demand, suppliers pay a higher share.* (150-152)

5. A price ceiling (a government-set price below market equilibrium price) is an implicit tax on producers and an implicit subsidy to consumers. (152-153)

6. A price floor (a government-set price above market equilibrium price) is in essence an implicit tax on consumers and an implicit subsidy to producers. (152-153)

7. An important similarity between taxes and price controls (which include price ceilings and price floors) is that they all create a loss of consumer and producer surplus shown graphically by a welfare loss triangle. An important difference between taxes and price controls is that price controls create surpluses (in the case of a price floor) and shortages (in the case of a price ceiling), while taxes do not create surpluses or shortages. (152-153)

8. Rent seeking is an activity designed to transfer surplus (consumer or producer surplus) from one group to another. The more inelastic the demand, the greater the incentive suppliers have to drive the price up because this will increase their revenue and lower their cost, which raises their profits. The more inelastic supply, the greater the incentive consumers have to lobby government to set a price ceiling because it will result in a larger transfer of surplus to themselves. (153-157)

9. The general rule of political economy in a democracy is that small groups that are significantly affected by a government policy will lobby more effectively than large groups that are equally affected by that same policy. (155)

■ ANSWERS ■

MATCHING

1-h; 2-d; 3-a; 4-j; 5-e; 6-g; 7-i; 8-b; 9-f; 10-c.

■ ANSWERS ■

PROBLEMS AND APPLICATIONS

1. **a.** Area A + B + C represents consumer surplus at the market equilibrium price. (144-147 and Figure 7-1)
    b. Area D + E + F represents producer surplus at the market equilibrium price. (144-147 and Figure 7-1)
    c. Area A is consumer surplus after the tax. (144-147 and Figure 7-1)
    d. Area B is what consumers pay in tax revenues to government. This represents lost consumer surplus gained by government. (144-147 and Figure 7-2)
    e. Area C is lost consumer surplus not gained by government. (144-147 and Figure 7-2)
    f. Area F is producer surplus after the tax. (144-147 and Figure 7-2)
    g. Area D is what producers pay in tax revenues to government. This represents lost producer surplus gained by government. (144-147 and Figure 7-2)

h. Area E represents lost producer surplus not gained by government. (144-147 and Figure 7-2)

i. Area C + E is the deadweight loss from a tax. This area is the welfare loss triangle. (144-147 and Figure 7-2)

2. **a.** The consumers now have to pay 44,000 takas per car, which is 4,000 takas more than before. Their tax burden is (4,000 × 250) = 1,000,000 takas. Suppliers now receive 34,000 takas (44,000-10,000) on each car they sell, which is 6,000 takas less per car than before the tax. Their tax burden is (6,000 × 250) = 1,500,000 takas. (148-151, especially Figure 7-3)

b. The graph above shows the relative taxes paid by consumers and producers. The upper shaded portion is consumers' tax burden. The lower shaded portion is suppliers' tax burden. (148-151, especially Figure 7-3)

c. Since the supplier's tax burden is greater, the supply curve is more inelastic than the demand curve. (148-151, especially Figure 7-3)

3. The deadweight loss of a tax is shown by a welfare loss triangle. In this case that triangle has a base of 10,000 takas and a height of 50 cars (when the triangle is turned on its side). The area of that triangle = ½ x base x height = ½ x 10,000 x 50 = 250,000 takas. (147)

4. The tax borne by buyers equals the price elasticity of supply divided by the sum of the price elasticities of supply and demand (0.5/2)= .25 or 1/4. Producers bear the other 75 percent or 3/4 of the tax. Producers pay the larger fraction (percentage) of a tax when demand is elastic and supply is inelastic. The one with the greater inelasticity bears the larger burden of a tax. (150)

5. **a.** Government should tax goods with *elastic* demand if it wishes to have as large an effect on individual actions as possible. This is because an elastic demand means there are many substitutes buyers can turn to in response to the higher price as a result of the tax. Buyers will cut back on their consumption rather dramatically. (148)

b. Government should tax goods with *inelastic* demand or supply if it wishes to raise revenues and minimize welfare loss. Revenues to government will rise because an inelastic demand or supply means there are few substitutes or alternatives for buyers and sellers to turn to. Graphically, an inelastic demand or supply will minimize welfare loss because the welfare loss triangle will be smaller the steeper (the more inelastic) the demand or supply curves. (148-150, Figure 7-3, and the "Reminder" box on page 148)

6. **a.** Market equilibrium is P_e and Q_e. Consumer surplus is area A + B + C. Producer surplus is area D + E + F. (145, especially Figure 7-1)

b. As a result of the price ceiling, the quantity supplied falls from Q_e to Q_1 and the quantity demanded rises from Q_e to Q_2. This creates a shortage of $Q_2 - Q_1$. (152-153, especially Figure 7-4)

c. Consumer surplus becomes area A + B + D. Producer surplus becomes area F. (152-153, especially Figure 7-4)

d. The welfare loss triangle is area C + E. (152-153, especially Figure 7-4)

e. A price ceiling is equivalent to a tax on producers and a subsidy to consumers because area D is transferred from producers to consumers as a result of the price ceiling. (152-153, especially Figure 7-4)

f. The welfare loss would be the same (the welfare loss triangle would still be area C + E). However, an essential difference between the two is that a price ceiling creates a shortage, while a tax would not. Another difference is who gets the surplus. In the case of the tax, government gets areas B and D as tax revenue. (152-153, especially Figure 7-4)

7. Because the demand for agricultural goods is inelastic, farmers have an incentive to get government to restrict supply or create a price floor, thereby raising their revenue (their income). This is rent seeking because farmers are attempting to shift consumer surplus to themselves. (155-156)

8. Price ceilings and price floors create greater shortages and surpluses over time because in the long run, supply and demand tend to be more elastic than in the short run. (157-158)

▬▬▬ ANSWERS ▬▬▬

MULTIPLE CHOICE

1. b   The consumer surplus triangle has a base of 6 (the equilibrium quantity) and a height of $3 (6 - 3). Since the area of a triangle is ½ (base x height), the consumer surplus is ½(3 x 6) = $9. See pages 144-146 and Figure 7-1.

2. a   The lost consumer and producer surplus when price rises to $4 is the triangle that has a height (looked at sideways) of 2 (6 – 4) and a base of 2 (4 - 2). Since the area of a triangle is ½ (base x height), the lost surplus is ½(2 x 2) = $2. See pages 144-146 and Figure 7-1.

3. b   Consumer surplus is the area under the demand curve above the equilibrium price. See page 147 and Figure 7-2.

4. d   The loss to consumers is *E* and *C* (but C is gained by producers). The loss to producers is *F*. So the total loss is *E* + *F*. See pages 152-153 and Figure 7-2.

5. c   The incorrect options have consumer and producer surplus confused. Deadweight loss is surplus lost by consumers and producers but not gained by anyone. It is a net loss to society because of deviation from market equilibrium. See pages 146-148 and Figure 7-2.

6. a   While total tax is areas B+D, consumers pay only B. Suppliers pay D. Tax revenue is the tax per unit times the units sold, area B + D. To be correct, option b should read "is *greater* than." See pages 146-148 and Figure 7-2.

7. c   Deadweight loss is the loss of consumer and producer surplus from a tax. See pages 146-147.

8. a   The welfare loss triangle is the cost of taxation in *excess* of the revenue paid to government. Moreover, it represents the *loss* of consumer *and* producer surplus from a tax. See pages 146-147.

9. a   Those with inelastic demand or supply are less able to change their behavior and therefore bear a greater share of the tax. See page 148.

10. b   The fraction of a tax borne by consumers equals the price elasticity of supply divided by the sum of the price elasticity of demand and supply (2/5= 0.4). 4/10 or 40 percent of $100 is $40. See page 150.

11. b   The fraction of a tax borne by consumers equals the price elasticity of supply divided by the sum of the price elasticity of demand and supply (2/6 = 1/3). One third of $100 is $33.33. See page 150.

12. d   Government divides the taxes among employees and employers equally. However, since the supply of labor is relatively more inelastic, employees bear the greater burden of Social Security taxes. See pages 150-151.

13. b   A price ceiling is a government-set price *below* equilibrium and creates a *shortage*. A price ceiling reduces consumer and producer surplus, but a portion of the lost producer surplus is transferred to consumers. A price ceiling creates welfare loss just like taxes do. See pages 152-153.

14. b   A price ceiling creates a shortage equal to $Q_2 - Q_1$. Producer surplus D is transferred to consumers because of the lower price.

Producer and consumer surplus *falls* by areas C and E (the welfare loss triangle). See pages 152-153, especially Figure 7-4.

15. d   Rent-seeking activity is designed to transfer surplus from one group to another—whether it be from producers to consumers or the other way around. See pages 153-154.

16. a   Congress may always be inefficient, but this is not the general rule of political economy. See page 155.

17. b   When both parties have the greatest possibility of change, there will be the greatest surplus. This occurs in the long run when both demand and supply are more elastic. See pages 157-158.

━━━━━━ ANSWERS ━━━━━━

POTENTIAL ESSAY QUESTIONS

The following are annotated answers. They indicate the general idea behind the answer.

1. The general rule about elasticities and tax burden is this: if demand is more inelastic than supply, consumers will pay a higher percentage of the tax. If supply is more inelastic than demand, suppliers will pay a higher share.

2. Price controls and taxes are similar in that they both create welfare loss. They differ in that price controls create shortages (in the case of a price ceiling) and surpluses (in the case of a price floor), while taxes do not. Another difference is who gets the surplus. For a tax, government gets some of the surplus as tax revenue.

MARKET FAILURE VERSUS GOVERNMENT FAILURE

8

CHAPTER AT A GLANCE

1. An externality is an effect of a decision on a third party not taken into account by the decision maker. (169-167)

   Externalities can either be negative (have undesirable social side effects in which case society would want less of the good) or positive (have desirable social side effects in which case society would want more of the good). Externalities are only one source of market failure.

   3 sources of market failure:
   - *Externalities*
   - *Public goods*
   - *Imperfect information*

   Any time a market failure exists there is a reason for possible government intervention to improve the outcome. However, government failure is always a possibility.
   Economic policy is often a choice between market failure and government failure.

2. Ways to deal with externalities include: (1) direct regulation, (2) incentive policies (tax incentive policies and market incentive policies), and (3) voluntary solutions. (167-171)

   Economists tend to like incentive policies to deal with externalities.

   The optimal policy is one in which the marginal cost of undertaking the policy equals the marginal benefit of that policy.

3. A public good is a good that is nonexclusive (no one can be excluded from its benefits) and nonrival (consumption by one does not preclude consumption by others). (171-174)

   The public/private good differentiation is seldom clear-cut.

   Public goods suffer from the free rider problem.

4. Market failure can occur when buyers and sellers have different amounts of information about the good for sale or when people don't bear the negative consequences of their actions. (174-178)

   When there is a lack of information or buyers and sellers don't have equal information, markets in some goods may not work well. Lack of information can lead to the adverse selection problems which can be partially resolved by signaling and screening.

   The health insurance sector suffers from the moral hazard problem.

   Signaling and screening are two ways individuals can resolve informational problems.

   2 general policies to deal with informational problems are:
   - *Regulatory approach*
   - *Market approach*

5. Should government intervene in the market? It depends. (178-179)

   One needs to weigh the benefits against the costs of government intervention on a case-by-case basis and remain as objective as possible in the measurement of those benefits and costs.

   Know 5 reasons why government failure may occur.

● **SHORT-ANSWER QUESTIONS**

1. What are three sources of market failures?

2. Suppose a steel plant begins production near your home. The resulting smoke pollutes the air you breathe. You bring a complaint to the local town board saying, "I didn't ask for that factory to be built, but I'm having to endure polluted air." The basis of your complaint is an example of what concept in economics?

3. Briefly describe the three methods of dealing with externalities.

4. Which of the methods you stated in Question #3 do most economists prefer to use when dealing with externalities?

5. What is an optimal policy?

6. Define "public good." Why is it difficult for government to decide the efficient quantity of a public good to provide?

7. Why does medical insurance lead to the moral hazard problem?

8. What are two ways individuals can partially resolve informational problems?

9. What are two ways society can deal with informational problems that lead to market failures?

10. When should the government intervene in the economy?

MATCHING THE TERMS
Match the terms to their definitions

____ **1.** adverse selection problem

____ **2.** direct regulation

____ **3.** efficient

____ **4.** effluent fee

____ **5.** externality

____ **6.** free rider problem

____ **7.** government failure

____ **8.** inefficient

____ **9.** marginal social benefit

____ **10.** marginal social cost

____ **11.** market failure

____ **12.** market incentive plan

____ **13.** moral hazard problem

____ **14.** negative externality

____ **15.** optimal policy

____ **16.** positive externality

____ **17.** public good

____ **18.** screening

____ **19.** signaling

____ **20.** tax incentive program

a. A situation in which the invisible hand pushes in such a way that individual decisions do not lead to socially optimal outcomes.

b. Equals the marginal private costs of production plus the cost of the negative externalities associated with that production.

c. The effect of a decision on a third party that is not taken into account by the decision maker.

d. The amount of a good people are allowed to use is directly limited by the government.

e. When the effect of a decision not taken into account by the decision maker is detrimental to others.

f. A charge imposed by government on the level of pollution created.

g. When the effect of a decision not taken into account by the decision maker is beneficial to others.

h. A plan requiring market participants to certify that they have reduced total consumption—not necessarily their own individual consumption—by a specified amount.

i. A good that is nonexclusive (no one can be excluded from its benefits) and nonrival (consumption by one does not preclude consumption by others).

j. Achieving a goal at the lowest cost in total resources without consideration as to who pays that cost.

k. A problem that occurs when buyers and sellers have different amounts of information about the good for sale.

l. When government intervention in the market to improve a market failure makes the situation worse.

m. Individuals' unwillingness to share in the cost of a public good.

n. Equals the marginal private benefit of consuming a good plus the benefit of the positive externalities resulting from consuming that good.

o. Achieving a goal in a more costly manner than necessary.

p. A policy in which the marginal cost of undertaking the policy equals the marginal benefit.

q. A program using a tax to create incentives for individuals to structure their activities in a way that is consistent with the desired ends.

r. An action taken by an informed party that reveals information to an uninformed party that offsets the false signal that caused the adverse selection problem in the first place.

s. An action taken by the uninformed party that induces the informed party to reveal information.

t. A problem that arises when people don't have to bear the negative consequences of their actions.

⬤ PROBLEMS AND APPLICATIONS

1. Secondhand cigarette smoke is believed to have a negative effect on the health of non-smokers. These people have not chosen to smoke, but nevertheless are negatively affected by the choice of others to smoke. Draw the market for cigarettes showing the marginal cost and marginal social cost of smoking cigarettes if this belief is correct.

    a. Demonstrate graphically the market price and quantity of cigarettes.

    b. Demonstrate graphically the efficient level of cigarettes. Explain your answer.

    c. Demonstrate graphically the tax the government would have to impose on cigarettes to arrive at the efficient level and price of cigarettes.

    d. Demonstrate graphically the tax revenue that government would collect from such a tax.

2. A small city located by a lake has been dumping its raw sewage into the lake. This has created a public outcry by those citizens who like to fish, swim, and water-ski in the lake. The city council has surveyed the community and has estimated the social benefits associated with different levels of pollution control. These benefits, as well as the costs associated with pollution control efforts for the community, are shown in the accompanying table. What is the optimal level of pollution control? Will there still be some pollution of the lake?

Pollution Control	Total Social Benefits	Total Social Costs
1	$200,000	$40,000
2	$275,000	$75,000
3	$330,000	$110,000
4	$375,000	$145,000
5	$410,000	$180,000
6	$435,000	$215,000

3. Assume a community has decided that there are some substantial social benefits associated with after-school organized recreational activities (such as basketball or soccer) provided to kids before many of their parents arrive home from work. The graph below shows the private demand (marginal private benefit) and society's demand (marginal social benefit) and the supply (marginal private plus social cost) of these recreational activities.

    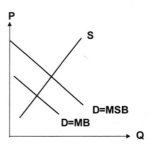

    a. Demonstrate graphically the efficient output level in the graph above. Why would this be an efficient output level?

    b. Assume the government is interested in a policy to increase the number of children spending time at these facilities. What policy would you recommend?

4. a. If you are willing to pay $7,000 for a used car that is a "cherry" and $2,000 for a used car that is a "lemon," how much will you be willing to offer to purchase a car if there is a 50 percent chance of purchasing a lemon?

    b. If many owners of cherry cars want $4,500 for their cherries, and you are still willing to offer the same dollar amount for a used car as in part *a*, how will your estimate of the chance of getting a cherry change?

5. Suppose there are just two individuals, Bob and Susie, in a community. Bob and Susie are both interested in using a public park (a public good). Below are Bob and Susie's individual demand tables for the use of the public park per month.

Bob		Susie	
Price per month	Qty Demanded in hours per month	Price per month	Qty Demanded in hours per month
$13	4	$10	4
9	6	6	6
7	8	4	8

    a. Construct a market demand table for the public park in this community.

    b. Construct individual demand curves for Bob and Susie as well as the market demand curve and place them on the same graph in the space below.

● MULTIPLE CHOICE

Circle the one best answer for each of the following questions:

1. All of the following are market failures *except:*
    a. positive externalities.
    b. imperfect information.
    c. negative externalities.
    d. the invisible hand.

2. An externality is:
    a. the effect of a decision on a third party not taken into account by a decision maker.
    b. another name for exports.
    c. an event that is external to the economy.
    d. the external effect of a government policy.

3. Refer to the graph below. The S curve represents the marginal private cost of production, and the D curve represents the marginal private benefit to consumers of the good. If there is a negative externality of production, and one wants to adjust the curves so that the equilibrium demonstrates the appropriate marginal social costs, either:

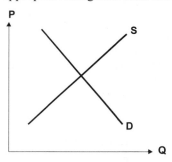

    a. the S curve should be shifted in to the left or the D curve should be shifted out to the right.
    b. the S curve should be shifted out to the right or the D curve should be shifted in to the left.
    c. the S curve should be shifted out to the right or the D curve should be shifted out to the right.
    d. the S curve should be shifted in to the left or the D curve should be shifted in to the left.

4. Refer to the graph on the following page. The S curve represents the marginal private cost of production, and the D curve represents the marginal private benefit to consumers of the good. If there is a positive externality of consumption, and one wants to adjust the

curves so that the equilibrium demonstrates the appropriate marginal social benefits, either:

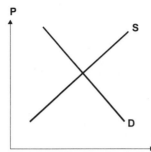

a. the S curve should be shifted in to the left or the D curve should be shifted out to the right.

b. the S curve should be shifted out to the right or the D curve should be shifted in to the left.

c. the S curve should be shifted out to the right or the D curve should be shifted out to the right.

d. the S curve should be shifted in to the left or the D curve should be shifted in to the left.

5. Which of the following is *not* one of the ways to deal with negative externalities?
    a. Regulation.
    b. Subsidizing producers.
    c. Creating a market in the externality.
    d. Voluntary solutions.

6. Refer to the graph below. If the government were attempting to set an effluent fee, the amount of that effluent fee should be:
    a. P_1.
    b. P_2.
    c. $P_1 - P_2$.
    d. $P_1 - P_3$.

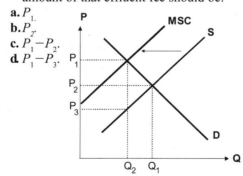

7. Mr. A is using 10 gallons of gas a day and Mr. B is using 20 gallons of gas a day. The marginal cost of reducing gas consumption by 3 gallons a day is $8 for Mr. A and $4 for Mr. B. The government places a tax on the use of gasoline. Economists would expect:

a. Mr. A to reduce his consumption by the same amount as Mr. B.

b. Mr. A to reduce his consumption by more than Mr. B.

c. Mr. B to reduce his consumption by more than Mr. A.

d. both to reduce their consumption to zero.

8. Refer to the graph below, which shows the marginal private and social cost of fishing and the demand for fishing. The socially efficient price for consumers of fishing would be:
    a. 0.
    b. P_1.
    c. P_2.
    d. P_3.

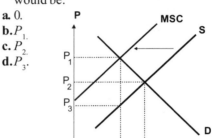

9. In addressing pollution problems, economists would most likely prefer:
    a. direct regulation.
    b. subsidies provided to suppliers.
    c. a market incentive plan.
    d. banning the production of those products that pollute.

10. Voluntary policies to resolve externalities:
    a. have historically been effective in addressing externalities.
    b. are generally favored by economists as the optimal policy to address externalities.
    c. are generally opposed by economists because of the free rider problem.
    d. are generally opposed by economists because of government failure.

11. A public good is:
    a. any good traded in markets.
    b. a good that is nonexclusive and nonrival.
    c. a good provided only to those who pay for it.
    d. rarely provided by government.

12. The optimal level of pollution control, or any other government policy, exists when the marginal benefit:

a. exceeds the marginal cost.
b. equals the marginal cost.
c. is less than the marginal cost.
d. is maximized.

13. The market demand curve for a public good is:
a. the vertical sum of the individual demand curves at every quantity.
b. the horizontal sum of the individual demand curves at every price.
c. vertical at the quantity desired.
d. always horizontal.

14. If health insurers cannot distinguish between people who have a high risk and low risk of medical needs, but those buying the health insurance can, the price at which insurers are willing to provide insurance to cover health care costs will be:
a. low enough so that at least one half of all those covered are low insurance risks.
b. set with the expectations that high risk people will not purchase coverage.
c. at a level where insurers will be unwilling to provide health coverage.
d. at a level where many of those in good health may be unwilling to buy insurance.

15. The moral hazard problem in medical insurance:
a. leads to higher insurance premiums.
b. leads to lower insurance premiums.
c. has no effect on insurance premiums.
d. is unrelated to insurance premiums.

16. Two actions individuals can take to offset the information problem are:
a. withdraw from the market and externalize the problem.
b. direct and indirect regulation.
c. screening and signaling.
d. tax and regulate.

17. Offering a money-back guarantee is an example of:
a. signaling.
b. screening.
c. adverse selection.
d. moral hazard.

18. Government failure:
a. always outweighs market failure.
b. sometimes outweighs market failure.
c. never outweighs market failure.
d. is the same as market failure.

POTENTIAL ESSAY QUESTIONS

You may also see essay questions similar to the "Problems & Applications" exercises.

1. Evaluate the benefits and costs of the regulatory versus the market approach to resolving informational problems that lead to market failure.

2. Discuss five reasons why government's solution to a market failure could worsen the market failure.

ANSWERS

SHORT-ANSWER QUESTIONS

1. Three sources of market failures are: externalities, public goods, and imperfect information. (165)

2. The pollution that you endure is an example of a negative externality. An externality is an effect of a decision not taken into account by the decision maker. In this case, the air pollution is the effect of steel production not taken into account by the firm. (164-167)

3. Ways to deal with externalities include (1) direct regulation, (2) incentive policies (tax incentive policies and market incentive policies), and (3) voluntary solutions. In a program of direct regulation, the government directly limits the amount of a good people are allowed to use. A tax incentive program is a program using a tax to create incentives for individuals to structure their activities in a way that is consistent with the desired ends. A market incentive program is a plan requiring market participants to certify that they have reduced total consumption—not necessarily their own individual consumption—by a specified amount. Voluntary solutions leave individuals free to choose whether to follow what is socially optimal or what is privately optimal. (167-170)

4. Economists tend to like incentive policies to deal with externalities. Direct regulation tends to be more costly to society in achieving the desired end. Voluntary policies will tend to fail because a small number of free riders often undermine the social consciousness of many in society. (167-171)

5. An optimal policy is one in which the marginal cost of undertaking the policy equals the marginal benefit of that policy. (170-171)

6. A public good is a good that is nonexclusive (no one can be excluded from its benefits) and nonrival (consumption by one does not preclude consumption by others). It is difficult for government to decide the efficient quantity of a public good because of the free rider problem. If the public good is to be financed by a tax on citizens who benefit from it, individuals have an incentive to conceal their willingness to pay for it. Similarly, if citizens think they will not be the ones taxed to fund the public good, but will benefit from it, they have an incentive to exaggerate their willingness to pay. (170-173)

7. If someone has health insurance then doctors' visits and prescriptions cost less or are free. The person has less incentive to make healthy choices in order to avoid seeing a doctor or taking medicine. (174-175)

8. Signaling and screening can partially resolve informational problems. Signaling is an action by the informed party to offset false signals. Screening is an action taken by the uninformed party designed to get the informed party to reveal information. (175)

9. Two general policies to deal with informational problems include the regulatory approach and the market approach. The regulatory approach would have government regulate the market and see that individuals provide the right information, or the government could license individuals in the market, requiring those with licenses to reveal full information about the good being sold or service provided. The market approach is for government to not regulate so that markets in information develop. (175-178)

10. The government should intervene in the economy only if the benefits outweigh the costs. One needs to weigh the benefits against the costs on a case-by-case basis and to remain as objective as possible. Government failure (government intervention only making matters worse) is always a real possibility. (178-179)

ANSWERS

MATCHING

1-k; 2-d; 3-j; 4-f; 5-c; 6-m; 7-l; 8-o; 9-n; 10-b; 11-a; 12-h; 13-t; 14-e; 15-p; 16-g; 17-i; 18-s; 19-r; 20-q.

ANSWERS

PROBLEMS AND APPLICATIONS

1. a. When there is a negative externality, as with the case of secondhand cigarette smoke, the supply curve which represents the marginal private cost, *S*, is lower than the marginal social cost, *MSC*. The supply curve represents the private costs of smokers who chose to smoke. The cost for society is higher, and the marginal social cost is higher, because cigarette smoke hurts those who do not smoke. The demand curve represents marginal social benefits. These curves are drawn on the graph below.

Because the market does not take into account the third-party effects, equilibrium quantity is Q_e and equilibrium price is P_e. (166 and Figure 8-1)

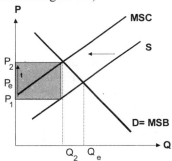

b. The efficient level of cigarettes is where marginal social costs equal marginal social benefits. This is at Q_2 and P_2. (166 and Figure 8-1)

c. The tax the government would have to impose on cigarettes to arrive at the efficient level of cigarettes is *t* equal to $P_2 - P_1$; it's the tax sufficient to shift the supply curve back to the marginal social cost curve. (168-169 and Figure 8-3)

d. This is *t* times the quantity of cigarettes in the market after the tax. This is shown by the shaded boxed region in the graph above. (168-169 and Figure 8-3)

2. See the table below. The optimal level of pollution control is 5 units, because this is the quantity of pollution control at which the marginal social benefit of the control just equals its marginal social cost. There will still be some pollution of the lake as evidenced by the increased marginal benefits associated with the 6th unit of pollution control—but that amount of pollution control is not worth it to the community given its marginal cost. (170-171)

Pollution Control	Total Benefits	Total Costs	Marginal Benefit	Marginal Cost
1	$200,000	$40,000	$200,000	$40,000
2	275,000	75,000	75,000	35,000
3	330,000	110,000	55,000	35,000
4	375,000	145,000	45,000	35,000
5	410,000	180,000	**35,000**	**35,000**
6	435,000	215,000	25,000	35,000

3. a. The efficient level of output (services provided in the community) is where the marginal social benefit equals the marginal social cost. This occurs at that output level, Q*, where the MSB curve intersects the supply curve as shown below. (It is reasonable to assume there is no difference between the private and social costs, so marginal social costs are given by the supply curve.) (167 and Figure 8-2)

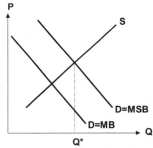

b. The private demand and/or the supply needs to be increased. This could be accomplished by subsidizing parents (increasing demand) and/or subsidizing the facilities (increasing supply). Either one of these options would increase the output level toward the efficient level where MSB = MSC. It may be much easier to administer the subsidization of the facilities. (167-169 and Figure 8-2)

4. a. Knowing that you have a 50 percent chance of buying a lemon, you will offer $4,500 (the average of $2,000 and $7,000). Given that offer price, individuals with cherries will be very hesitant to sell and will begin to exit the market, while individuals with lemons will be anxious to sell. (174)

b. If many owners of cherries want $4,500 and you are still willing to pay $4,500 for a used car then there will be more owners of cherries left in the market, increasing the chances you will be able to purchase a cherry used car. (174)

5. a. The market demand table for the public park is shown below. Notice that to derive the market demand table for a public good one needs to add the marginal benefit each individual receives from the public good (the price they are willing to pay) at each quantity. (This is just the opposite from deriving a demand table for a private good where one would have to add the quantity demanded at each price.) (171-174)

Price per month	Quantity Demanded in hours per month
$23	4
$15	6
$11	8

b. The lowest curve is Susie's demand curve. The middle curve is Bob's demand curve. The highest curve is the market demand curve. Notice that we vertically sum the individual demand curves to construct the market demand curve for a public good. (171-174 and Figure 8-4)

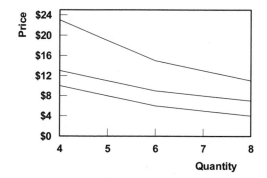

ANSWERS

MULTIPLE CHOICE

1. d An outcome where individual buyers and sellers do not have any control over price (the invisible hand) is a desirable competitive market outcome. See page 164.

2. a An externality occurs when there is an effect of a trade on a third party. See page 165.

3. d A negative externality of production makes the marginal social cost higher than the marginal private cost. Equilibrium price must be raised. See page 166 and Figure 8-1.

4. c A positive externality of consumption makes the marginal social benefit higher than the marginal private benefit. See page 167 and Figure 8-2.

5. b Subsidizing producers would increase the production of the product. Instead, we would want to restrict the production of a product that has a negative externality. See pages 168-169.

6. d The effluent fee should be set to equate marginal social cost with marginal social benefit (which, in absence of any information to the contrary, the marginal social benefit can be assumed to be represented by the demand curve). To achieve this equality, the effluent fee needs to be sufficient to shift the supply curve up to the marginal social cost curve. See pages 168-169 and Figure 8-3.

7. c The amount of reduction will be based on the marginal costs of reduction. Since the marginal costs of reduction are higher for Mr. A, economists would expect Mr. B to reduce his consumption by more than Mr. A. See pages 169-170.

8. b The socially efficient price is where the marginal social cost equals the marginal social benefit (which, in absence of any information to the contrary, can be assumed to be represented by the demand curve). See page 166 and Figure 8-1.

9. c   Economists prefer market incentive plans because they are more efficient. See pages 169-170.

10. c   Economists believe a small number of free riders will undermine the social consciousness of many in society and that eventually a voluntary policy will fail. Generally, the results of voluntary programs have not been positive. Government failure can exist only if government intervenes. The optimal government intervention exists when the marginal benefits equal the marginal costs. See page 170.

11. b   A public good is a good that is nonexclusive and whose consumption by one does not preclude its consumption by others. See page 171.

12. b   Whenever the marginal benefit exceeds the marginal cost, do more of that activity. Do less whenever the marginal benefit is less than the marginal cost. See pages 170-171.

13. a   To arrive at the market demand curve for a public good we vertically add the price that each individual is willing to pay for each unit since each receives a benefit when the good is supplied. See pages 171-173 and Figure 8-4.

14. d   With certainty, insurers would not offer to provide health insurance at a price low enough so that low-risk people would purchase insurance. The only people left looking for health insurance are high-risk people. The price will rise even further until very few will buy health insurance. This is known as adverse selection. See pages 174-175.

15. a   The moral hazard problem leads people to make riskier choices since they don't suffer the consequences of their actions. Premiums go up because health care costs rise. See pages 174-175.

16. c   Screening and signaling are designed to reveal information. They are actions taken by individuals. Options b and d are government actions. See page 175.

17. c   Offering a guarantee reveals information about the condition of a car to offset lack of information of the buyer. This is known as signaling. Screening is an action taken by the uninformed party. Sellers are the informed party. See page 175.

18. b   Government failure occurs when government intervention does not improve the market failure. As with almost all economic issues, there is always an "on the other hand" so the "sometimes" is the right answer. See pages 178-179.

ANSWERS

POTENTIAL ESSAY QUESTIONS

The following are annotated answers. They indicate the general idea behind the answer.

1. The regulatory approach would have government regulate the market and see that individuals provide the right information, or the government could license individuals in the market, requiring those with licenses to reveal full information about the good being sold. Although regulatory solutions have their benefits they may also create government failure. The market approach suggests that allowing markets for information to develop may be the best approach because it may at least avoid some government failure.

2. Government intervention may worsen the problems created by market failure. Government failure may occur because (1) governments don't have an incentive to correct the problem, (2) governments don't have enough information to deal with the problem, (3) intervention is more complicated than it initially seems, (4) the bureaucratic nature of government precludes fine-tuning, and (5) government intervention often leads to more government intervention.

COMPARATIVE ADVANTAGE, EXCHANGE RATES, AND GLOBALIZATION

9

CHAPTER AT A GLANCE

1. The principle of comparative advantage states that as long as the relative opportunity costs of producing goods differ among countries, there are potential gains from trade. (186-187)

    When countries specialize in the production of those goods for which each has a <u>comparative advantage</u> and then trade, all economies involved benefit.

    A country has a comparative advantage in producing good "x" if its opportunity cost of producing good "x" is lower.

2. Three determinants of the gains of trade are: (189-190)
    *   The more competition, the less the trader gets.
    *   Smaller countries get a larger proportion of the gain than larger countries.
    *   Countries producing goods with economies of scale get a larger gain from trade.

    Also: countries which specialize and trade along the lines of comparative advantage are able to consume more than if they did not undertake trade (they are able to escape the confines of their own production possibility curves).

3. Four reasons for differences between economists' and laypeople's views of trade are: (1) gains from trade are often stealth gains, (2) opportunity cost is relative, (3) nations trade more than just manufactured goods, and (4) trade affects distribution of income. (190-192)

    The gains from trade in the form of low consumer prices tend to be widespread and not easily recognizable, while the costs in jobs lost tend to be concentrated and readily identifiable. This affects the distribution of income. But, the gains outweigh the costs over

time. *Convincing the public of this remains a challenge, especially for policymakers.*

4. Transferable comparative advantages will tend to erode over time; inherent comparative advantages will not. (192-195)

    The law of one price and the convergence hypothesis will work to erode any transferable comparative advantages over time. The degree to which, and how quickly, the United States loses some of its comparative advantages depends on how transferable they are.

    Rising wages in China relative to the United States and a decline in the exchange rate value of the dollar are two ways the United States will gain comparative advantages.

5. The foreign exchange (forex) market is the market for foreign currencies. It can be analyzed using the supply and demand model to determine the price of one country's currency in terms of another country's currency; the rate at which one country's currency can be traded for that of another is the exchange rate. The graph below shows the market for euros. The equilibrium price is $1.30 per euro and 100 euros. (196-198)

A *currency depreciation* is *a change in the exchange rate so that one currency buys fewer units of a foreign currency*. A *currency appreciation* is *a change in the exchange rate so that one currency buys more units of a foreign currency.*

When comparing two currencies with the supply and demand model, the supply of one currency equals the demand for the other currency. To demand one currency, you must supply another. For example, if a European citizen wants to purchase a US product, she must supply euros in order to demand dollars to buy the product.

6. The exchange rate plays a major role in the demand for a country's domestic goods. If a country's currency depreciates, its goods become more competitive in the global market; on the other hand, if a country's currency appreciates, its goods become less competitive in the global market. (198-199)

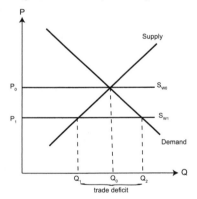

In the graph above, the nation's trade is balanced when the world supply is S_{w0} and the domestic price is P_0. If the country's currency appreciates, the world price level shifts down, in this case to S_{w1}. The nation will develop a trade deficit shown by Q_2-Q_1.

With free trade, if producers want to sell their goods, they must match the world price, and if consumers have the ability to buy all the goods they want at the world price, they will not pay more than that price.

7. The resource curse occurs when a country discovers a large amount of natural resources, which raises foreign demand for the resource and thus causes the country's currency to appreciate. (199-200)

While there is increased foreign demand for the discovered resources, the appreciation of the country's currency causes other goods lose their comparative advantage.

● SHORT-ANSWER QUESTIONS

1. What is the principle of comparative advantage?

2. What are three determinants of the gains of trade?

3. What are four reasons laypeople's and economists' views of trade differ?

4. How does trade today affect the distribution of income within the United States?

5. What are four sources of comparative advantages for the United States?

6. How do transferable comparative advantages differ from inherent advantages?

7. Why is the United States losing some of its comparative advantages?

8. What does it mean for the dollar to appreciate relative to the yuan?

9. How will an appreciation of the dollar affect the U.S. trade deficit? Explain your answer.

10. What is the resource curse? What impact does it have on exchange rates and the trade deficit?

MATCHING THE TERMS
Match the terms to their definitions

___	1. Balance of trade	a.	The difference between the value of exports and imports
___	2. Comparative advantage	b.	When a nation's exports exceed its imports
___	3. Currency appreciation	c.	As long as the relative opportunity costs of producing goods differ among countries, there are potential gains from trade, even if one country has an absolute advantage in everything
___	4. Currency depreciation		
___	5. Exchange rate		
___	6. Inherent comparative advantage	d.	A change in the exchange rate so that one currency buys fewer units of a foreign currency
___	7. Resource curse	e.	When a nation's imports exceed its exports
___	8. Trade deficit	f.	The rate at which one country's currency can be traded for another country's currency
___	9. Trade surplus		
___	10. Transferable comparative advantage	g.	Comparative advantage based on factors that are relatively unchangeable
		h.	Comparative advantage based on factors that can be changed relatively easily
		i.	The paradox that countries with an abundance of resources tend to have lower economic growth and more unemployment than countries with fewer resources
		j.	A change in the exchange rate so that one currency buys greater units of a foreign currency

PROBLEMS AND APPLICATIONS

1. **a.** State whether there is a basis for trade in the following:

Case 1: In Country A the opportunity cost of producing one widget is two wadgets. In Country B the opportunity cost of producing two widgets is four wadgets.

Case 2: In Country C the opportunity cost of producing one widget is two wadgets. In Country D the opportunity cost of producing two widgets is one wadget.

Case 3: In Country E the opportunity cost of producing one widget is two wadgets. In Country F the opportunity cost of producing one widget is four wadgets.

b. On what general principle did you base your reasoning?

c. Assume that in Case 3 there are constant economies of scale. Country E is currently producing 10 widgets and 4 wadgets. Country F is currently producing 20 widgets and 20 wadgets. Can you make an offer involving trade that will make both countries better off?

d. How would your answer differ if each country experiences economies of scale?

2. Suppose Country A and Country B are potential trading partners. Each country produces two goods: fish and wine. If Country A devotes all of its resources to producing fish, it can produce 1,000 fish, and if it devotes all of its resources to producing wine, it can produce 2,000 bottles of wine. If Country B devotes all of its resources to producing fish, it can produce 3,000 fish, and if it devotes all of its resources to producing wine it can produce 3,000 bottles of wine. For simplicity, assume the production possibility curves of these countries are straight lines.

    a. Draw the production possibility curve for Country A on the axes below. In Country A, what is the opportunity cost of one bottle of wine in terms of fish?

    b. Draw the production possibility curve for Country B on the axes for part *a*. In Country B, what is the opportunity cost of one bottle of wine in terms of fish?

    c. Does Country A have a comparative advantage in producing either wine or fish? Does Country B have a comparative advantage in producing either wine or fish?

d. Suppose Country A specialized in that good for which it has a comparative advantage and Country B specialized in that good for which it has a comparative advantage. Each country would then trade the good it produced for the good the other country produced. What would be a fair exchange of goods?

3. Suppose two countries A and B have the following production possibility tables:

% Resources devoted to Machines	Country A Production Machines	Country A Production Food	Country B Production Machines	Country B Production Food
A	100	200	0	40	0
B	80	160	8	32	40
C	60	120	16	28	80
D	40	80	24	24	120
E	20	40	32	16	160
F	0	0	40	0	200

    a. Draw the production possibility curves for Country A and Country B on the axes below.

    b. Which country has the comparative advantage in the production of food?

c. Suppose each country specializes in the production of one good. Explain how Country A can end up with 50 food units and 150 machines and Country B can end up with 150 food units and 50 machines. Both points are outside the production possibility curve for each country without trade.

4. The currency of Norway is the krone. State whether the following would cause the krone to appreciate or depreciate.

a. Drilling in the north of Norway leads to the discovery of a huge reservoir of oil. Norway now has more oil than any other nation.

b. A national recession causes interest rates and income to decrease.

c. Unprecedented civil war breaks out and causes foreign investors to doubt the stability of Norwegian assets.

5. Using a supply and demand curve for domestic goods with a world price level show a country with a trade balance:

P
|
|
|
|
|
|
|_____→ Q

a. Show the effect of a currency appreciation on the trade balance.

b. Show the effect of a currency depreciation on the trade balance.

⬤ MULTIPLE CHOICE

Circle the one best answer for each of the following questions:

1. Refer to the graph below. Given these production possibility curves, you would suggest that:

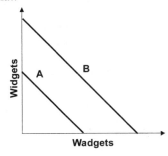

a. Country A should specialize in widgets and Country B in wadgets.
b. no trade should take place.
c. Country A should specialize in wadgets and Country B in widgets.
d. Both countries should produce an equal amount of each.

2. Refer to the graph below. The graph demonstrates Saudi Arabia's and the United States' production possibility curves for widgets and wadgets. Given these production possibility curves, you would suggest that:

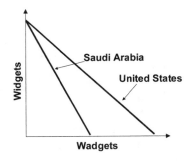

a. Saudi Arabia specialize in widgets and the United States in wadgets.
b. no trade should take place.
c. Saudi Arabia specialize in wadgets and the United States in widgets.
d. both countries should produce an equal amount of each.

3. If a nation has a comparative advantage in the production of good X then:
a. it can produce good X at the lowest opportunity cost.
b. it will import good X.

c. it can produce more of good X than any other nation.

d. the opportunity cost of producing an additional unit of good X is greater than for any other nation.

4. A widget has an opportunity cost of 4 wadgets in Saudi Arabia and 2 wadgets in the United States. Given these opportunity costs, you would suggest that:

a. Saudi Arabia specialize in widgets and the United States in wadgets.

b. no trade should take place.

c. Saudi Arabia specialize in wadgets and the United States in widgets.

d. both countries should produce an equal amount of each.

5. Country A's cost of widgets is $4.00 and cost of wadgets is $8.00. Country B's cost of widgets is 8 euros and cost of wadgets is 16 euros. Which of the following would you suggest?

a. Country A should specialize in widgets and Country B in wadgets.

b. Trade of widgets for wadgets would not benefit the countries.

c. Country A should specialize in wadgets and Country B in widgets.

d. Both countries should produce an equal amount of each.

6. In considering the distribution of the gains from trade:

a. smaller countries usually get a larger proportion of the gains from trade.

b. larger countries usually get a larger proportion of the gains from trade.

c. the gains are generally split equally between small and large countries.

d. no statement can be made about the general nature of the split.

7. Which of the following statements correctly summarizes a difference between the layperson's and the economist's views of the net benefits of trade?

a. Economists often argue that the gains from trade in the form of low consumer prices tend to be widespread and not easily recognizable while the costs in jobs lost tend to be concentrated and readily identifiable.

b. Economists often argue that most U.S. jobs are at risk of outsourcing while laypeople intuitively recognize that inherent in comparative advantage is that each country has a comparative advantage in the production of some good.

c. Economists focus on trade in manufactured goods while laypeople also focus on trade involving the services of people who manage the trade.

d. Economists most often argue that the costs of trade outweigh the benefits while laypeople often argue that the benefits of trade outweigh the costs.

8. In the United States, globalization has caused workers in the education, healthcare, and government sectors to face:

a. lower wages.

b. higher prices on consumer goods.

c. little or no downward pressure on their wages.

d. longer hours to compete with the higher production levels abroad.

9. Transferable comparative advantages are:

a. based on factors that are relatively unchangeable.

b. based on factors that can change relatively easily.

c. becoming more like inherent comparative advantages with technological innovations.

d. rarely eroded over time.

10. Which of the following is eroding the U.S. comparative advantage?

a. The spread of technology.

b. The law of one price.

c. A depreciating dollar.

d. Intellectual property rights.

11. The foreign exchange rate is the rate at which:

a. taxes are imposed on foreign imports.

b. foreign good are traded between domestic consumers.

c. one country's currency can be traded for another country's currency.

d. immigrants are exchanged between countries.

12. If civil war broke out in China, causing interest rates and income to drop:
   a. the demand for yuan would decrease and the supply of yuan would increase.
   b. the demand for yuan would increase and the supply of yuan would increase.
   c. the demand for yuan would decrease and the supply of yuan would decrease.
   d. the demand for yuan would increase and the supply of yuan would decrease.

13. In the graph below, the value of the dollar is:

   a. appreciating because the dollar buys more yuan.
   b. depreciating because the dollar buys more yuan.
   c. appreciating because the dollar buys fewer yuan.
   d. depreciating because the dollar buys fewer yuan.

14. All of the following would cause the yen (currency of Japan) to appreciate *except*:
   a. the discovery of a vegetable only grown in Japan that could be used as biofuel.
   b. increased interest rates on Japanese financial assets.
   c. a decrease in Japanese income.
   d. a new, global trend for Japanese sushi.

15. In the following graph, the country has a trade:

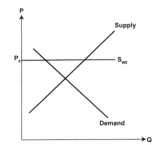

   a. deficit.
   b. surplus.
   c. balance.
   d. appreciation.

16. Which of the following would raise the world price level facing the United States?
   a. The dollar appreciates.
   b. The dollar depreciates.
   c. The trade deficit rises.
   d. The trade deficit falls.

17. The resource curse is when:
   a. a nation only has an inherent comparative advantage for one resource.
   b. a nation only has a transferrable comparative advantage for one resource.
   c. the discovery of a resource in a nation causes its currency to appreciate and thus causes the nation to lose comparative advantages in other sectors.
   d. a nation has neither an inherent nor a transferrable comparative advantage for any resource.

● POTENTIAL ESSAY QUESTIONS

You may also see essay questions similar to the "Problems & Applications" exercises.

1. What are two complications in exchange rate determination? What is the effect of each on the value of a country's currency?

2. If you were a trader would you look for potential trades between countries where production costs fall as output rises, or where production costs rise as output rises? Why?

━━━━ ANSWERS ━━━━

SHORT-ANSWER QUESTIONS

1.   The principle of comparative advantage is that as long as the relative opportunity costs of production differ among countries, there are potential gains from trade, even if one country has an absolute advantage in everything. (187)

2.   Three determinants of the gains of trade are (1) the more competition, the less the trader gets and the more will go to the countries who are trading; (2) smaller countries get a larger proportion of the gain than larger countries; and (3) countries producing goods with economies of scale get a larger gain from trade. (188)

3.   Four reasons for differences between economists' and laypeople's views of trade are: (1) gains from trade are often stealth gains, (2) opportunity cost is relative therefore comparative advantage is determined by more than wages, (3) nations trade more than just manufactured goods, and (4) trade affects the distribution of income. (190-192)

4.   Currently trade has made the distribution of income in the United States more unequal. Production in the tradable sector such as manufacturing has become less competitive. Some workers in this sector have received lower wages and lost their jobs, which lowers their overall income. At the same time, people with intellectual property and workers in high tech and financial sectors have seen their incomes rise because the market for high-tech products has expanded beyond the United States and globalization has increased the demand in the financial and trade-facilitation sectors. (191-192)

5.   The United States has comparative advantages due to: (1) skills of the U.S. labor force, (2) U.S. governmental institutions, (3) U.S. physical and technological infrastructure, (4) English as the international language of business, (5) wealth from past production, (6) U.S. natural resources, (7) cachet, (8) inertia, (9) U.S. intellectual property rights, and (10) a relatively open immigration policy. (The question asks for four of these.) (192-193)

6.   Transferable comparative advantages are comparative advantages based on factors that can change relatively easily. Inherent comparative advantages are comparative advantages that are based on factors that are relatively unchangeable. (194)

7.   The United States is losing some of its comparative advantage because economic forces are pushing to spread capital and technology to other countries. (194-195)

8.   The appreciation of the dollar relative to the yuan means that one dollar buys more yuans. (198)

9.   The appreciation of the dollar will increase the U.S. trade deficit. The appreciation causes the relative price of U.S. goods to increase, causing U.S. goods to become less competitive in the global market. As a result, the quantity of goods exported by the United States decreases and the quantity of foreign goods imported by the United States increases, both of which cause the trade deficit to increase. (198-199)

10. The resource curse is the paradox that countries with an abundance of resources tend to have lower economic growth and more unemployment than countries with fewer resources. This occurs because the large quantity of resources or discovery of resources in the country raises foreign demand for that resource and causes the country's currency to appreciate. The appreciation of the country's currency causes other goods to lose their comparative advantage and become less competitive in the global market, thus, one industrial sector gains a comparative advantage while others lose their comparative advantage. As a result, the trade deficit rises. (199-200)

━━━━ ANSWERS ━━━━

MATCHING

1-a; 2-c; 3-j; 4-d; 5-f; 6-g; 7-i; 8-e; 9-b; 10-h.

■ ANSWERS ■

PROBLEMS AND APPLICATIONS

1. **a.** There is a basis for trade in Cases 2 and 3 because opportunity costs differ. (186-188)

    b. The general principle is that there are gains from trade to be made when each country has a comparative advantage in a different good. That is, the opportunity costs differ. (186-188)

    c. I would have country E specialize in widgets and country F specialize in wadgets. Since country E is currently producing 10 widgets and 4 wadgets, I would have it produce 12 widgets and no wadgets, promising that I will give it 5 wadgets for the extra two widgets it produced. I would have Country F produce 28 wadgets and 18 widgets, promising that I will give it 2 widgets in return for 7 of its wadgets. After I made this trade both countries are one widget better off. I am two widgets better off. (These two widgets are the return to me for organizing the trade.) (186-188)

    d. If there were economies of scale, there would be an even stronger argument for trade. (186-188)

2. **a.** The production possibility curve for Country A is the curve labeled A in the graph below. In Country A the opportunity cost of one bottle of wine is 1/2 fish. Each fish forgone frees up resources sufficient to make two bottles of wine. (186-188)

    b. The production possibility curve for Country B is the curve labeled B in the graph above. In Country B the opportunity cost of one bottle of wine is one fish. Each fish forgone frees up resources sufficient to make one bottle of wine. (186-188)

    c. Country A has a comparative advantage in wine because it has to give up only 1/2 a fish for each bottle of wine while Country B has to give up 1 fish for each bottle of wine. Country B must necessarily have a comparative advantage in fish. (186-188)

    d. A fair exchange for B would be giving up one fish for one bottle of wine or better because that is its opportunity cost of producing one fish. A fair exchange for A would be giving up two bottles of wine for 1 fish or better since its opportunity cost of producing two bottles of wine is one fish. Any exchange that reflects a ratio between these two values would be fair. (186-188)

3. **a.** The production possibility curves for Country A and Country B are drawn below. (186-188)

    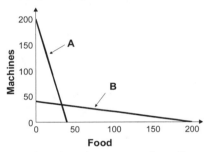

    b. Country B has the comparative advantage in the production of food since it has to give up only 1/5 of a machine to produce one unit of food while Country A has to give up 5 machines to produce one unit of food. (186-188)

    c. Country A would be willing to supply 5 machines for 1 unit of food. Country B would be willing to supply 5 units of food for one machine. Let's suppose they trade 1 for 1. Country A would produce 200 machines, selling 50 to Country B for 50 units of food. Country B would produce 200 food units, and sell 50 to Country A for 50 machines. This way they each reach their higher desired level of consumption. (186-188)

4. **a.** The krone would be expected to appreciate. The demand for krones would shift to the right as foreign nations bought more oil from Norway; the supply of krones would shift to the left because Norwegians would shift their oil consumption back to Norwegian oil. This is shown on the accompanying graph. (196-198)

b. The krone would be expected to depreciate. The demand for krones would shift to
the left as foreign investors bought fewer
Norwegian assets and bonds; the supply
of krones would shift to the right as
Norwegian investors shifted from buying
Norwegian assets to buying foreign
assets. This is shown on the graph below.
(196-198)

c. The krone would be expected to depreciate. The demand for krones would shift to
the left as foreign investors bought fewer
Norwegian assets and bonds due to the
war; the supply of krones would shift to
the right as Norwegian investors shifted
from buying Norwegian assets to buying
foreign assets. This is shown on the
graph below. (196-198)

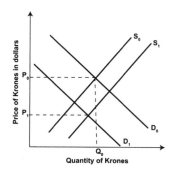

5. The world price level intersects the demand
and supply curves at their equilibrium as
shown in the graph below. There is no trade
deficit.
   a. The world price level falls below the
domestic price level, which causes a trade
deficit shown by $Q_1 - Q_2$. (196-198)
   b. The world price level rises above the
domestic price level, which causes a trade
surplus shown by $Q_2 - Q_1$. (196-198)

━━━━━━ ANSWERS ━━━━━━

MULTIPLE CHOICE

1. **b**   Since the curves have the same slope, no
country has a comparative advantage in
either good and there is no basis for trade.
See pages 186-188 and Figure 9-1.

2. **a**   The opportunity cost for Saudi Arabia of
wadgets in terms of widgets is higher than
the opportunity cost for the United States.
So Saudi Arabia should specialize in
widgets and the United States in wadgets.
See pages 186-188 and Figure 9-1.

3. **a**   A comparative advantage in the production of X means the nation can produce
that good with a lower opportunity cost.
Because the nation is relatively more
efficient at producing X, it will specialize in
its production and export that good.
Answer c may be true, but it is also
possible to have a comparative advantage
in X without being able to produce more of
X than any other nation. See pages 186-
188.

4. **c**   The opportunity cost for the United States
of wadgets in terms of widgets is higher
than the opportunity cost for Saudi

Arabia. So the United States should specialize in widgets and Saudi Arabia in wadgets. See pages 186-188.

5. b The opportunity cost of widgets and wadgets is equal in both countries so neither country has a comparative advantage in either good and there is no basis for trade. See pages 186-188.

6. a Smaller countries usually find that their production possibilities are changed more, and hence they benefit more. See pages 188-189.

7. a It is because the costs of trade are more visible than the benefits that many laypeople oppose free trade. Switching "economists" and "laypeople" would make options b through d correct. See pages 190-192.

8. c Workers in education, healthcare, and government sectors felt little or no downward pressure on their wages from globalization because these sectors produce goods and services that cannot be easily traded on the global market. See pages 191-192.

9. b Transferable comparative advantages are based on factors that can change relatively easily and will tend to erode over time. Technological innovations are turning inherent comparative advantages into transferable comparative advantages. See page 194.

10. a As technology spreads, foreign countries can compete on a broader range of goods. As long as wages in foreign countries are lower than in the United States, this will erode U.S. comparative advantage. The law of one price describes why low wage countries will eventually lose comparative advantage. An depreciating dollar increases U.S. comparative advantage. See page 198.

11. c The foreign exchange rate is the rate at which one country's currency can be traded for another country's currency. See page 196.

12. a If civil war broke out in China and caused interest rates and income to drop, the yuan would depreciate. Thus, the demand for yuan would decrease and the supply for yuan would increase. See pages 196-198.

13. d Since the supply of dollars is shifting out to the right, it takes fewer yuan to buy one dollar. That means the dollar is depreciating. See page 198.

14. c A decrease in Japanese income would cause the yen to depreciate rather than appreciate. Fewer foreign investors and Japanese investors would invest in Japan due to the lower income, thus the demand for yen would decrease and the supply of yen would increase, causing the currency to depreciate. See pages 196-198.

15. b The graph shows a country with a trade surplus, for the world price is greater than the domestic price; therefore the nation will export more and import less. See pages 198-199.

16. b When the dollar depreciates, an American gets fewer foreign currency units for every dollar exchanged, making foreign goods cost more. See pages 198-199.

17. c The resource curse occurs when the discovery of a resource in a nation causes it's currency to appreciate and thus causes the nation to lose comparative advantages in other sectors. See pages 199-200.

━━━ ANSWERS ━━━

POTENTIAL ESSAY QUESTIONS

The following are annotated answers. They indicate the general idea behind the answer.

1. If the supply and demand for currencies applied only to tradable goods, trade between two countries would generally be in balance, and both countries would have roughly equal sectors of comparative advantages in producing goods. However, that doesn't always happen because of two main complications. (1) The demand for a country's currency reflects a demand for its assets as well as its produced goods. Therefore, when the demand for a country's assets is high, the value of its currency will also be high. With a higher exchange rate, the world price of tradable goods will be low, and the domestic country will have a comparative advantage in relatively fewer sectors than other countries. (2)Another complication to determining the exchange rate is known as the resource curse, which is when a resource is discovered that increases the demand for a nation's currency and thus causes its value to appreciate. When this happens, the natural resource sector of the country gains a comparative advantage while other sectors either do not gain a comparative advantage or lose a comparative advantage due to the higher value of the currency.

2. If I were a trader, I would look for potential trades between countries where production costs fall as output rises. If a nation's production costs fall as output rises, it exhibits economies of scale, therefore, an increase in production can lower the average cost of producing a good. With lower production costs, the nation produces more and reaps more benefits from trade in the form of higher profits. As a trader, the more the trading countries make, the more I make, so I would look for nations that exhibit economies of scale and generate greater profits.

INTERNATIONAL TRADE POLICY

10

CHAPTER AT A GLANCE

1. The primary trading partners of the United States are Canada, Mexico, the European Union, and the Pacific Rim countries. (206-208)

   A trade balance is the difference between a country's exports and imports. When imports exceed exports, a country has a trade deficit. When exports exceed imports a country has a trade surplus. Because the United States has had large trade deficits since the 1970s, it is a net debtor nation.

   The nature of trade is continually changing. The United States is importing more and more high-tech goods and services from India, China and other East Asian countries.

   Outsourcing is a type of trade. Outsourcing is a larger phenomenon today compared to 30 years ago because countries where jobs are outsourced today—China and India—are much larger.

2. Three policies used to restrict trade are: (210-213)
   - tariffs: taxes on internationally traded goods;
   - quotas: quantity limits placed on imports; and
   - regulatory trade restrictions: government-imposed procedural rules that limit imports.

   Countries can also restrict trade through: voluntary restraint agreements, embargoes, and nationalistic appeals.

3. A tariff operates in the same way as a tax. The difference between a tariff and a quota is who gets the revenue. Government collects the revenue with the tariff. Firms receive the revenue with a quota. (210-213)

   As seen in the following graph, a tariff, T, raises equilibrium price from P_0 to P_1 and equilibrium quantity declines from Q_0 to Q_1. Government collects the shaded region in tariffs. A quota of Q_1 has the same effect, except the shaded area goes to firms.

   When the domestic country is small and world price lower than domestic prices, tariffs lower a trade deficit. See Figure 10-5 for how.

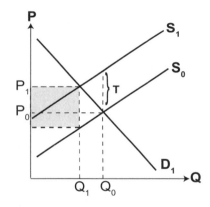

4. Arguments for restricting trade include: (213-219)
   - Unequal internal distribution of the gains from trade;
   - Haggling by companies over the gains from trade;
   - Haggling by countries over trade restrictions;
   - Specialized production; learning by doing; and economies of scale;
   - Macroeconomic aspects of trade;
   - National security;
   - International politics;
   - Increased revenue brought in by tariffs.

   Understand these motives for trade barriers and be able to explain why they may not be sound.

5.   Economists generally oppose trade restrictions because: (219-220)

- from a global perspective, free trade increases total output;
- international trade provides competition for domestic companies;
- restrictions based on national security are often abused or evaded; and
- trade restrictions are addictive.

Economists generally argue that the benefits of free trade outweigh the costs—especially over time.

Trade restrictions limit the supply of an imported good, increasing its price and decreasing quantity. Governments prefer tariffs over quotas because they generate tax revenues, while companies prefer quotas.

6.   Free trade associations help trade by reducing barriers to trade among member nations. Free trade associations could hinder trade by building up barriers to trade with nations outside the association. (220-222)

A free trade association is a group of countries that allow free trade among its members and puts up common barriers against all other countries' goods.

The WTO and GATT are important international economic organizations designed to reduce trade barriers among all countries.

● SHORT-ANSWER QUESTIONS

1. Who are the primary trading partners of the United States?

2. How has U.S. trade with the rest of the world changed in recent years?

3. What is the difference between a debtor and a creditor nation? Is the United States a creditor or debtor nation?

4. As a foreign firm, would you prefer a tariff or a quota in the country to which you export? Why?

5. In a talk to first-year members of Congress you are asked what they can do to restrict trade. You oblige.

6. You reveal to these first-year members of Congress that you believe in free trade. Hands fly up from people just waiting to tell you why they want to restrict trade. What are some of their reasons?

7. After listening to their remarks, you gather your thoughts and offer them reasons why you generally oppose trade restrictions. What do you say?

8. The first-year members of Congress ask you how joining a free trade association could help and hinder international trade. What do you say?

MATCHING THE TERMS
Match the terms to their definitions

___ 1.	economies of scale	a.	A tax governments place on internationally traded goods—generally imports.
___ 2.	embargo	b.	All-out restriction on the import or export of a good.
___ 3.	free trade association	c.	Costs per unit output go down as output increases.
___ 4.	General Agreement on Tariffs and Trade (GATT)	d.	A country that will pay as low a tariff on its exports as will any other country.
___ 5.	infant industry argument	e.	Demanding a larger share of the gains of trade than you might get normally.
___ 6.	learning by doing	f.	Government-imposed procedural rule that limits imports.
___ 7.	most-favored nation	g.	Group of countries that allow free trade among its members and put up common barriers against all other countries' goods.
___ 8.	quota	h.	Periodic international conference held in the past to reduce trade barriers.
___ 9.	regulatory trade restriction	i.	Program designed to compensate losers for reductions in trade restrictions.
___ 10.	strategic bargaining	j.	Quantity limit placed on imports.
___ 11.	strategic trade policy	k.	An organization whose functions are generally the same as were those of GATT—to promote free and fair trade among countries.
___ 12.	tariff	l.	With initial protection, an industry will be able to become competitive.
___ 13.	trade adjustment assistance program	m.	You become better at a task the more you perform it.
___ 14.	World Trade Organization (WTO)	n.	Threatening to implement tariffs to bring about a reduction in tariffs or some other concessions from the other country.

● PROBLEMS AND APPLICATIONS

1. State whether the trade restriction is a quota, tariff, or regulatory trade restriction.

   a. The EU (European Union) requires beef to be free of growth-inducing hormones in order to be traded in EU markets.

   b. Hong Kong has maintained rice import controls on quantity since 1955 in order to keep local rice importers in business and to secure a steady wartime food supply.

   c. To encourage domestic production of automobile parts, Japan limits the importation of automobile parts according to a rigid schedule of numbers.

   d. The United States charges French wineries 10% of the value of each case of French wine imported into the United States.

2. Suppose the U.S. is considering trade restrictions against EU-produced hams. Given the demand and supply curves drawn below, show a tariff and a quota that would result in the same exports of ham to the United States.

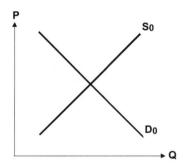

a. Would a tariff or a quota result in higher government revenue?

b. Which would the EU prefer?

c. Which would American ham producers prefer?

d. Which would American consumers prefer?

3. Refer to the graph below. The world price for a pound of coconuts is $3.00. The government of Fiji imposes a 50 cent tariff on the coconut imports to raise revenue and protect domestic producers as shown in the graph below. Assume the country is so small it takes the world price as given.

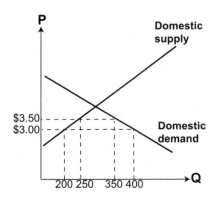

a. What are imports when the world price is $3.00?

b. What are imports if government imposes a 50-cent tariff?

c. Shade in the government revenue as a result of the tariff. What is the value of this revenue?

d. What quota would have the same effect on price and quantity as the tariff? Label the quota on the graph.

4. Coconut producers in Fiji politically lobby to get the tariff changed to a quota.

a. Why would the firms lobby for a quota instead of a tariff?

b. Why might the Fijian government resist changing the tariff to a quota?

c. What difference does the quota make for Fijian consumers compared to the tariff?

d. A member of Congress argues to eliminate restrictions altogether. What are some of the reasons she gives?

MULTIPLE CHOICE

Circle the one best answer for each of the following questions:

1. The prime trading partners of the United States by dollar volume are:
   a. India, China, and Indonesia.
   b. Canada, Mexico, the European Union, and the Pacific Rim countries.
   c. Saudi Arabia, Israel, and Iran.
   d. South American and West African nations.

2. If a nation is a debtor nation it:
   a. is currently running a trade deficit.
   b. is currently running a trade surplus.
   c. has run trade deficits in the past.
   d. has run trade surpluses in the past.

3. Compared to the past, the United States is now:
   a. importing more high-tech goods and services from India and China and other East Asian countries.
   b. importing more goods and services that are lower down the technological ladder.
   c. outsourcing less to newly emerging industrialized countries like China and India.
   d. facing less competition from newly emerging industrialized countries like China and India.

4. If a country has a trade deficit, it is:
   a. consuming more than it is producing.
   b. lending to foreigners.
   c. buying financial assets.
   d. buying real assets.

5. A most-favored nation is a country that:
   a. pays no tariffs on exports.
   b. has a policy of no regulatory trade restrictions.
   c. prefers regulatory trade restrictions to tariffs and quotas.
   d. pays as low a tariff on its exports as will any other country.

6. Trade restrictions tend to:
   a. increase competition.
   b. increase prices to consumers.
   c. benefit consumers.
   d. have economic benefits that outweigh the economic costs.

7. A tariff is a:
   a. tax government places on imports.
   b. quantity limit placed on imports.
   c. total restriction on imports.
   d. government-imposed procedural rule that limits imports.

8. An embargo is:
   a. a tax government places on imports.
   b. a quantity limit placed on imports.
   c. a total restriction on imports.
   d. a government-imposed procedural rule that limits imports.

9. The value T on the graph below represents?

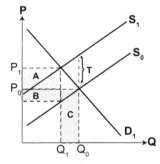

   a. an embargo.
   b. a tariff.
   c. a quota.
   d. a regulatory trade restriction.

10. In the graph for Question #9, which area represents the revenue collected by government?
    a. A.
    b. B.
    c. B and C.
    d. A and B.

11. For governments:
    a. tariffs are preferred over quotas because tariffs can help them collect revenues.
    b. quotas are preferred over tariffs because quotas can help them collect revenues.
    c. neither quotas nor tariffs can help collect revenues.
    d. both because quotas and tariffs are sources of revenues.

12. Trade adjustment assistance programs are designed to:
    a. compensate losers for trade restrictions.
    b. assist importers to conform to regulatory trade restrictions.
    c. educate firms how to trade on the global level.
    d. subsidize research on the most effective strategic trade policies.

13. Reasons for restricting trade include all of the following *except:*
    a. the existence of learning by doing and economies of scale.
    b. national security reasons.
    c. the increased revenue brought in from tariffs.
    d. the fact that trade decreases competitive pressures at home.

14. Economists generally oppose trade restrictions for all of the following reasons *except:*
    a. from a global perspective, free trade increases total output.
    b. the infant industry argument.
    c. trade restrictions lead to retaliation.
    d. international politics.

15. Free trade associations tend to:
    a. reduce restrictions on trade and thereby always expand free trade.
    b. lower trade barriers for all countries.
    c. replace multinational negotiations, and thereby always hurt free trade.
    d. expand, but also reduce, free trade.

● POTENTIAL ESSAY QUESTIONS

You may also see essay questions similar to the "Problems & Applications" exercises.

1. What is the difference between a tariff and a quota? Why do governments prefer tariffs while foreign producers prefer quotas? What is the result of tariffs and quotas on the price and equilibrium quantity of the imported good?

2. What are six ways in which a country may restrict trade? Why do most economists support free trade and oppose trade restrictions?

ANSWERS

SHORT-ANSWER QUESTIONS

1. The primary trading partners of the United States are Canada, Mexico, the European Union, and Pacific Rim countries. (206-208)

2. The kinds of goods and services the U.S. imports have shifted from primarily basic manufacturing goods and raw commodities to high-tech manufacturing goods and services from developing countries such as India, China, and other East Asian countries. In addition, more and more production of more sophisticated goods and services is being outsourced to these countries because their economies are much larger. (207-208)

3. A debtor nation is a nation that accumulated more trade deficits than trade surpluses. The United States is currently a debtor nation. A creditor nation is a nation that is running a trade surplus; its accumulated trade surpluses exceed accumulated trade deficits. (209-210)

4. I would prefer a quota to a tariff because, while in both cases the quantity I sell is lower, with a quota I collect the revenue and with a tariff, government collects the revenue. (211)

5. Three policies countries use to restrict trade are (1) tariffs, (2) quotas, and (3) regulatory trade restrictions. There are others. (211-215)

6. Answers might include: (1) although foreign competition might make society better off, some people may lose their jobs because of foreign competition (unequal internal distribution of the gains from trade); (2) some foreign companies are taking tough bargaining positions, and restricting trade is our only weapon (haggling by companies over trade restrictions); (3) some foreign countries are threatening us with trade restrictions (haggling by countries over the gains from trade); (4) trade restrictions will protect new U.S. industries until they learn to be competitive (learning by doing and economies of scale); (5) imports hurt U.S. domestic income in the short run, and the economy needs to grow in the short run (trade can reduce domestic output in the short run); (6) some restrictions are needed to

protect our national security; (7) we do not want to trade with countries who violate our human rights standards or whose ideology conflicts with our democratic ideals (international politics may dominate trade considerations); and (8) tariffs bring in revenue for the U.S. government. (213-219)

7. I would say that I generally oppose trade restrictions because (1) from a global perspective, free trade increases total output, (2) international trade provides competition for domestic companies, (3) restrictions based on national security are often abused, and (4) trade restrictions are addictive. (219-220)

8. Free trade associations promote trade among members by reducing barriers to trade among the member nations. However, free trade associations could hinder trade by building up barriers to trade with nations outside the association. (220-222)

ANSWERS

MATCHING

1-c; 2-b; 3-g; 4-h; 5-l; 6-m; 7-d; 8-j; 9-f; 10-e; 11-n; 12-a; 13-i; 14-k.

ANSWERS

PROBLEMS AND APPLICATIONS

1. a. Regulatory trade restriction because this is a regulation that has the final effect of reducing imports without a tax or numerical limitation. (210-213)
    b. Quota. It is a numerical restriction on the amount of rice entering the country. (210-213)
    c. Quota because it is a numerical restriction on imports. (210-213)
    d. Tariff because it is a tax on imports. (210-213)

2. A tariff would shift the supply curve up by the amount of the tariff. A quota with the same result would be at Q_1. Equilibrium quantity

would fall from Q_0 to Q_1. Equilibrium price would rise from P_0 to P_1. This is shown on the graph below. (210-211 and Figure 10-4)

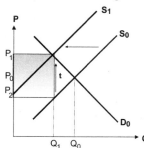

a.   The government receives no revenue from the quota, but receives the shaded region as revenue from the tariff as shown on the graph above. (210-211 and Figure 10-4)

b.   The EU would prefer the quota since it will receive a higher price, P_1, for the same quantity of goods, Q_1 as it would with a tariff. With a tariff it would receive P_2, for Q_1. (210-211 and Figure 10-4)

c.   American ham producers prefer the quota because any increase in domestic demand would be met by domestic supply. (210-211)

d.   American consumers do not prefer either since the resulting price and quantity is the same with both. If, however, the tariff revenue were to lead to lower taxes or higher government services, they might prefer the tariff over the quota. They also might prefer the tariff to the quota because any increase in domestic demand will be partially met with imports, keeping domestic producers more efficient than under a quota system. (210-211)

3.   a.   At a world price of $3.00 the domestic quantity demanded is 400 pounds of coconuts and imports are 200. Thus, imports are 200. (210-212)

b.   The tariff leads to a decline in domestic quantity demanded to 350 pounds of coconuts and an increase in domestic quantity supplied to 250 pounds of coconuts. Net imports are now 100. (210-212)

c.   The government of Fiji earned $50 as a result of the tariff. ($0.50x100) (210-212)

d.   The quota would be a limit of 100 pounds of coconut. See the accompanying graph. (210-211)

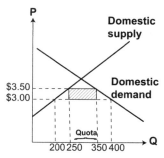

4.   Considering the graph for Question #3 above;

a.   Fijian coconut producers prefer a quota to a tariff because in the case of a quota, they receive the benefits from trade in the form of additional corporate revenue as domestic demand must then be met with domestic supply. (210-212)

b.   The government may resist changing the tariff to a quota because they would lose tariff revenue. (210-212)

c.   Fijian consumers have no preference. Both result in higher prices. (210-212)

d.   She might say that free trade increases total output and provides competition to domestic companies. She might also add that trade restrictions are addictive and soon they might be placing tariffs on all types of goods, not just coconuts. (210-212)

ANSWERS

MULTIPLE CHOICE

1.   b   Though the United States has recently expanded trade with China and India, the prime trade partners of the United States are Canada, Mexico, the European Union, and the Pacific Rim countries. See Figure 10-1.

2.   c   A debtor nation may currently be running a surplus or a deficit. Debt is accumulated deficits. A debtor nation could be running a surplus if it ran deficits in the past. See pages 209-210.

3.   a   The U.S. is importing more and more high-tech goods and services that are higher up the technological ladder from India and China and other East Asian countries. The

U.S. is outsourcing more to these newly emerging industrialized countries and is therefore facing more competition from these nations. See page 208.

4. a   If a country has a trade deficit, it is importing (consuming) more than it is exporting (producing). See page 208.

5. d   Most-favored nations might pay tariffs, but they receive the lowest tariffs compared to all other countries. See page 222.

6. b   Trade restrictions reduce competition and therefore increase prices to consumers. Thus, consumers are hurt. The benefits of trade restrictions go to the domestic producers that do not have to compete as aggressively. The economic costs of trade restrictions (in the form of higher prices consumers must pay) far outweigh their benefits (which go to the protected domestic industries in the form of higher profits and more secure jobs). See pages 210-211.

7. a   A tariff is a tax placed on imported goods. See page 210.

8. c   An embargo is an all-out restriction on the trade of goods with another country. See page 212.

9. b   A tariff is a tax on goods, in this graph represented by T. Quotas are quantity restrictions. Regulatory trade restrictions cannot be illustrated with this graph. See pages 210-211.

10. d   The revenue to government is represented by the tariff times the quantity imported, Areas A+B. Area A does not reflect the entire amount of the tariff revenue. The tariff is T. Area C does not make sense. See pages 210-212.

11. a   Governments prefer tariffs because they generate revenues, quotas do not. See pages 210-212.

12. a   Trade adjustment assistance programs compensate people who have lost their jobs as a result of an increase in trade restrictions. Governments try to use trade adjustment assistance programs to facilitate free trade, but in practice, it is difficult to determine who is actually hurt by free trade. See page 215.

13. d   Trade increases competitive pressures at home and increases competitiveness. See pages 210-218.

14. b   The infant industry argument is an argument in favor of trade restrictions. Economists' response to the infant industry argument is that history shows that few infant industries have ever grown up. See pages 213-220.

15. d   While free trade associations may work toward lowering trade barriers among member nations, they may result in higher trade barriers for nonmember countries. See pages 220-222.

━━━━━━━   ANSWERS   ━━━━━━━

POTENTIAL ESSAY QUESTIONS

The following are annotated answers. They indicate the general idea behind the answer.

1. A tariff is a tax on an imported item. A quota is a quantity limitation. Tariffs are preferred by governments because they raise revenues and are disliked by foreign producers because they require tax payments to the imposing government. However, notice that both tariffs and quotas raise prices and decrease the quantity of imported goods bought and sold.

2. Countries use a variety of policies to restrict trade. These include:
   • Tariffs.
   • Quotas.
   • Voluntary restraint agreements.
   • Embargoes.
   • Regulatory trade restrictions.
   • Nationalistic appeals.

Economists generally oppose trade restrictions because: (1) from a global perspective, free trade increases total output—it raises standards of living; (2) international trade provides competition for domestic companies; (3) restrictions based on national security are often abused or evaded; and (4) trade restrictions often become addictive for domestic firms that benefit. Free trade forces domestic firms to be efficient—to provide higher quality goods at cheaper prices. Economists argue that trade restrictions may create some short-run benefits, but the costs (or harm done, which includes higher prices domestic consumers must pay) outweigh the benefits over time.

PRODUCTION AND COST ANALYSIS I

CHAPTER AT A GLANCE

1. Accounting profit is explicit revenue less explicit cost. Economists include implicit revenue and cost in their determination of profit. (227-228)

   Economic profit = (explicit and implicit revenue) – (explicit and implicit cost).

   Implicit revenue includes the increases in the value of assets owned by the firm.

   Implicit costs include the opportunity cost of time and capital provided by the owners of the firm. Accountants do not include these implicit revenues and costs in their calculations of profit.

2. A long-run decision is a decision in which the firm can choose among all possible production techniques. A short-run decision is a decision in which the firm is constrained in regard to what production decisions it can make. (229-230)

   Long run → all inputs are variable → all costs are variable.

   Short run → at least one input is fixed → some costs are fixed and some are variable (vary with the production level).

3. The law of diminishing marginal productivity states that as more and more of a variable input is added to an existing fixed input, at some point the additional output one gets from the additional input will fall. (231-232)

   Sometimes called "flowerpot law." Its existence eventually causes costs of production to rise.

   Study all tables and figures in this chapter! Marginal product is the extra output from an additional unit of an input.

   Marginal productivity declines because of the law of diminishing marginal productivity. It is because of diminishing marginal productivity that costs of production eventually rise.

4. The most important categories of costs are shown in Table 11-1. Notice total costs, marginal costs, average fixed costs, average variable costs, and average total costs can be calculated given fixed costs and variable costs at each level of output. (232-235)

✓ *Know how to calculate all 7 short-run cost figures! (FC, VC, TC, MC, AFC, AVC, and ATC). Notice the two ways to calculate each:*

$$
\begin{aligned}
TC &= FC + VC\ (= ATC \times Q) \\
VC &= TC - FC\ (= AVC \times Q) \\
FC &= TC - VC\ (= AFC \times Q) \\
MC &= \Delta TC/\Delta Q\ (= \Delta TVC/\Delta Q) \\
ATC &= TC/Q\ (= AFC + AVC) \\
AVC &= VC/Q\ (= ATC - AFC) \\
AFC &= FC/Q\ (= ATC - AVC)
\end{aligned}
$$

5. The marginal cost curve goes through the minimum point of the average total cost curve and average variable cost curve; each of these curves is U-shaped. The average fixed cost curve slopes down continuously. (235-239)

   See Figure 11-2(b). Remember that all cost curves (except FC and AFC) are shaped the way they are because of increasing and diminishing marginal productivity!

6. When marginal and average productivity are rising, marginal and average cost curves are falling. When marginal and average productivity are falling, marginal and average cost curves are rising. (237-238)

   Figure 11-3 in the textbook on page 237 shows how marginal productivity and marginal costs are mirror images of one another. The same is true for average productivity and average cost.

✓ *Study the "Reminder" box "Review of Costs."*

● SHORT-ANSWER QUESTIONS

1. What are three roles of the firm?

2. What is the difference between accounting profit and economic profit?

3. Suppose you are the president of a corporation who is designing a 2-year plan of operations and a 10-year plan of operations. How would those plans differ?

4. Suppose you are a novice gardener. You plant one seed in a flower pot and watch it grow into a stalk of wheat with plump wheat berries. The next year, you plant two seeds in that pot and harvest double the amount of wheat berries. You deduce that at this rate, you can provide the world's supply of wheat berries in your little pot. Why is this obviously not true? What principle is your answer based on?

5. What is the algebraic relationship between total cost, total variable cost, and total fixed cost? What is the algebraic relationship between average total cost, average variable cost, and average fixed cost? What is marginal cost equal to?

6. What does the marginal cost curve measure?

7. What does the average variable cost curve measure?

8. What does the average fixed cost curve measure?

9. What does the average total cost curve measure?

10. How does the law of diminishing marginal productivity affect the shape of short-run cost curves?

11. Where does the marginal cost curve intersect the average total cost and average variable cost curves? Explain why the relationship between marginal cost and average cost is how you have described it.

12. Draw typical *AFC*, *AVC*, *ATC,* and *MC* curves on the same graph, making sure to maintain the relationships among them.

MATCHING THE TERMS
Match the terms to their definitions

____ 1. average fixed cost

____ 2. average product

____ 3. average total cost

____ 4. average variable cost

____ 5. economic profit

____ 6. firm

____ 7. fixed costs

____ 8. law of diminishing marginal productivity

____ 9. long-run decision

____ 10. marginal cost

____ 11. marginal product

____ 12. production

____ 13. production function

____ 14. production table

____ 15. profit

____ 16. short-run decision

____ 17. total cost

____ 18. total revenues

____ 19. variable costs

a. A decision in which the firm can choose among all possible production techniques.

b. Additional output forthcoming from an additional input, other inputs constant.

c. As more and more of a variable input is added to an existing fixed input, after some point the additional output one gets from the additional input will fall.

d. Total revenue minus total cost, (excluding implicit revenue and cost).

e. Costs that are spent and cannot be changed in the period of time under consideration.

f. Equation that describes the relationships between inputs and outputs, telling the maximum amount of output that can be derived from a given number of inputs.

g. Firm is constrained in regard to what production decisions it can make.

h. Fixed cost divided by quantity produced.

i. Sum of fixed and variable costs.

j. Variable cost divided by quantity produced.

k. The costs of variable inputs.

l. The cost of changing the level of output by one unit.

m. Total output divided by the quantity of the input.

n. Total cost divided by the quantity produced.

o. Explicit and implicit revenue minus explicit and implicit cost.

p. The transformation of factors into goods and services.

q. An economic institution that transforms factors of production into goods and services.

r. The amount a firm receives for selling its product or service plus any increase in the value of assets owned by the firm.

s. A table showing the output resulting from various combinations of factors of productions or inputs.

PROBLEMS AND APPLICATIONS

1. Suppose you and a friend are thinking about opening a fast food vending service at a nearby resort during your summer break. This will entail serving pizzas out of a vendor's truck. This venture is an alternative to working at a factory job where you could each earn $7,000 over the summer break. A fully equipped truck could be leased for $10,000. Insurance and other miscellaneous operating expenses total $1,000. Given your projected sales revenues of $33,000 you anticipate your variable costs to total $8,000. Together, you and your friend have just enough money in the bank to cover all of the summer's fixed and variable costs of the business. If you pull that money out of the bank, you will have to collectively forgo $500 in interest income for the summer.

    a. What would be the accounting profit for your business?

    b. What would be the economic profit for your business?

2. Find *TC, AFC, AVC, ATC,* and *MC* for the following table. Also, graph the TC curve on one graph and graph AFC, AVC, ATC, and MC on another graph.

Units	FC	VC	TC	MC	AFC	AVC	ATC
0	50	0					
1	50	90					
2	50	120					
3	50	165					
4	50	220					
5	50	290					

3. You are presented with the following table on average productivity. Labor is your only variable cost. The price of labor is $20 per hour, and the fixed cost is $50.

Labor	TP	MP	AP	TC	MC	AVC
1	2					
2	6					
3	15					
4	20					
5	23					
6	24					

    a. Fill in the table above for marginal product (MP), average product (AP), total cost (TC), marginal cost (MC), and average variable costs (AVC).

    b. Graph the average variable cost curve.

    c. Show that the graph you drew in part *3b* is the approximate mirror image of the average productivity curve.

    d. Graph the marginal cost and the marginal productivity curves. Show that they are approximate mirror images of each other.

e. What is the relationship between marginal cost (*MC*) and average cost (*AVC* and *ATC*)? What is the relationship between marginal product (*MP*) and average product (*AP*)?

4. A firm has fixed cost of $50. Variable costs are as follows:

Units	VC
1	75
2	110
3	150
4	200
5	260
6	335

a. Graph *AFC*, *ATC*, *AVC,* and *MC* curves on the axes below from the information provided in the table above (all on the same graph).

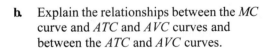

b. Explain the relationships between the *MC* curve and *ATC* and *AVC* curves and between the *ATC* and *AVC* curves.

c. Suppose fixed costs fall to $20. Graph new *AFC, ATC, AVC,* and *MC* curves.

d. Which curves shifted? Why?

5. A box of Wheaties cereal with a wholesale price of $1.60 has the following costs:

Labor:	$ 0.15
Materials:	0.30
Sales cost:	0.30
Advertising:	0.15
Research and Development:	0.15
Rent on factory building and equipment:	0.15
Owner's profit:	0.40

a. Which are likely variable costs?

b. Which are likely fixed costs?

c. If output were to rise, what would likely happen to *ATC*?

MULTIPLE CHOICE

Circle the one best answer for each of the following questions:

1. Economic profit:
   a. equals explicit and implicit revenues minus explicit and implicit costs.
   b. is the same as accounting profit.
   c. will always be larger than an accounting profit.
   d. does not include the opportunity cost of the entrepreneur in the total revenue calculation.

2. The difference between the short run and the long run in the cost model is that:
   a. the short run pertains to a period of time less than one year; the long run is longer than one year.
   b. in the short run at least one input (factor of production) is fixed; in the long run all inputs are variable.
   c. in the short run some costs are fixed; in the long run all costs are fixed.
   d. in the short run all costs are variable; in the long run all costs are fixed.

3. In a short-run decision:
   a. a firm has more options than in the long run.
   b. a firm has the same number of options as in the long run.
   c. a firm has fewer options than in the long run.
   d. there is no relationship between the number of options a firm has and whether it is a short-run decision or a long-run decision.

4. If a firm can produce 560 units of output with 5 workers and 600 units of output with 6 workers then the:
   a. marginal product of the 6th worker is 100 units.
   b. marginal product of the 6th worker is 40 units.
   c. average product of 6 workers is 70 units.
   d. average product of 5 workers is 100 units.

5. Refer to the graph below. The range marked "A" shows:

   a. increasing marginal productivity.
   b. diminishing marginal productivity.
   c. diminishing absolute productivity.
   d. diminishing absolute marginal productivity.

6. The law of diminishing marginal productivity:
   a. states that as more and more of a variable input is added to an existing fixed input, after some point the additional output one gets from the additional input will fall.
   b. states that as more and more of a variable input is added to an existing fixed input, after some point the additional output one gets from the additional input will rise.
   c. explains why marginal costs of production fall as additional units of output are produced.
   d. explains why average productivity always rises.

7. When the law of diminishing marginal productivity is operating:
   a. increasing returns to scale are realized.
   b. marginal productivity is falling and average productivity is rising.
   c. marginal productivity is falling and marginal costs are rising.
   d. marginal productivity is rising and marginal costs are rising.

8. Five workers are producing a total of 28 units of output. A worker's marginal product:
   a. is 5.
   b. is 28.
   c. is 28 divided by 5.
   d. cannot be determined from the information provided.

9. The firm is producing an output of 24 and has total costs of 260. Its marginal cost:
   a. equals 10.83.
   b. equals 8.75.
   c. equals 260.
   d. cannot be determined from the information provided.

10. Fixed costs:
    a. are costs that do not change with the output level.
    b. equal total costs plus variable costs.
    c. equal average fixed costs divided by the output level.
    d. rise at first then decline as output rises.

11. Concerning costs of production, it is true that:
    a. if a firm shuts down for a month its total costs for the month will equal its fixed costs for the month.
    b. average variable costs equal total variable costs multiplied by the output level.
    c. marginal costs equal the change in total costs divided by the change in variable costs.
    d. marginal cost equals average total cost multiplied by the output level.

12. A firm is producing 100 units of output at a total cost of $800. The firm's average variable cost is $5 per unit. The firm's:
    a. marginal cost is $8.
    b. total variable cost is $300.
    c. average fixed cost is $3.
    d. average total cost is $500.

13. The only variable input used in the production of pickles in a small factory is labor. Currently 5 workers are employed; each works 40 hours per week and is paid $15 per hour. If fixed costs are $4,000 per week and total output is 4,000 jars of pickles per week, then:
    a. average fixed cost is $16,000.
    b. total costs are $7,000.
    c. total variable costs are $4,000.
    d. average total costs are $0.75.

14. A firm's total fixed costs are $100; total variable costs are $200; and average fixed costs are $20. The firm's total output:
    a. is 1.
    b. is 5.
    c. is 10.
    d. cannot be determined from the information provided.

15. Refer to the graph below. The curves in the graph are:

a. correctly drawn.
b. incorrectly drawn because the average total cost curve is above the average variable cost curve.
c. incorrectly drawn because the marginal cost curve is positioned wrong.
d. incorrectly drawn because marginal cost and average variable costs are confused.

16. Refer to the graph below. The curve represented is most likely:

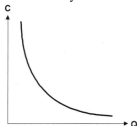

a. an average total cost curve.
b. an average variable cost curve.
c. an average fixed cost curve.
d. a total cost curve.

17. Concerning costs and cost curves for a firm, it is true that:
    a. if a firm increases its output from 100 to 101 and total costs increase from $55 to $60 then marginal cost of producing the 101st unit of output is $115.
    b. if marginal cost exceeds average total cost then average total cost is falling.
    c. the vertical distance between the average total and average variable cost curves at any given output level equals average fixed cost at that output level.
    d. the marginal cost curve intersects the average variable and average total cost curves when they are sloping downward.

18. If marginal cost exceeds average total cost then:
    a. average total cost is falling.
    b. average total cost is at its low point.
    c. average total cost is rising.
    d. marginal cost is at its low point.

19. Marginal cost reaches its minimum at a production level in which:
    a. average total cost is at its minimum.
    b. average variable cost is at its minimum.
    c. average productivity is at its maximum.
    d. marginal productivity is at its maximum.

20. Robbie owns a bike shop; given the table below, what is the total cost of producing 25 bikes?

Quantity	AVC	AFC
25	65	25

  a. $90.
  b. $625.
  c. $1625.
  d $2250.

21. If marginal cost equals average total cost then the average total cost curve is:
  a. rising.
  b. falling.
  c. at its maximum.
  d at its minimum.

22. Which one of the following is most likely a variable cost?
  a. Rent.
  b. Utilities.
  c. Wages.
  d Machinery.

23. Which of the following is impossible to calculate if you have only the total cost and the variable cost of producing 10 footballs?
  a. Fixed cost.
  b. Average variable cost.
  c. Marginal cost.
  d Average fixed cost.

POTENTIAL ESSAY QUESTIONS

You may also see essay questions similar to the "Problems & Applications" exercises.

1. Describe the relationship between the law of diminishing marginal productivity and costs of production in the short run.

2. Distinguish the various kinds of cost curves and describe the relationship between them.

ANSWERS

SHORT-ANSWER QUESTIONS

1. A firm (1) organizes factors of production, (2) produces goods and services, and (3) sells produced goods and services. A firm is the basis of production because it organizes factors of production into goods and services. (237)

2. Accounting profit = explicit revenue – explicit cost. Economic profit = (explicit *and* implicit revenue) – (explicit *and* implicit cost). Implicit revenue includes the increases in the value of assets owned by the firm. Implicit costs include the opportunity cost of time and capital provided by the owners of the firm. Accountants do not include these implicit revenues and costs in their calculations of profit. (227-229)

3. In a long-run planning decision, a firm chooses among all possible production techniques. In a short-run planning decision, the firm has fewer options. (229-230)

4. This is obviously not true because eventually each additional seed you add will produce fewer and fewer berries. At some point, the plants will choke one another out. This follows from the law of diminishing marginal productivity: as more and more of a variable input is added to an existing fixed input, after some point the additional output one gets from the additional input will fall. (231-232)

5. $TC = VC + FC. ATC = AVC + AFC. MC = \Delta TC/\Delta Q (= \Delta TVC/\Delta Q).$ (232-235)

6. A marginal cost curve measures the change in cost associated with a change in output. It is the extra cost of producing an additional unit of output. (234-236)

7. An average variable cost curve measures variable cost averaged over total output. (235-237)

8. An average fixed cost curve measures fixed costs averaged over total output. (235-237)

9. An average total cost curve measures total cost (variable plus fixed cost) averaged over total output. (235-237)

10. The law of diminishing marginal productivity means that eventually marginal productivity falls. When that happens, short-run costs (except fixed costs) begin to rise. When marginal and average productivity are rising, marginal and average cost curves are falling. When marginal and average productivity are falling, marginal and average cost curves are rising. (236-238)

11. The marginal cost curve intersects the average total and average variable cost curves at their minimum points. The marginal cost curve intersects these average cost curves at their minimum points because when marginal cost exceeds average cost, average cost must be rising; when marginal cost is less than average cost, average cost must be falling. (237-239)

12. Typical *AFC, AVC, ATC,* and *MC* curves are graphed below. Since fixed costs are the same for all levels of output, the *AFC* curve is always falling as the same fixed costs are spread over larger and larger levels of output. The *MC* curve first declines because of increasing marginal productivity but then rises because decreasing marginal productivity eventually sets in. The *MC* curve intersects the *AVC* and *ATC* curves at their minimum points. This is true because if marginal cost is below average cost, average cost must be falling and if marginal cost is above average cost, average cost must be rising. (237-239, especially Figure 11-2(b) and Figure 11-4)

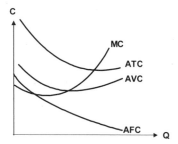

ANSWERS

MATCHING

1-h; 2-m; 3-n; 4-j; 5-o; 6-q; 7-e; 8-c; 9-a; 10-l; 11-b; 12-p; 13-f; 14-s; 15-d; 16-g; 17-i; 18-r; 19-k.

ANSWERS

PROBLEMS AND APPLICATIONS

1. **a.** Accounting profit = explicit revenue − explicit cost = $33,000 − ($10,000 + $1,000 + $8,000) = $14,000 accounting profit. (227-229)

    b. Economic profit = (explicit and implicit revenue) − (explicit and implicit cost) = ($33,000) − ($7,000 + $7,000 + $10,000 + $1,000 + $8,000 + $500) = − $500; $500 economic loss. (277-279)

2. By definition, $TC = FC + VC$, $AFC = FC/Q$, $AVC = VC/Q$, $ATC = AFC + AVC$, and $MC =$ the change in TC per unit of output. Using this information, we completed the following table. (Marginal cost refers to the marginal cost of increasing output to that row, e.g., the marginal cost of going from 0 to 1 is 90.) (232-237)

Units	TC	MC	AFC	AVC	ATC
0	50	—	—	—	—
1	140	90	50.00	90	140.00
2	170	30	25.00	60	85.00
3	215	45	16.67	55	71.67
4	270	55	12.50	55	67.50
5	340	70	10.00	58	68.00

The total cost curve is shown below. The *ATC, AVC, MC,* and *AFC* curves are also shown below. (232-237; Figure 11-2)

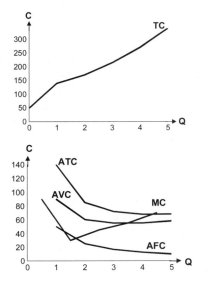

3. **a.** $AP = TP/Q$, $MP =$ change in TP, TC is (Labor × $20) + FC, $MC =$ change in TC divided by the change in TP (or Q). *AVC*

is VC/Q. Using these definitions, we completed the following table. (Marginal cost refers to the marginal cost of increasing to that row, e.g., the marginal cost of increasing total product from 2 to 6 is 5.00.) (281-283; Figure 11-1 and Table 11-1)

Labor	TP	MP	AP	TC	MC	AVC
1	2	—	2.0	70	—	10.00
2	6	4	3.0	90	5.00	6.67
3	15	9	5.0	110	2.22	4.00
4	20	5	5.0	130	4.00	4.00
5	23	3	4.6	150	6.67	4.35
6	24	1	4.0	170	20.00	5.00

b. The average variable cost curve is shown below. (235-237; Figure 11-2)

c. The *AP* and *AVC* curves are shown below. They are the mirror images of one another in that the maximum point on the *AP* curve occurs at the same quantity as the minimum point on the *AVC* curve. Also, when the *AP* curve is falling, *AVC* is rising, and vice versa. This is because as productivity falls, costs per unit rise, and as productivity increases, costs per unit decrease. (237-238; Figure 11-3)

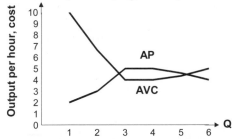

d. The marginal cost and marginal productivity curves are shown below. The maximum point on the *MP* curve occurs at the same quantity as the minimum point on the *MC* curve. When the *MP* curve is falling *MC* is rising, and vice versa. This is because as productivity falls, costs per unit rise and as productivity increases, costs per unit decrease. (237-238, Figure 11-3)

e. When the *MC* curve is below the *AVC* (or *ATC*) curve, the *AVC* (or *ATC*) curve is falling. The *MC* curve intersects with the *AVC* (or *ATC*) curve at its minimum point. When the *MC* curve is above the *AVC* (or *ATC*) curve, the *AVC* (*ATC*) curve is rising. The same goes for marginal product and average product. When marginal product is below average product, average product is falling and when marginal product is above average product, average product is rising. (237-238)

4. a. To graph the *ATC*, *AFC*, *AVC*, and *MC* curves, first determine the values of these curves for units 1 through 6. *TC = FC + VC*, *AFC = FC/Q*, *AVC = VC/Q*, *ATC = AFC + AVC*, and *MC* = the change in *TC*. These values are shown in the table below. The curves are also shown below. (Marginal cost refers to the marginal cost of increasing to that row, e.g., the marginal cost of going from 0 to 1 is 75.) (232-237)

Units	VC	ATC	AVC	AFC	MC
1	75	125	75	50	75
2	110	80	55	25	35
3	150	66.67	50	16.67	40
4	200	62.5	50	12.5	50
5	260	62	52	10	60
6	335	64.17	55.83	8.33	75

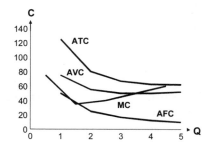

b. The *MC* curve goes through the minimum points of both the *ATC* and *AVC* curves, which are rising when they are below the

MC curve, and falling when they are above the *MC* curve. *ATC* and *AVC* curves are both U-shaped. Because of fixed costs, the *AVC* curve is always below the *ATC* curve, but the two curves converge as output increases (because AFC equals ATC – AVC, and AFC decreases as output increases). (237-239)

c. The curves are shown below. (232-237)

Units	VC	ATC	AVC	AFC	MC
1	75	95	75	20	75
2	110	65	55	10	35
3	150	56.67	50	6.67	40
4	200	55	50	5	50
5	260	56	52	4	60
6	335	59.17	55.83	3.33	75

d. Only the *AFC* and *ATC* curves shifted because they are the only curves that depend on fixed costs. All the others are based only on variable costs. Because the fixed cost falls to $20, the average fixed cost must fall as well. (235-237)

5. a. Labor and material costs are variable costs since they will rise and fall as production of Wheaties rises and falls. (232-233)

b. Sales, advertising, R&D, and rent on factory building and equipment are fixed costs since they are most likely independent of the level of Wheaties produced. (232-233)

c. Because fixed cost is high in this production process, almost equal to half of the revenue, an increase in output is likely to reduce *AFC*. If *AVC* does not rise more then *ATC* would likely fall as well. (232-233)

ANSWERS

MULTIPLE CHOICE

1. a   Economic profit is explicit and implicit revenue minus explicit and implicit costs. Economists include opportunity costs in total cost. Since implicit revenue might be positive and greater than implicit cost, economic profit could be higher than accounting profit but that is not always the case. Indeed, economic profit is typically smaller than an accounting profit because implicit costs usually exceed implicit revenue. See pages 237-239.

2. b   There is no set calendar time associated with the short run or the long run. In the short run some costs are fixed; in the long run all costs are variable costs—because nothing is fixed in the long run. See pages 229-230.

3. c   The longer the time period, the more numerous the options. See pages 229-230.

4. b   Marginal product is the change in total product. That is, $600 - 560 = 40$. Average product is total product divided by the number of workers. Average product of 5 workers is 112 and the average product of 6 workers is 100. See pages 229-231, especially Figure 11-1.

5. b   A bowed downward production function has marginal product decreasing marginal productivity as output increases. See Figure 11-1 on page 231.

6. a   Because of diminishing marginal productivity, marginal costs of production rise as additional units are produced. In addition, diminishing marginal productivity causes average productivity to fall. See pages 231-232.

7. c   When marginal productivity is falling, more inputs are necessary to increase production by the same amount. Thus, marginal costs are rising. See pages 231-233 and 237-238.

8. d   To determine marginal product you need to know the change in total product as you add a worker. See pages 231-232.

9. d   To determine marginal costs one must know the change in costs associated with a change in quantity. See pages 234-235.

10. a   Fixed costs remain constant no matter what output is. Also, fixed costs equal total costs minus variable costs. Moreover, fixed costs equal average fixed costs multiplied by the output level. See pages 233-234.

11. a   Total costs equal fixed costs when a firm shuts down. This is because there are no variable costs when a firm shuts down. Average variable costs equal total variable costs *divided* by the output level. Marginal costs equal the change in total costs divided by the change in *the output level. Total cost* equals average total cost multiplied by the output level. See pages 232-235.

12. c   Average total cost equals total cost divided by output ($\$800/100 = \$8$). Average fixed cost equals average total cost minus average variable cost ($\$8–\$5 = \$3$). See pages 233-234.

13. b   5 workers times 40 hours times $15 is $3,000. These are variable costs. Add this to fixed cost to get total cost. Average total cost is $7,000 divided by 4,000, or $1.75. Average fixed cost is $4,000 divided by 4,000, or $1. See pages 233-234.

14. b   Average fixed costs equal total fixed costs divided by output. If the firm's total fixed costs are $100 and average fixed costs are $20, the quantity must be $100/20 = 5$. See pages 232-234.

15. a   The *ATC* curve is above the *AVC* curve and the *MC* curve goes through the minimum points of the *AVC* and the *ATC* curves. The *AFC* curve is always falling. See Figure 12-2 on page 235.

16. c Only the average fixed cost curve falls continuously. See Figure 11-2 on page 235.

17. c $AFC = ATC - AVC$. See pages 233-235.

18. c If marginal cost exceeds average total cost, average total cost is rising. Marginal cost reaches a minimum well below average total cost. See pages 237-239 and Figure 11-4.

19. d Marginal cost and marginal product are mirror images. When marginal productivity is at its maximum then the extra cost of producing an additional unit (marginal cost) reaches its minimum. See page 237-238 and Figure 11-3.

20. d Given the AVC and AFC, you can then find the VC and FC curves and add those values to determine the total cost of making 25 bikes; $2250. See pages 232-235.

21. d The marginal cost curve only intersects the average total cost curve at its minimum. This is because when MC>ATC, ATC is rising and when MC<ATC, ATC is falling. See pages 238-239.

22. c The cost of rent, utilities, and machinery are all fixed costs - you still have to pay the same amount for them whether you are producing 1 product or 1000 products. However, wages are a variable cost; the amount you pay for wages depends on how many workers you hire which depends on how much you want to produce. See page 232.

23. c You cannot determine the marginal cost because the marginal cost is the change in total cost as a result of an additional unit of output. As we only know the costs of producing 10 footballs, we cannot calculate this change. See pages 232-235.

■■■■■■ ANSWERS ■■■■■■

POTENTIAL ESSAY QUESTIONS

The following are annotated answers. They indicate the general idea behind the answer.

1. When marginal productivity is increasing, costs of production (except fixed cost, which do not vary with the output level) are falling. When marginal productivity is decreasing, costs of production (except fixed cost, which do not vary with the output level) are rising.

2. The average fixed cost curve graphs FC/Q. The AVC curve graphs VC/Q. The ATC graphs TC/Q. The MC curve graphs the change in TC. The AFC is not related to the other cost curves. The ATC curve is always above the AVC curve. The MC curve intersects the ATC and AVC curves at their minimum.

✓ *Know how to calculate all 7 short-run costs!* They appear in Table 11-1 on page 233.

PRODUCTION AND COST ANALYSIS II

CHAPTER AT A GLANCE

1. Technical efficiency is producing with as few inputs as possible. It does not consider costs of inputs. The least-cost technically efficient process is the economically efficient process. (246)

   Firms try to be economically efficient because they want to minimize costs to maximize profits.

2. In the long run all inputs are variable, so only economies and diseconomies of scale can influence the shape of the long-run cost curve. (246-247)

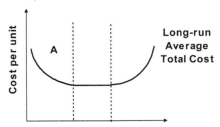

   Output
   Note that in the long run, as the quantity of production increases, the firm is using ever-larger scales of operation (larger plant or factory sizes).

   If you double all inputs and __per-unit__ costs fall (rise), the firm is experiencing economies (diseconomies) of scale.

   If per-unit (or average) costs do not change, the firm is experiencing constant returns to scale.

   Don't get short-run costs confused with long-run costs. The U-shape of __short-run__ average variable and average total cost curves reflects increasing and diminishing marginal productivity. The U-shape of the __long-run__ average total cost curve reflects economies and diseconomies of scale.

3. The envelope relationship is the relationship showing that, at the planned output level, short-run average total cost equals long-run average total cost, but at all other levels of output, short-run average total cost is higher than long-run average total cost. (301-302)

   See Figure 12-2 in the textbook (pages 250-251).

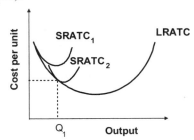

   SRATC$_2$ is the appropriate plant size to produce Q$_1$ because cost per unit is lower.

4. The expected price per unit must exceed the opportunity cost of supplying the good for a good to be supplied. (252-253)

   Potential economic profit motivates entrepreneurs to supply those goods demanded by consumers. The greater the demand, the greater the price, the greater the profit potential, and the greater the quantity supplied.

5. Some of the problems of using cost analysis in the real world include: (253-258)
   ● Economies of scope;
   ● Learning by doing and technological change;
   ● Many dimensions; and
   ● Unmeasured costs such as opportunity costs.

   See also, Appendix A: "Isocost/Isoquant Analysis."

SHORT-ANSWER QUESTIONS

1. You are consulting for a firm. Through analysis the firm has determined that the best it can do is produce 100 tons of wheat per day with 10 workers and 1 acre of land, or 100 tons of wheat per day with 10 acres of land and 1 worker. You are asked to choose the most efficient method of production. What do you advise?

2. After having read your report, the executives come running after you. They tell you that they have forgotten to tell you that an acre of land costs $40 an acre per day and workers can be hired for $100 a day. They wonder whether your answer to Question #1 changes.

3. The cost of developing a typical introductory economics textbook is well over $1 million. Once the textbook is developed and ready to print, the actual print costs for large runs are about $6 per book. What do these facts suggest about the shape of the long-run average total cost curve of producing textbooks?

4. What is the envelope relationship between short-run cost curves and long-run cost curves?

5. Why does an entrepreneur start a business? How are the decisions by the entrepreneur central to all supply decisions?

6. Suppose you are giving a talk on costs to decision-makers of firms. Without caveat, you have presented the cost curves as taught to you in this text. What are some likely problems your audience might have with your presentation?

MATCHING THE TERMS
Match the terms to their definitions

____ 1. constant returns to scale

____ 2. depreciation

____ 3. diseconomies of scale

____ 4. economically efficient

____ 5. economies of scale

____ 6. economies of scope

____ 7. entrepreneur

____ 8. indivisible setup cost

____ 9. learning by doing

____ 10. minimum efficient level of production

____ 11. monitoring costs

____ 12. team spirit

____ 13. technical efficiency

____ 14. technological change

a. A decrease in per-unit costs as a result of an increase in output.

b. An increase in per-unit costs as a result of an increase in output.

c. An increase in the range of production techniques that provides new ways of producing existing goods and new goods.

d. Becoming more proficient at doing something by actually doing it.

e. Where long-run average total costs do not change with an increase in output.

f. Individual who sees an opportunity to sell an item at a price higher than the average cost of producing it.

g. The costs of producing products are interdependent so that producing one good lowers the cost of producing another.

h. The level of production run that spreads out setup costs sufficiently for a firm to undertake production profitably.

i. The cost of an indivisible input for which a certain minimum amount of production must be undertaken before the input becomes economically feasible to use.

j. Using the method of production that produces a given level of output at the lowest possible cost.

k. A situation in which as few inputs as possible are used to produce a given output.

l. Costs incurred by the organizer of production in seeing to it that the employees do what they're supposed to do.

m. The feelings of friendship and being part of something that bring out people's best efforts.

n. A measure of the decline in value of an asset that occurs over time.

● PROBLEMS AND APPLICATIONS

1. In some developing countries relatively primitive labor-intensive production processes are often used. Farming is an example. Why might a firm be economically efficient by not using the latest technology in the production process?

2. The following table represents long-run total costs:

Q	TC	LRATC
1	60	
2	66	
3	69	
4	72	
5	75	
6	90	
7	126	
8	184	
9	297	
10	600	

   a. Calculate the long-run average total cost in the column provided.

b. Graph the *LRATC* curve on the graph below.

c. Label the area of economies of scale and the area of diseconomies of scale on the graph.

3. How can the extent to which economies and diseconomies of scale are present in an industry help account for the size and the number of firms in that industry? That is, if economies of scale were quite extensive in a particular industry, would you expect a large number of relatively small firms, or a small number of relatively large firms to be operating within that industry? What if diseconomies of scale set in at a relatively small output level?

4. What could help account for computer hardware manufacturers getting increasingly more involved with the development and production of computer software? Or, the airline passenger service businesses getting involved in air parcel and small package delivery service, and soft drink manufacturers buying up fast food restaurants (e.g. Pepsi-Cola company buying up Kentucky Fried Chicken and Pizza Hut—to name just a few)?

A1. Suppose the following table depicts the combinations of factors of production that result in the production of 100 units of a jeweled bhindi, a painted dot or decorative item worn by Hindu women.

	Labor	Machinery
A	25	4
B	20	5
C	10	10
D	5	20
E	4	25

a. Graph the isoquant curve for this table on the graph below, with machinery on the vertical axis and labor on the horizontal axis.

b. What is the marginal rate of substitution between combinations C and D?

A2. Suppose you had $120 available to produce the same product (bhindi) as in the previous question. Labor costs are $4 per person and machinery costs are $8 per unit. Draw the isocost line with machinery on the vertical axis and labor on the horizontal axis.

a. What is the slope of the line?

b. What happens to the isocost line if you frivolously spend $40 of your $120 on entertaining your good-for-nothing boyfriend Kyle? What is the slope of your new isocost line? Show this graphically.

c. Suppose the labor union raises labor costs to $10 per person. What happens to the isocost line? Show this graphically.

d. Combine the isoquant curve from *A1* with the original isocost line from *A2* on the graph below. What combination of labor and machinery will you choose for the economically efficient point of production?

● MULTIPLE CHOICE

Circle the one best answer for each of the following questions:

1. Kathleen and Fritz both produce 500 pairs of jeans. Kathleen produces her jeans with 4 workers and 400 bolts of denim while Fritz produces 500 pairs with 8 workers and 300 bolts of denim. With the information given, is Kathleen or Fritz more technically efficient?
   a. Both could be technically efficient.
   b. Neither can be technically efficient.
   c. Kathleen is more technically efficient.
   d. Fritz is more technically efficient.

2. Using the same information in Question #1, assuming workers are equally efficient, wages are $12/hour and fabric costs $10 a bolt. Who is more economically efficient?
   a. Both are economically efficient.
   b. Neither are economically efficient.
   c. Kathleen is more economically efficient.
   d. Fritz is more economically efficient.

3. The long-run average total cost of production:
   a. rises as output increases when we experience economies of scale.
   b. is explained by decreasing marginal productivity.
   c. passes through the minimum point of each short-run average total cost curve.
   d. is considered to be an envelope curve because each short-run average total cost curve touches it at only one level of output.

4. Indivisible setup costs refer to:
   a. the cost of an indivisible input for which a certain minimum amount of production must be undertaken before production becomes economically feasible.
   b. the cost of an indivisible input for which a certain maximum amount of production must be undertaken before production becomes economically feasible.
   c. the cost of an indivisible input whose cost is invisible.
   d. the cost of an indivisible input whose cost of production is lower because an interdependent good is also being produced.

5. Economies of scale:
   a. account for the upward-sloping portion of the long-run average total cost curve.
   b. exist because of the difficulties in coordinating and managing a large business enterprise.
   c. imply an increase in per-unit costs of production associated with an increase in output.
   d. arise because large indivisible setup costs are spread out among a larger level of output and because of the efficiencies of greater labor and management specialization.

6. If production were purely a technical phenom-
    enon and has no social components, in the
    long run, a firm would never experience:
    a. economies of scale.
    b. constant returns to scale.
    c. diseconomies of scale.
    d. any of the above.

7. Refer to the graph below. The section of the
    long-run average total cost curve marked as
    "A" represents:

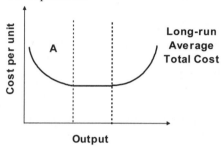

    a. economies of scale.
    b. diseconomies of scale.
    c. diminishing marginal productivity.
    d. increasing marginal productivity.

8. Explanations for diseconomies of scale include
    all of the following *except:*
    a. as firm size increases, monitoring costs
    generally increase.
    b. as firm size increases, team spirit or morale
    generally decreases.
    c. as firm size increases, monitoring costs
    generally decrease, thereby increasing other
    costs.
    d. All of the above are explanations.

9. Which of the following is associated with
    diseconomies of scale?
    a. Producing 1,000 lawn mowers costs $100,000
    while producing 2,000 lawn mowers costs
    $220,000.
    b. 50 workers and 5 machines produce 1,000
    units of output while 100 workers and 10
    machines produce 2,500 units of output.
    c. 50 workers and 5 machines produce 1,000
    units of output while 60 workers and 5
    machines produce 1,200 units of output.
    d. Producing 1,000 lawn mowers costs $100,000
    while producing 2,000 lawn mowers costs
    $150,000.

10. Refer to the graph below. Which of the
    following statements about the graph is
    true?

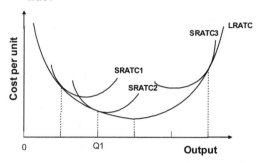

    a. The scale of operation associated with
    $SRATC_3$ is realizing some economies of
    scale.
    b. $SRATC_2$ is a smaller scale of operation than
    $SRATC_1$.
    c. The lowest-cost scale of operation to
    produce Q_1 is $SRATC_1$.
    d. The lowest-cost scale of operation to
    produce Q_1 is $SRATC_2$.

11. Constant returns to scale:
    a. refer to the upward sloping portion of the
    long-run ATC curve.
    b. refer to the downward sloping portion of the
    long-run ATC curve.
    c. mean long-run average total costs do not
    change with an increase in output.
    d. are a result of rising monitoring costs and a
    loss of team spirit.

12. The envelope relationship refers to the fact
    that the:
    a. short-run average cost curve forms an
    envelope around long-run average cost
    curves.
    b. long-run average cost curve forms an
    envelope around short-run average cost
    curves.
    c. average cost curve forms an envelope
    around the marginal cost curve.
    d. marginal cost curve forms an envelope
    around the average cost curve.

13. Economies of scope occur when:
    a. firms increase production of a good, and that
    good's cost falls.
    b. firms increase their long-run vision and costs
    fall.

c. the costs of production of one product fall when the firm increases the production of another product.

d. technological change lowers cost of production.

14. Learning by doing and increases in technology cause the long-run:
   a. average cost curve to be downward sloping.
   b. average cost curve to be upward sloping.
   c. average cost curve to shift down.
   d. marginal cost curve to be downward sloping.

15. A cost that economists include when calculating profit which accountants do not is:
   a. explicit cost.
   b. opportunity cost.
   c. scope cost.
   d. monitoring cost.

16. A business owner makes 400 items by hand in 500 hours. She could have earned $20 an hour working for someone else. If the items sell for $50 each and the explicit costs total $12,000, then:
   a. total revenue equals $10,000.
   b. implicit costs equal $20,000.
   c. the accounting profits equal $10,000.
   d. the economic loss equals $2,000.

A1. Refer to the graph below. The isocost line represents a price of machinery (in terms of labor) of:

   a. one-eighth unit of labor.
   b. one-fourth unit of labor.
   c. one-half unit of labor.
   d. two units of labor.

A2. Refer to the graph for Question #A1. If the price of machinery increases, the isocost line will rotate:
   a. in and become flatter.
   b. in and become steeper.
   c. out and become flatter.
   d. out and become steeper.

A3. The economically efficient point in the isoquant model in the graph below is at point:

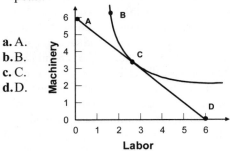

   a. A.
   b. B.
   c. C.
   d. D.

● POTENTIAL ESSAY QUESTIONS

You may also see essay questions similar to the "Problems & Applications" exercises.

1. What are economies and diseconomies of scale? Why do they exist?

2. Discuss some of the problems of using cost analysis in the real world.

ANSWERS

SHORT-ANSWER QUESTIONS

1. You tell them that both methods are of equal technical efficiency, but you cannot determine which is more economically efficient. To make this decision you would need to know the relative cost of each input. (246)

2. You smile and say that is exactly the information you need to tell them the most economically efficient method of production. At these prices, the first method of production costs $1,040 per 100 tons and the second method costs $500 per 100 tons. The second method is the economically efficient method. Technical efficiency means as few inputs as possible are used to produce a given output. It does not consider the costs of inputs. Economic efficiency means using that combination of inputs with the lowest possible cost for a given output. (246)

3. Because of the large indivisible setup costs, large economies of scale are possible in printing books. These economies of scale suggest that the long-run average total cost curve is steeply downward sloping. As production expands, economies of scale dominate and cost per unit declines. After some point, as output increases, however, diseconomies could set in and cost per unit could rise. This would lead to a U-shaped average total cost curve in the long run. (246-251)

4. The envelope relationship is the relationship between short-run and long-run average total costs. At the planned output level, short-run average total cost equals long-run average total cost, but at all other levels of output, short-run average total cost is higher than long-run average total cost. (250-251)

5. An entrepreneur will supply a good if the expected price of the good exceeds the cost of producing it. This difference is the entrepreneur's expected profit. It is the profit incentive that underlies production in an economy. (252-253)

6. Since your audience is working with the real world, they will see that actual production processes diverge from textbook analysis.

Some of the problems the audience might list are (1) economies of scope; (2) learning by doing and technological change; (3) the supply decision is multidimensional; and (4) the relevant costs are not always the ones you find in a firm's accounts. (253-258)

ANSWERS

MATCHING

1-e; 2-n; 3-b; 4-j; 5-a; 6-g; 7-f; 8-i; 9-d; 10-h; 11-l; 12-m; 13-k; 14-c.

ANSWERS

PROBLEMS AND APPLICATIONS

1. Using the latest technology in combination with the required inputs may be a more costly production process than using more primitive techniques—especially when labor is cheap. What a firm wants to do is to use whatever combination of inputs that minimizes costs of production so that it can remain price competitive in the market. (246)

2. Before graphing *LRATC*, first calculate the figures. $LRATC = TC/Q$. (246-249)

   a.
Q	TC	LRATC
1	60	60
2	66	33
3	69	23
4	72	18
5	75	15
6	90	15
7	126	18
8	184	23
9	297	33
10	600	60

   b. The graph shown below plots the values from the table above to show the *LRATC* curve. (See Figure 12-1 on page 248)

c. As shown in the figure, economies of scale is to the left of $Q = 5$, where *LRATC* is falling. Diseconomies of scale is to the right of $Q = 6$, where *LRATC* is rising. (See Figure 12-1 and page 248)

3. If economies of scale are quite extensive in an industry (i.e., larger and larger scales of operation result in lower and lower long-run average total costs of production) one would expect a relatively small number of very large firms. This is because all firms will be trying to reduce their costs by expanding, to lower their prices, and to gain a greater share of the market. You have to "get big or get out"or be driven out of business by your competitor's lower prices. If diseconomies of scale set in at a relatively small output level, however, then you would expect a relatively large number of relatively small firms. (246-251)

4. Economies of scope can explain this. It is cheaper for these firms to produce, market, or distribute these goods or services when they are already involved in producing the other. Indeed, this concept seems to explain best why firms produce multiple rather than single products. (253-254)

A1. a. To graph the isoquant curve, plot each of the combinations of labor and machinery which generate the same (100) units of production of bhindi, as is done in the graph below. (262-263)

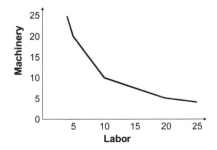

b. The marginal rate of substitution between combinations C and D is equal to the absolute value of the slope between C and D, $MP_{labor}/MP_{machinery} = 2$. (263)

A2. a. The x-axis (labor axis) intercept is 30 ($120/$4), and the y-axis (machinery axis) intercept is 15 ($120/$8). The slope of the line is $-P_{labor}/P_{machinery} = -4/8 = -1/2$. It is shown in the graph below. (264-265).

b. The isocost line shifts in to the left as money available for production is reduced to $80. Now maximum 20 units of labor or 10 units of machinery can be purchased. Since the relative price of labor and machinery doesn't change, the slope of the isocost line remains $-1/2$. This is shown in the graph below. (264-265)

c. Now because relative prices change, the isocost line rotates. To find the new isocost line, find first how many units of labor can be purchased for $120 at the new price $10. The isocost line rotates along the labor axis and intersects it at 12 units of labor. The y intercept remains the same at 15 since the price of machinery did not change. Since labor becomes more expensive, the slope becomes steeper. The slope of the line now is $-P_{labor}/P_{machinery} = -10/8 = -1.25$. This is shown in the graph below. (264-265)

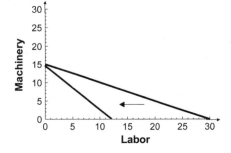

d To find the most economically efficient combination of inputs, find that point where the slope of the isocost line equals the slope of the isoquant curve (which is the marginal rate of substitution between labor and machinery). This is at points between B and C where $-MP_{labor}/MP_{machinery} = -1/2 = -P_{labor}/P_{machinery}$. The isocost line is tangent to the isoquant curve at points between B and C. This implies that any other isoquant curve that intersects the isocost line is less economically efficient. This is shown in the graph below. (265)

━━━━━━━━━ ANSWERS ━━━━━━━━━

MULTIPLE CHOICE

1. **a** Both Kathleen and Fritz can be technically efficient since neither involves more of both inputs (workers and bolts of denim) to produce the same output (500 pairs of jeans). See page 246.

2. **d** Fritz is more economically efficient. His total costs are $3,096 and Kathleen's costs are $4,048. See page 246.

3. **d** Economies of scale cause the LRATC curve to decrease (slope downward). Long run costs are *not* related to marginal productivity. The curve is not tangent to the low points of all SRATC curves. See pages 246-251.

4. **a** This is the definition of indivisible setup costs found on page 247. Note that huge setup costs require high levels of production to get per-unit production costs down to a level where production is profitable.

5. **d** Economies of scale cause the LRATC curve to slope downward. Per unit production costs fall. Difficulties in coordinating and managing a large business cause *dis*economies of scale. See pages 246-249.

6. **c** If a production process is purely technical, it can be repeated over and over without increasing costs. It could still experience economies of scale due to large set-up costs. See pages 246-251.

7. **a** Economies of scale cause the LRATC curve to slope downward. The law of diminishing marginal productivity relates to short-run curves only. See Figure 12-1 on page 248.

8. **c** Monitoring costs generally rise as a firm enlarges. Moreover, there is no reason to assume that decreasing monitoring costs will cause other costs to increase. See page 249.

9. **a** Economies and diseconomies of scale relate to instances where all inputs are varied. That eliminates the option where only the number of workers is increased as a possibility. Diseconomies of scale exist when *average* costs rise. Average costs rise in a from $100 to $110. See pages 246-249.

10. **d** The lowest-cost scale of operation is on the SRATC curve that is tangent to the LRATC curve at that level of output. The scale of operation represented by SRATC$_3$ suffers from diseconomies of scale. See pages 250-251, especially Figure 12-2.

11. **c** Constant returns to scale refer to the flat portion of the LRATC curve where long-run average total costs remain constant when output increases. See page 250.

12. **b** As discussed on pages 250-251 (including Figure 12-2), the long-run average cost curve forms an envelope around short-run average cost curves.

13. c   As discussed on pages 253-254, c is the definition of economies of scope. Economies of scope play an important role in firms' decisions about what combinations of goods to produce.

14. c   Learning by doing reduces average costs at every level of output. This is shown by a downward shift in the average cost curve. See pages 254-255.

15. b   Both include explicit costs, an example of which is monitoring cost. Scope cost makes no sense. See pages 257-258.

16. d   Total revenue equals $20,000 ($50 \times 400$). Implicit costs ($20 \times 500 = $10,000$) plus explicit costs ($12,000) equal $22,000. Economic loss is $2,000. Accounting profit equals $8,000. See pages 257-258.

A1. c   To get one unit of machinery one must give up one-half unit of labor. See pages 264-265.

A2. a   A rise in the price of machinery means that the same amount of funds will purchase less machinery, so the isocost line rotates down from the intersection of the labor axis, hence becoming flatter. See pages 264-265.

A3. c   The economically efficient point is where the isoquant curve is tangent to the isocost line. See page 265.

ANSWERS

POTENTIAL ESSAY QUESTIONS

The following are annotated answers. They indicate the general idea behind the answer.

1. Economies of scale have lower average total costs of production as larger scales of operation are used. They result from greater specialization of labor and management.

Diseconomies of scale arise when larger scales of operation are associated with and higher average total costs of production.

Diseconomies of scale arise because management loses control over operations. That is, monitoring costs rise and there is a loss of team spirit.

2. Some of the problems of using cost analysis in the real world include: (1) economies of scope; (2) learning by doing and technological change; (3) many dimensions; and (4) unmeasured costs such as opportunity cost.

Pretest
Chapters 6 - 12

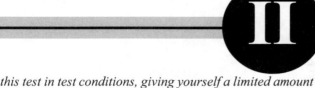

Take this test in test conditions, giving yourself a limited amount of time to complete the questions. Ideally, check with your professor to see how much time he or she allows for an average multiple choice question and multiply this by 30. This is the time limit you should set for yourself for this pretest. If you do not know how much time your teacher would allow, we suggest 1 minute per question, or 30 minutes.

1. When the price of a good was raised from $10 to $11, the quantity demanded fell from 100 to 99. The price elasticity of demand is approximately:
   a. .1.
   b. 1.
   c. 10.
   d. 100.

2. As a manager, you have determined that the demand for your good is quite elastic. Therefore:
   a. increasing the price of your good will increase revenues.
   b. decreasing the price of your good will increase revenues.
   c. increasing the price of your good will have no impact on the quantity demanded.
   d. any change in your price will not impact revenues.

3. In the graph below, point A on the supply curve, S, is:

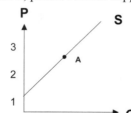

   a. elastic.
   b. inelastic.
   c. unit elastic.
   d. unknown because one cannot say from the graph.

4. A significant price rise with virtually no change in quantity would most likely be caused by a highly:
   a. elastic demand and supply shifts to the right.
   b. inelastic supply and a shift in demand to the right.
   c. inelastic demand and supply shifts out.
   d. elastic supply and demand shifts in.

5. Assume equilibrium in the graph below. What area represents consumer surplus?
   a. A + B + C.
   b. D + C + E.
   c. E.
   d. E + F.

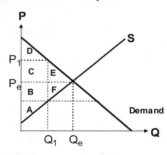

6. Refer to the graph below. If a per unit tax, t, is paid by sellers:

   a. producer surplus is represented by areas A, B, and C before the tax and area A after the tax.
   b. consumer surplus is represented by areas D, E and F before the tax and B after the tax.
   c. the tax, t, imposes a deadweight loss represented by the welfare loss triangle–areas C and E.
   d. consumers lose surplus given by area E while producers lose surplus given by area C.

7. The burden of a tax is:
    a. most heavily borne by those with the more inelastic demand or supply.
    b. most heavily borne by those with the more elastic demand or supply.
    c. usually equally split between buyers and sellers.
    d. usually passed on to consumers in the form of a higher price.

8. How much of a $100 tax will consumers pay if the price elasticity of demand is 3 and the price elasticity of supply is 2?
    a. $50.
    b. $40.
    c. $30.
    d. $20.

9. In which case will a price floor result in the greatest excess supply?
    a. When both demand and supply are highly inelastic.
    b. When both demand and supply are highly elastic.
    c. When demand is elastic and supply is inelastic.
    d. When demand is inelastic and supply is elastic.

10. An externality is:
    a. the effect of a decision on a third party not taken into account by a decision maker.
    b. another name for exports.
    c. an event that is external to the economy.
    d. the external effect of a government policy.

11. Refer to the graph below. The S curve represents the marginal private cost of production, and the D curve represents the marginal private benefit to consumers of the good. If there is a positive externality of consumption, and one wants to adjust the curves so that the equilibrium demonstrates the appropriate marginal social benefits, either:

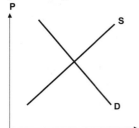

a. the S curve should be shifted in to the left or the D curve should be shifted out to the right.
b. the S curve should be shifted out to the right or the D curve should be shifted in to the left.
c. the S curve should be shifted out to the right or the D curve should be shifted out to the right.
d. the S curve should be shifted in to the left or the D curve should be shifted in to the left.

12. Refer to the graph below. If the government were attempting to set an effluent fee, the amount of that effluent fee should be:
    a. P_1.
    b. P_2.
    c. $P_1 - P_2$.
    d. $P_1 - P_3$.

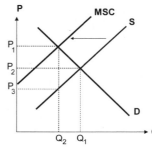

13. A public good is:
    a. any good traded in markets.
    b. a good that is nonexclusive and nonrival.
    c. a good provided only to those who pay for it.
    d. rarely provided by government.

14. Government failure:
    a. always outweighs market failure.
    b. sometimes outweighs market failure.
    c. never outweighs market failure.
    d. is the same as market failure.

15. Country A's cost of widgets is $4.00 and cost of wadgets is $8.00. Country B's cost of widgets is 8 euros and cost of wadgets is 16 euros. Which of the following would you suggest?
    a. Country A should specialize in widgets and Country B in wadgets.
    b. Trade of widgets for wadgets would not benefit the countries.
    c. Country A should specialize in wadgets and Country B in widgets.
    d. Both countries should produce an equal amount of each.

16. In the United States, globalization has caused workers in the education, healthcare, and government sectors to face:
    a. lower wages.
    b. higher prices on consumer goods.
    c. little or no downward pressure on their wages.
    d. longer hours to compete with the higher production levels abroad.

17. Transferable comparative advantages are:
    a. based on factors that are relatively un-changeable.
    b. based on factors that can change relatively easily.
    c. becoming more like inherent comparative advantages with technological innovations.
    d. rarely eroded over time.

18. In the graph below, the value of the dollar is:

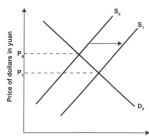

    a. appreciating because the dollar buys more yuan.
    b. depreciating because the dollar buys more yuan.
    c. appreciating because the dollar buys fewer yuan.
    d. depreciating because the dollar buys fewer yuan.

19. Which of the following would raise the world price level facing the United States?
    a. The dollar appreciates.
    b. The dollar depreciates.
    c. The trade deficit rises.
    d. The trade deficit falls.

20. If a country has a trade deficit, it is:
    a. consuming more than it is producing.
    b. lending to foreigners.
    c. buying financial assets.
    d. buying real assets.

21. In the graph below, which area represents the revenue collected by government?
    a. A.
    b. B.
    c. B and C.
    d. A and B.

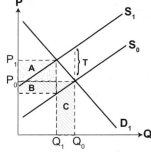

22. Economists generally oppose trade restrictions for all of the following reasons *except*:
    a. from a global perspective, free trade increases total output.
    b. the infant industry argument.
    c. trade restrictions lead to retaliation.
    d. international politics.

23. Refer to the graph below. The range marked "A" shows:

    a. increasing marginal productivity.
    b. diminishing marginal productivity.
    c. diminishing absolute productivity.
    d. diminishing absolute marginal productivity.

24. Five workers are producing a total of 28 units of output. A worker's marginal product:
    a. is 5.
    b. is 28.
    c. is 28 divided by 5.
    d. cannot be determined from the information provided.

25. A firm is producing 100 units of output at a total cost of $800. The firm's average variable cost is $5 per unit. The firm's:
    a. marginal cost is $8.
    b. total variable cost is $300.
    c. average fixed cost is $3.
    d. average total cost is $500.

26. Refer to the graph below. The curves in the graph are:

   a. correctly drawn.
   b. incorrectly drawn because the average total cost curve is above the average variable cost curve.
   c. incorrectly drawn because the marginal cost curve is positioned wrong.
   d. incorrectly drawn because marginal cost and average variable costs are confused.

27. Kathleen and Fritz both produce 500 pairs of jeans. Kathleen produces her jeans with 4 workers and 400 bolts of denim while Fritz produces 500 pairs with 8 workers and 300 bolts of denim. With the information given, is Kathleen or Fritz more technically efficient?
   a. Both could be technically efficient.
   b. Neither can be technically efficient.
   c. Kathleen is more technically efficient.
   d. Fritz is more technically efficient.

28. Economies of scale:
   a. account for the upward-sloping portion of the long-run average total cost curve.
   b. exist because of the difficulties in coordinating and managing a large business enterprise.
   c. imply an increase in per-unit costs of production associated with an increase in output.
   d. arise because large indivisible setup costs are spread out among a larger level of output and because of the efficiencies of greater labor and management specialization.

29. Constant returns to scale:
   a. refer to the upward sloping portion of the long-run ATC curve.
   b. refer to the downward sloping portion of the long-run ATC curve.
   c. mean long-run average total costs do not change with an increase in output.
   d. are a result of rising monitoring costs and a loss of team spirit.

30. The envelope relationship refers to the fact that the:
   a. short-run average cost curve forms an envelope around long-run average cost curves.
   b. long-run average cost curve forms an envelope around short-run average cost curves.
   c. average cost curve forms an envelope around the marginal cost curve.
   d. marginal cost curve forms an envelope around the average cost curve.

━━━━━━━   ANSWERS   ━━━━━━━

1.	a	(6:2)	**16.**	c	(9:8)
2.	b	(6:6)	**17.**	b	(9:9)
3.	a	(6:10)	**18.**	d	(9:13)
4.	b	(6:19)	**19.**	b	(9:16)
5.	b	(7:3)	**20.**	a	(10:4)
6.	c	(7:5)	**21.**	d	(10:10)
7.	a	(7:9)	**22.**	b	(10:14)
8.	b	(7:10)	**23.**	b	(11:5)
9.	b	(7:17)	**24.**	d	(11:8)
10.	a	(8:2)	**25.**	c	(11:12)
11.	c	(8:4)	**26.**	a	(11:15)
12.	d	(8:6)	**27.**	a	(12:1)
13.	b	(8:11)	**28.**	d	(12:5)
14.	b	(8:18)	**29.**	c	(12:11)
15.	b	(9:5)	**30.**	b	(12:12)

Key: The figures in parentheses refer to multiple choice question and chapter numbers. For example (1:2) is multiple choice question 2 from chapter 1.

PERFECT COMPETITION

CHAPTER AT A GLANCE

1. A perfectly competitive market is a market in which economic forces operate unimpeded. (267)

    The model of a perfectly competitive market serves as a reference point to those of the non-competitive markets such as monopoly, oligopoly, and monopolistic competition (See the next two chapters for these other markets.)

2. Three conditions for a market to be perfectly competitive include: (267-268)

    1. Both buyers and sellers are price takers.
    2. No barriers to entry.
    3. Identical products.

    Compare these with the non-competitive markets (next 2 chapters).

3. If marginal revenue does not equal marginal cost, a firm can increase profit by changing output. Therefore, profit is maximized when MC = MR = P. (268-271)

    P = MR for a perfectly competitive firm.

    In general, for any firm, if
    MR > MC, increase Q.
    MR = MC, profit is maximized.
    MR < MC, decrease Q.

4. Because the marginal cost curve tells us how much of a produced good a firm will supply at a given price, the marginal cost curve is the firm's supply curve. (271, 276)

    A firm's short-run supply curve is its MC curve above minimum AVC. This is because at any P greater than minimum AVC, a competitive firm will produce where P = MR = MC.

5. The profit-maximizing output can be determined in a table (as in Table 13-1 on page 269) or in a graph (as in Figure 13-4 on page 274).

    Just find that output level at which MR = MC. This is shown graphically where the two curves intersect. (Remember: the demand curve facing the firm is also its MR curve and it is horizontal at the market price).

    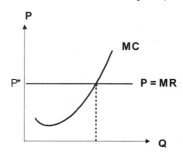

6. The market supply curve is the horizontal sum of all the firms' marginal cost curves, taking account of any changes in input prices that might occur. (276-277)

    At each price, draw a vertical line from the marginal cost curve to the quantity axis to determine the quantity supplied by each firm in the market. Then add the quantity supplied by each firm at each price to obtain the market supply curve.

7. Since profits create incentives for new firms to enter, output will increase, and the price will fall until zero profits are being made. (277-279)

    Over time if economic profits are earned, the number of sellers increases, increasing market supply and decreasing market price. The lower market price decreases firms' profits until the economic profits are competed away. Note that competitive firms earn no profit in the long run.

8.   The long-run market supply curve may be upward sloping, horizontal, or downward sloping, depending on what happens to input prices as an industry expands. (279-281)

If the demand for an industry's product increases, the industry will expand (more of the good is produced) and:

- *An increasing-cost industry has an upward-sloping long-run market supply curve reflecting higher input prices as the industry expands.*

- *A constant-cost industry has a horizontal long-run market supply curve reflecting no change in input prices as the industry expands.*

- *A decreasing-cost industry has a downward-sloping long-run market supply curve reflecting lower input prices as the industry expands.*

● SHORT-ANSWER QUESTIONS

1. How is competition as a process different from competition as a state?

2. What are three necessary conditions for perfect competition?

3. You are advising a vendor of ice cream at a beach. There are plenty of vendors on the beach and plenty more waiting to begin selling. Your client can't seem to change the market price for ice cream, but she still wants to make sure she maximizes profits. What do you advise she do? She knows all her costs of doing business.

4. You are given a competitive firm's marginal cost curve and asked to determine the supply curve for that firm. What do you say?

5. Given the following table, what is the profit-maximizing output and profit of a perfect competitor?

P=MR	Q	FC	VC
35	0	10	0
35	1	10	20
35	2	10	38
35	3	10	50
35	4	10	77
35	5	10	112
35	6	10	156

6. On the graph below, show the output and short-run profit for a perfect competitor.

7. When should a firm shut down?

8. How are firms' marginal cost curves and the market supply curve related?

9. Given the graph below, showing a representative firm in a competitive market, what will happen in the long run? Explain, using the graph and words.

10. Suppose the owners of a small drug store decided to close their store after Walmart opened a store nearby. Assuming the market was competitive before and after Walmart opened its store, show graphically and explain with words the likely conditions for the small drug store before and after Walmart opened.

11. What does the long-run market supply curve look like in an increasing-cost industry? Why? What about the constant-cost and decreasing-cost industries?

MATCHING THE TERMS
Match the terms to their definitions

___ 1. barriers to entry
___ 2. marginal cost
___ 3. marginal revenue
___ 4. market supply curve
___ 5. normal profit
___ 6. perfectly competitive market
___ 7. price taker
___ 8. profit-maximizing condition
___ 9. shutdown point

a. Firm or individual who takes the market price as given.
b. Anything that prevents other firms from entering a market.
c. The change in total cost associated with a change in quantity.
d. The change in total revenue associated with a change in quantity.
e. Market in which economic forces operate unimpeded.
f. Point at which the firm will gain more by temporarily shutting down than it will by staying in business.
g. The horizontal sum of all the firms' marginal cost curves, taking account of any changes in input prices that might occur.
h. The amount of money the owners of a business would have received in their next-best alternative.
i. Produce where MC = MR.

● PROBLEMS AND APPLICATIONS

1. The following table shows the total cost for a
    product that sells for $20 a unit.

Q	TC
0	30
1	55
2	75
3	85
4	100
5	120
6	145
7	185
8	240
9	310
10	395

    a. What is the output level for a profit-
        maximizing firm? Use the space to the right
        of the table to work out your answer.

    b. How does your answer change if price
        rises to $25?

    c. Calculate profit in part *a* and *b* above.

    d. Should the firm stay in business at $P =$
        $20? At $25?

    e. Suppose $P = \$15$, what output level
        maximizes profit? What is the profit?
        Should the firm stay in business?

2. The following cost curves are for a representa-
    tive firm in a competitive market.

    a. Label the minimum point of the *ATC* and
        AVC curves as A and B respectively.
        Explain your answer.

    b. Draw a demand curve for this firm on that
        same graph, assuming the market is in
        equilibrium. Explain why you have drawn it
        this way.

    c. Illustrate the long-run equilibrium price
        and quantity for the firm on that same
        graph. Is the firm earning economic profit?
        Explain your answer.

3. Consider the market demand and supply
    curves below on the left and a representative
    firm's cost curves below on the right.

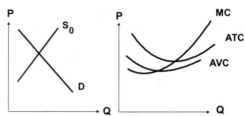

    a. Is this representative firm earning eco-
        nomic profit, loss, or zero profit? Shade the
        area for profit or loss, or label the point of
        zero profit.

b. In the long run, what will happen?

c. Beginning with the long-run equilibrium in part *b*, show the effect of a decrease in demand on profit. What will happen in the long run to supply, price, and profit?

4. What is wrong with each of the following graphs?

a.

b.

c.

d.

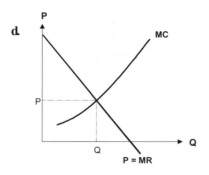

● **MULTIPLE CHOICE**

Circle the one best answer for each of the following questions:

1. Which of the following is a requirement of a perfectly competitive market?
   a. Buyers and sellers are price takers.
   b. There are barriers to entry.
   c. There are indivisible setup costs.
   d. Selling firms maximize sales.

2. In a perfectly competitive market:
   a. firms sell a differentiated product where one firm's output can be distinguished from another firm's output.
   b. there are so many firms selling output in the market that no one individual firm has the ability to control the market price.
   c. economic profits can be earned in the long run.
   d. there are very strong barriers to entry that can prevent potential competitors from entering the market.

3. Barriers to entry:
   a. are required for a firm to be perfectly competitive.
   b. prevent other firms from entering a market.
   c. prevent existing firms from earning profits.
   d. are economic impediments created by profits.

4. Refer to the graph below. The perceived demand curve faced by an individual firm in a competitive market is best represented by which of the following?
   a. A.
   b. B.
   c. C.
   d. D.

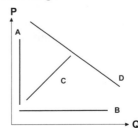

5. Refer to the graph below. The market demand
    curve in a competitive market is best
    represented by which of the following?
    a. A.
    b. B.
    c. C.
    d. D.

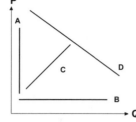

6. Refer to the graph below. A competitive firm is
    producing at output A.

    a. It could increase profits by increasing
       output.
    b. It could increase profits by decreasing
       output.
    c. It cannot increase profits.
    d. One can say nothing about profits from the
       diagram.

7. Refer to the graph below. A competitive firm is
    producing at output A.

    a. It could increase profits by increasing output.
    b. It could increase profits by decreasing output.
    c. It cannot increase profits.
    d. One can say nothing about profits from the
       diagram.

8. Refer to the graph below. How much should a
    firm produce to maximize profits?

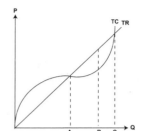

    a. A.
    b. B.
    c. C.
    d. It cannot be determined with the information
       given.

9. In order to maximize profits (or minimize losses)
    a firm should produce at that output level at
    which:
    a. total revenue is maximized.
    b. average total costs are minimized.
    c. marginal revenue equals marginal cost.
    d. marginal revenue exceeds marginal cost by
       the greatest amount.

10. Price in a competitive market is $6. The firm's
    marginal cost is $4 and the marginal cost
    curve has the normal shape. What would
    you advise the firm to do?
    a. Raise its price.
    b. Increase its output.
    c. Decrease its output.
    d. Lower its price.

11. In a competitive market, which of the following
    is the firm's supply curve?
    a. The average variable cost curve.
    b. The marginal cost curve.
    c. The average total cost curve.
    d. The average revenue curve.

12. If a firm is producing at an output level at which:
    a. marginal revenue exceeds marginal cost, then
       the firm should reduce its output level to
       maximize profits.
    b. marginal revenue is less than marginal cost,
       then the firm should expand its output level
       to maximize profits.
    c. price exceeds average total costs, then the
       firm is earning an economic profit.
    d. price is less than minimum average total cost
       but greater than average variable cost, then
       the firm should shut down.

13. Refer to the graph below. The firm's profit in this case will be measured by:

  a. the rectangle ABEF.
  b. the rectangle ACDF.
  c. the rectangle ABHG.
  d. the rectangle BCDE.

14. A firm should shut down in the short run when it is:
  a. neither making a profit nor a loss.
  b. covering variable costs but not fixed costs.
  c. covering neither variable nor fixed costs.
  d. producing at a point where marginal cost in maximized.

15. Refer to the graph below. How low must the price fall before the firm will decide to shut down?

  a. Approximately $40.
  b. Approximately $35.
  c. Approximately $18.
  d. Approximately $12.

16. Refer to the graph below. This firm:

  a. is earning an economic profit equal to $2,000.
  b. should produce 100 units of output and charge a price of $40.
  c. is incurring total costs equal to $80.
  d. should shut down because price is less than minimum average variable cost.

17. In the graph below for a perfectly competitive firm:

  a. at P_2 the firm is incurring an economic loss but should remain in operation to minimize losses.
  b. at P_3 a zero economic profit is being earned.
  c. at P_4 an economic profit is earned.
  d. all of the above.

18. Refer to the graph below. Which demand curve illustrates a competitve firm in long-run equilibrium?

  a. D1.
  b. D2.
  c. D3.
  d. D4.

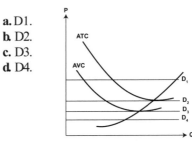

19. Normal profits are:
  a. approximately 6 percent of costs.
  b. approximately 8 percent of costs.
  c. returns to the owners of business for the opportunity cost of their implicit inputs.
  d. generally larger than accounting profits.

20. In the long-run competitive equilibrium the average firm:
  a. will be going out of business.
  b. will be expanding.
  c. will be making only a normal profit.
  d. won't even be making a normal profit.

21. In an increasing-cost industry, the long-run
 market supply curve will be:
 a. upward sloping.
 b. horizontal.
 c. vertical.
 d. downward sloping.

POTENTIAL ESSAY QUESTIONS

*You may also see essay questions similar to the "Problems
& Applications" exercises.*

1. Describe how to find a competitive firm's price,
 level of output, and profit given the firm's
 marginal cost curve and average total cost
 curve.

2. According to the textbook author, there are
 four major things to remember when considering a perfectly competitive industry. What are
 these four things?

ANSWERS

SHORT-ANSWER QUESTIONS

1. Competition as a process is a rivalry among firms, with one firm trying to take away market share from another firm. Competition as a state is the end result of the competitive process under certain conditions. (268)

2. The three onditions necessary for perfect competition include (1) buyers and sellers are both price takers, (2) there are no barriers to entry, and (3) firms' products are identical. (267-268)

3. It is clear that she is in a competitive market. She has no control over prices—she is a price-taker. I would advise that she calculate her marginal cost at various levels of output and sell the number of ice creams where marginal cost equals price. This will maximize her profit. To see why, for a perfect competitor, producing where $MC = P$ maximizes total profit, you must first understand that $MR = P$ for a perfect competitor. By definition a competitive firm takes price as given, so the incremental revenue, marginal revenue, of selling an additional unit is that unit's price. If we prove that a perfect competitor maximizes profit when $MC = MR$, we simultaneously prove that profit is maximized at output where $MC = P$. If marginal revenue does not equal marginal cost, a firm can increase profit by changing output. If a firm produces where $MC < MR$, it is earning a profit per unit and the firm can increase total profits by producing more until MC is no longer less than MR. If $MC > MR$, the firm is incurring a loss for that last unit; it can increase profits by reducing output until MC is no longer greater than MR. Given these conditions, the firm maximizes profit where $MC = MR$ or $MC = P$. (268-271)

4. The marginal cost curve (above the AVC curve) is the supply curve for a perfectly competitive firm because the marginal cost curve tells us how much of a produced good a firm will supply at a given price. (271, especially Figure 13-2 and 276)

5. To find where the profit-maximizing competitive firm produces, we need to know MR and MC.

We know MR. We need to calculate MC, the change in TC. We do this in column 5 in the table below. To calculate profit we need to know ATC. It is the sum of FC and VC divided by Q and is shown in column 7. (Marginal cost refers to the marginal cost of increasing to that row, e.g., the marginal cost of going from 0 to 1 is 20.)

P= MR	Q	FC	VC	MC	TC	ATC	TR	Profit
35	0	10	—	—	10	—	0	−10
35	1	10	20	20	30	30	35	5
35	2	10	38	18	48	24	70	22
35	3	10	50	12	60	20	105	45
35	4	10	77	27	87	21.75	140	53
35	5	10	112	35	122	24.4	175	53
35	6	10	156	44	166	27.67	210	44

Looking at the table, we see that $MC = MR$ at Q = 5. Profit is $(P - ATC) \times Q = 10.6 \times 5 = 53$. Alternatively, profit = TR − TC = $(P \times Q) - TC = (35 \times 5) - 122 = 175 - 122 = 53$. Notice that when producing where MR = MC, profit is as high or higher than at any other level of output. Increase output until MR = MC. This way you know you will be maximizing profits (minimizing losses). (268-271, especially Table 13-1)

6. The output of a perfect competitor is shown by the intersection of the marginal cost curve and the marginal revenue curve. On the graph below it is at Q^*. Profit for a perfect competitor is the profit per unit, the difference between the price for which each unit is sold and the average total cost of each unit, times the number of units sold. Graphically, profit per unit is the vertical distance from the MR curve to the ATC curve. Multiply this by Q^* to get profit. It is the shaded region in the graph. (274-275)

7. A firm should shut down if P ≤ minimum AVC. (Alternatively, a firm should shut down if

losses are greater than total fixed costs; or, total revenue is less than total variable costs. (276)

8. The market supply curve is the horizontal sum of all firms' marginal cost curves, taking account of any changes in input prices that might occur. (276-277)

9. The graph below shows a representative firm in a competitive market making an economic profit when price is P^*. Since profits create incentives for new firms to enter, output will increase and the price will fall to P_1 until zero profits are being made. (277-279)

10. Before Walmart opened a store, the small drug store produced Q^* at a given competitive price of P^* and earned normal profits. Since Walmart is a discount drug store, opening its store in the market most likely pushed prices down to P_1. Given the new price level, the small drug store now reduced output to Q_1 and incurred a loss. Eventually, all costs are variable and the ATC curve becomes the AVC curve and prices now are below the shutdown point. This is shown in the graph below. (276-279)

11. In an increasing-cost industry the long-run market supply curve is upward sloping because of higher input prices as the industry expands. The constant-cost industry's long-run market supply curve is horizontal because of constant input prices as the industry expands. The decreasing-cost industry's long-run market supply curve is downward sloping because of lower input prices as the industry expands. (280-281)

ANSWERS

MATCHING

1-b; 2-c; 3-d; 4-g; 5-h; 6-e; 7-a; 8-i; 9-f.

ANSWERS

PROBLEMS AND APPLICATIONS

1. To find the profit-maximizing level of output, first we determine marginal costs for the firm. We also show the values for a number of other costs. We use the formulas for these costs: MC = change in total cost, FC = \$30 (costs when $Q = 0$); $VC = TC - FC$, $AVC = VC/Q$. (Marginal cost refers to the marginal cost of increasing to that row, e.g., the marginal cost of going from 0 to 1 is 25.) (268-271, especially Figure 13-1)

Q	TC	MC	VC	FC	AVC
0	30	0	0	30	0
1	55	25	25	30	25
2	75	20	45	30	22.5
3	85	10	55	30	18.3
4	100	15	70	30	17.5
5	120	20	90	30	18
6	145	25	115	30	19.2
7	185	40	155	30	22.1
8	240	55	210	30	26.25
9	310	70	280	30	31.1
10	395	85	365	30	36.5

a. A profit-maximizing firm will produce at the output level where $MC = MR$. Since MR = market price for the competitive firm, MR = \$20. MC = 20 at 2 units and 5 units. It will not choose to produce 2 units because marginal costs are declining and the firm would make additional profit by increasing output above 2. So, the profit-maximizing output level is at 5 units. (268-271)

b. If price rises to $25, so does *MR*. *MC = 25* at 6 units. (268-271)

c. In part *a*, profit = total revenue − total costs at 5 units: (5 × $20) − $120 = −$20, an economic loss. In part *b*, profit = total revenue − total costs at 6 units: (6 × $25) − $145 = $5. (273-276)

d. The firm will stay in business at *P* = $20 and $25, since *P* > *AVC* at both these prices. (276)

e. At *P* = $15, the profit-maximizing level of output is 4 units. The profit in this case is −$40 (loss of $40). Since *P* < *AVC* in this case, the firm should temporarily shut down its business. (268-276)

2. a. As shown in the graph below, points A and B are the minimum of the *ATC* and *AVC* curves. It is where they intersect the *MC* curve. From an earlier chapter, we know that the *MC* curve goes through the *ATC* and *AVC* curves at their minimum points. (Figure 13-4 on page 274)

b. A demand curve for the representative firm is drawn in the graph above. It is a horizontal line because an individual firm in a competitive market is a price taker; the demand for its product is perfectly elastic. (274)

c. As illustrated above, the long-run equilibrium position occurs when the demand curve is tangent to the *ATC* curve because it is only at this point that economic profit for the firm is equal to zero. There is no incentive for new firms to enter the market, nor would existing firms exit the market. The long-run equilibrium is reached. (Figure 13-5 on page 277)

3. a. As shown by the shaded region on the following graph, the representative firm is earning an economic profit. (274-275)

b. Refer to the graphs below. More firms will enter the market to share the profit. But as market supply increases from S_0 to S_1, the market price falls which in turn reduces the profit margin for all the firms. This process continues until price falls to P_1 where there is no more economic profit. This assumes a constant-cost industry. (276-277)

c. As shown on the graphs below, a decrease in market demand from D_0 to D_1, results in a fall of market price from P_0 to P_1 which in turn causes each firm in the market to make a loss. The losses will cause some firms to exit the market. Hence, market supply shrinks from S_0 to S_1, until prices rise from P_1 to P_0. In the long run, price returns to the original level. Each firm still has zero economic profit. This assumes a constant-cost industry. (279-281)

4. a. The curve labeled *AVC* is really an *AFC* curve. The correct *AVC* curve would intersect the *MC* at the minimum point of the *AVC* curve and rise thereafter. (Figure 13-4 on page 274)

b. Loss is mislabeled in the graph. Loss and profit are measured by the vertical difference between price and average total costs, not average variable costs. Here, economic profit is zero (there is no loss). (Figure 13-4 on page 274)

c. Output should be where $MC = MR = P$, not where $ATC = MC$. A competitive firm will maximize profits where $MC = MR = P$. (Figure 13-4 on page 274)

d. A competitive firm faces a horizontal demand curve since it cannot affect prices. Here it is downward sloping. (Figure 13-4 on page 274)

——— ANSWERS ———

MULTIPLE CHOICE

1. a In a competitive market, firms are profit-maximizing, not sales-maximizing firms. Buyers and sellers are price takers because each one cannot affect the market. See pages 267-268.

2. b Competitive firms sell a homogenous product, there are no barriers to entry, and they cannot earn economic profits in the long run. See pages 267-268.

3. b Barriers to entry are anything that prevents other firms from entering a market. They can be a consequence of political, economic, or social forces. There cannot be barriers to entry in a competitive market. See page 268.

4. b Although the market demand curve is downward sloping, individual firms are so small in relation to the market that they perceive their demand curves as horizontal. See page 269 and Figure 13-1.

5. d The market demand curve is downward sloping. See page 279 and Figure 13-6.

6. a For the perfectly competitive firm $P = MR$. If $P > MC$, increase output to increase profits. See pages 268-270, especially Figure 13-1.

7. b For the perfectly competitive firm $P = MR$. If $P < MC$, decrease output to increase profits. See pages 268-270, especially Figure 13-1.

8. b A profit-maximizing firm will produce where the difference between TR and TC is greatest. This is at a quantity B. Where the two intersect, profits are zero. See pages 272-273, especially Figure 13-3.

9. c Any firm maximizes profit by producing where marginal revenue equals marginal cost. Also note, for the perfectly competitive firm, price equals marginal revenue. See pages 270-271.

10. b Since $P > MC$, increase output until $MC = P = MR$, the profit-maximizing level of output. See pages 270-271.

11. b Since a perfect competitor chooses to produce where $P = MC$, the marginal cost curve is the firm's supply curve (above minimum average variable cost). See page 271.

12. c Profit per unit $= (P - ATC)$. Total profit equals profit per unit times quantity. To maximize profits (or minimize losses), firms will produce where marginal revenue equals marginal cost. Firms will shut down if price is less than average variable costs. See pages 270-275.

13. b Output is determined where marginal cost equals price (and price equals marginal revenue for the competitive firm). To determine profit one finds the rectangle formed by ATC at the output level and price is determined by where marginal cost equals price. See Figure 13-4, page 274.

14. c A firm should shut down in the short run when price is less than the minimum of the AVC curve. At this point the firm is covering neither its variable nor its fixed costs. If a firm shuts down when it is covering all its variable costs but not all its fixed costs, or when it is making zero profit and zero loss, it will end up losing more money by shutting down. See page 276.

15. c   The shutdown point is where the marginal cost equals minimum average variable cost. See page 276.

16. a   Quantity is where P = MR = MC. Profit is (P − ATC) times quantity produced. Total cost is ATC times quantity. See pages 274-276.

17. d   If P > ATC an economic profit is earned. If P = ATC a zero economic profit (a normal profit) is earned. If P < ATC but above minimum AVC, the firm is incurring an economic loss but should remain in operation to minimize losses. See pages 274-276.

18. b   D2 represents a competitive firm in long-run equilibrium where there is no profit or loss. If the firm is making a profit in the long run as in D1, other firms would enter the market, lowering market price until demand is D2. If the firm is making a loss as in D3 or D4, firms will exit the market until the market price is D2. See page 277.

19. c   See definition of normal profit in the textbook on page 277.

20. c   The zero profit condition for long-run competitive equilibrium discussed in the text includes a normal profit. See page 277.

21. a   If an industry expands and this increases input prices then the long-run market supply curve will be upward sloping. See page 277.

■■■■ ANSWERS ■■■■

POTENTIAL ESSAY QUESTIONS

The following are annotated answers. They indicate the general idea behind the answer.

1. To find a competitive firm's price, level of output, and profit given the firm's marginal cost curve and average total cost curve, do the following: (See the "A Reminder" box on page 278).
    1. Determine the market price where market supply and demand curves intersect. This is the price the competitive firm accepts for its products. Draw a horizontal marginal revenue (MR) curve at this market price.
    2. Determine the profit-maximizing level of output by finding the level of output where the MR and MC curves intersect.
    3. Determine profit by subtracting average total costs at the profit-maximizing level of output from the price and multiplying by the firm's output.

    If you are determining profit graphically, find the point at which MR = MC. Extend a line down to the ATC curve. Extend a line from that point to the vertical axis. To complete the box indicating profit, go up the vertical axis to the market price.

2. Four things to remember when considering a perfectly competitive industry: (See "A Reminder" box on page 281).
    1. The profit-maximizing condition for perfectly competitive firms is MC = MR = P.
    2. To determine profit or loss at the profit-maximizing level of output, subtract average total cost at that level of output from price and multiply the result by the output level.
    3. Firms will shut down production if price falls below the minimum of their average variable costs.
    4. A competitive firm is in long-run equilibrium only when it is earning zero economic profit, or where price equals the minimum of long-run average total costs.

MONOPOLY AND MONOPOLISTIC COMPETITION

14

● CHAPTER AT A GLANCE

1. A competitive firm produces where marginal revenue equals price. A monopolist does not. The monopolist takes into account the fact that its output decision can affect price. (289-292)

   The monopolist faces the market demand curve. It must reduce P to sell more. Hence, MR < P.

2. The general rule that any firm must follow to maximize profit is: Produce at an output level at which MC = MR. (291-292)

   If MR > MC then increase Q.

   If MR = MC then the firm is maximizing profit (minimizing loss).

   If MR < MC then decrease Q.

3. To find a monopolist's level of output, price, and profit, follow these four steps: (290-294 and especially Figures 14-1, 14-2, and 14-3, and "A Reminder" on page 294)

   a. Draw the marginal revenue curve.

   b. Determine the output the monopolist will produce: The profit-maximizing level of output is where MR and MC curves intersect. *(See the graph in the next column.)*

   c. Determine the price the monopolist will charge: Extend a line from where MR = MC up to the demand curve. Where this line intersects the demand curve is the monopolist's price. *(See the graph at the top of the next column.)*

   d. Determine the profit the monopolist will earn: Subtract the *ATC* from price at the profit-maximizing level of output to get profit per unit. Multiply profit per unit by quantity of output to get total profit. *(See the graph below.)*

4. The welfare loss from monopoly is the triangle in the graph below. It is not the loss that most people consider. They are often interested in normative losses that the graph does not capture. (295-296)

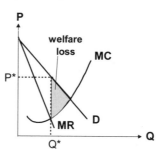

Because monopolists reduce output and charge a price that is higher than marginal cost, monopolies create a welfare loss to society.

5. When a monopolist price discriminates, it charges individuals high up on the demand curve higher prices and those low on the demand curve lower prices. (296-297)

    If a monopolist can (1) identify groups of customers who have different elasticities of demand, (2) separate them in some way, and (3) limit their ability to re-sell its product between groups, it can price discriminate.

    A price discriminating monopolist earns more profit than a normal monopolist because it can charge a higher price to those with less elastic demands and a lower price to those with more elastic demands. Price discrimination increases profits.

    It also eliminates welfare loss from monopoly.

6. If there were no barriers to entry, profit-maximizing firms would always compete away monopoly profits. (297-302)

    Economies of scale are a barrier to entry that creates natural monopolies. Know why.

✔ *Know the three different types of barriers to entry.*

    The stronger the barriers to entry, the stronger the monopoly power (the greater the ability to charge a higher price) and the greater the ability to earn economic profits over time.

7. Four distinguishing characteristics of monopolistic competition are: (302-304)

    1. Many sellers.
    2. Differentiated products.
    3. Multiple dimensions of competition.
    4. Easy entry of new firms in the long run.

✔ *Know these as well as the distinguishing characteristics of all 4 market models.*

8. The equilibrium of a monopolistic competitor is different than for a monopolist. (304-305)

    While monopolistic competitors face a downward-sloping demand curve, they make zero economic profit in the long run.

    In the long run, average total costs equal price.

    See also, Appendix A: "The Algebra of Competitive and Monopolistic Firms."

● SHORT-ANSWER QUESTIONS

1. What is the key difference between the
    decisions by monopolists and the collective
    decisions of competing firms with regard to
    setting price and production levels?

2. Calculate a monopolist's price, output, and
    profit using the following table:

Q	Price	Total cost
0	$36	$47
1	33	48
2	30	50
3	27	58
4	24	73
5	21	89
6	18	113
7	15	153
8	12	209
9	9	289

3. Show a monopolist's price, output, and profit
    using the graph below.

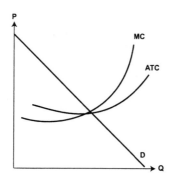

4. Show graphically the welfare loss from
    monopoly on the axes below.

5. Why will a price discriminating monopolist
    earn more profit than a normal monopolist?

6. Why, without barriers to entry, would there be
    no monopoly?

7. Show graphically the equilibrium of a
    monopolistic competitor.

8. How is a monopolistic competitor different
    from and similar to a perfect competitor in the
    long run?

MATCHING THE TERMS
Match the terms to their definitions

___ **1.**	monopolistic competition	**a.**	A legal protection of a technical innovation that gives the person holding it sole right to use that innovation.
___ **2.**	monopoly	**b.**	Monopolies that exist because economies of scale create a barrier to entry.
___ **3.**	natural monopoly	**c.**	To charge a different price to different individuals or groups of individuals.
___ **4.**	patent	**d.**	A market structure in which one firm makes up the entire market.
___ **5.**	price discriminate	**e.**	A market structure in which there are many firms selling differentiated products and few barriers to entry.

● PROBLEMS AND APPLICATIONS

1. What are some real-world examples of monopolies?

2. Consider the following graph for a monopoly.

    a. Indicate on the graph the monopolist's output and price. Shade the area representing any economic profit (or loss).

    b. If this monopolist earns economic profits, then what is expected to happen over time? What if economic losses were incurred?

3. Consider the following graph for a monopoly.

    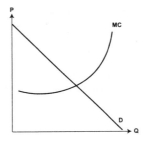

    a. Illustrate the output level and price charged by the monopoly on the graph.

    b. What would the price and output level be if this were a competitive market?

    c. Illustrate the area representing welfare loss on the graph. Explain what is meant by "welfare loss" associated with a monopoly.

4. The following table represents the market for Corning Fiberglass. Corning is the sole producer of fiberglass.

Q	Price	TC
0	—	60
1	46	65
2	42	81
3	38	111
4	34	145
5	30	189
6	24	249

a. Determine the profit-maximizing price and output.

b. What is the monopolist's profit?

c. Suppose the market is competitive, what is output and price? Would this company stay in business?

5. Given the following demand curve, add a marginal cost curve.

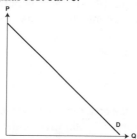

a. Label profit-maximizing price and output for a monopolist. Label profit-maximizing price and output for a monopolistically competitive firm.

b. Add an average total cost curve that is consistent with long-run equilibrium in a market characterized by monopolistic competition. What is the economic profit? Explain your answer.

6. For each of the following graphs state whether it characterizes perfect competition, monopoly, or monopolistic competition in the long run. Explain your answer.

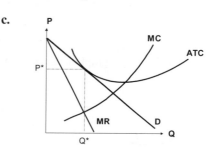

A1. Suppose the marginal costs, and therefore the market supply, for Mimi Chocolates is given by $P = Q_s/2 + 3$. The market demand is given by $Q_d = 10 - 2P$.

a. What is the equilibrium price and quantity if the market for chocolates is perfectly competitive?

b. If Mimi Chocolates has a monopoly in the market, what will be the price and the quantity produced in the market?

● **MULTIPLE CHOICE**

Circle the one best answer for each of the following questions:

1. Monopoly is the market structure in which:
   a. one firm makes up the entire market.
   b. two firms make up the entire market.
   c. the market is made up of a few big firms.
   d. firms make a supernormal profit.

2. Which of the following is *false*?
   a. A monopoly is a price maker, whereas a competitive firm is a price taker.
   b. The monopolist produces where MR = MC while the perfect competitor does not.
   c. The monopoly's marginal revenue curve lies below the demand curve whereas the competitive firm's marginal revenue curve is horizontal at the market price.
   d. A monopolist is protected by barriers to entry whereas a competitive firm is not.

3. A profit-maximizing monopolist will:
   a. produce an output level at which MR > MC.
   b. produce an output level at which P > MC.
   c. always earn an economic profit in the short run.
   d. increase production when MR < MC.

4. Refer to the graph below. Which curve is the marginal revenue curve for the market demand curve D faced by a monopolist?
   a. Curve A.
   b. Curve B.
   c. Curve C.
   d. Curve D.

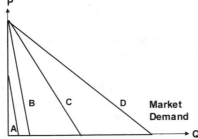

5. Refer to the graph below. A monopolist would most likely produce quantity shown by:
   a. A.
   b. B.
   c. C.
   d. D.

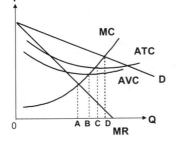

6. Refer to the graph below. Which rectangle represents the monopolist's profit?
   a. A.
   b. A + B + C.
   c. C + D.
   d. None of the above.

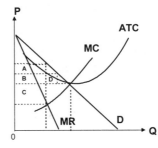

7. Refer to the graph below. The monopolist represented is:

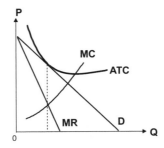

   a. making a profit.
   b. making a loss.
   c. making zero profit.
   d. unable to determine what kind of profit it is making.

8. Refer to the graph below. Which of the following statements about the market represented is true?

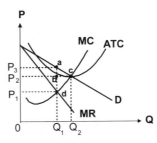

   a. A monopolist would charge price P_2 and produce output Q_2.
   b. A monopolist would charge price P_1 and produce output Q_1.
   c. A competitive market would charge price P_2 and produce output Q_2.
   d. A monopolist would earn a profit per unit equal to P_3 minus P_1.

9. Refer to the graph for Question #8. Which of the following statements about the effect of the monopolist represented is true?
    a. Triangle *bac* represents the lost producer surplus to society due to the monopoly.
    b. Triangle *dbc* represents the lost consumer surplus to society due to the monopoly.
    c. Triangle *dac* represents the welfare loss to society due to the monopoly.
    d. Lost production due to the monopoly is equal to Q_1.

10. Refer to the graph below. This monopolist is:

    a. earning a profit of $600.
    b. earning a profit of $800.
    c. breaking even.
    d. incurring a loss of $300.

11. Refer to the graph below. Which area represents the welfare loss due to a monopolist?
    a. A.
    b. A+B.
    c. B+C.
    d. A+B+C.

12. A price-discriminating monopolist:
    a. charges different prices to customers with different elasticities of demand.
    b. will earn a lower profit than a non-price-discriminating monopolist.
    c. will have a marginal revenue curve that lies above its demand curve.
    d. is trying to allow some people to purchase the good who could not normally afford to do so.

13. Price discrimination requires:
    a. identifying groups of customers with different elasticities.
    b. separating customers in some way.
    c. limiting customers' ability to re-sell the product between different groups.
    d. all of the above options listed to be successful.

14. A natural monopoly is a monopoly:
    a. that exists because of economies of scale.
    b. that is created by natural law.
    c. where natural legal barriers prevent entry.
    d. in which patents exist.

15. If the government forced a natural monopolist to charge consumers the price that a perfect competitor would charge, the monopolist would make a loss represented by rectangle:

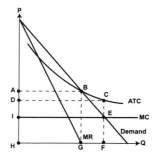

    a. ABGH.
    b. DCFH.
    c. IEFH.
    d. None of the above.

16. For a monopolist to earn an economic profit in the long run, which of the following must happen?
    a. There are barriers to entry.
    b. Average total costs must fall.
    c. Welfare loss due to monopoly must increase.
    d. Fixed costs must be eliminated.

17. At the equilibrium output for a monopolistic competitor:
    a. price equals marginal cost equals marginal revenue.
    b. price equals average total cost equals marginal revenue.
    c. marginal cost equals marginal revenue equals average total costs.
    d. price equals average total cost and marginal cost equals marginal revenue.

18. Refer to the graph below. Which of the following is the output chosen by the monopolistically competitive firm?

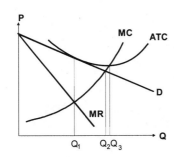

a. Q_1.
b. Q_2.
c. Q_3.
d. Output cannot be determined.

19. In long-run equilibrium, a monopolistically competitive firm:
a. makes a loss.
b. makes only a normal profit.
c. makes a monopolistic profit.
d. may make a loss or a profit.

20. A firm makes a profit in the long run. It is a:
a. perfect competitor.
b. monopolist.
c. monopolistic competitor.
d. This is true for all above.

21. A firm produces where marginal revenue equals marginal cost to maximize profits. It is a:
a. perfect competitor.
b. monopolist.
c. monopolistic competitor.
d. This is true for all above.

22. A firm sells a differentiated product and faces no barriers to entry in the long-run. It is a:
a. perfect competitor.
b. monopolist.
c. monopolistic competitor.
d. This is true for all above.

A1. Suppose the marginal costs, and therefore the market supply, for ketchup in Mexico is given by $P = Q_s/2 + 1$. The market demand is given by, $Q_d = 20 - 4P$. If there is a monopoly in the ketchup market the price and the quantity produced are:
a. $P = 11/3, Q = 16/3$.
b. $P = 11/3, Q = 4$.
c. $P = 3, Q = 4$.
d. $P = 4, Q = 4$.

● POTENTIAL ESSAY QUESTIONS

You may also see essay questions similar to the "Problems & Applications" exercises.

1. What is the objective of price discrimination? What conditions must be present for a firm to be able to price discriminate?

2. What are the monopolistic element and the competitive element of monopolistic competition?

━━━ ■ ANSWERS ■ ━━━

SHORT-ANSWER QUESTIONS

1. For a competitive firm, marginal revenue equals price regardless of output. But for a monopolist, price depends on output. A monopolist must take into account the fact that its output decisions can affect price. Its marginal revenue does not equal the price it charges. Instead, MR < P for the monopolist. (288-290)

2. To calculate a monopolist's output, first calculate total revenue ($P \times Q$) for each output level. Then calculate marginal revenue (the change in total revenue). Find where $MR = MC$. This is at 4 units and a price of $24. Profit is calculated as total revenue minus total cost: $23. Notice that profit is maximized at an output where $MR = MC$. Profits are as high or higher here than at any other output level. (Marginal cost refers to the marginal cost of increasing to that row, e.g., the marginal cost of going from 0 to 1 is 1. The same goes for marginal revenue.) (289-290)

Q	Price	Total revenue	Marginal revenue	Total cost	Marginal cost
0	$36	0	—	$47	—
1	33	33	33	48	1
2	30	60	27	50	2
3	27	81	21	58	8
4	24	96	15	73	15
5	21	105	9	89	16
6	18	108	3	113	24
7	15	105	−3	153	40
8	12	96	−9	209	56
9	9	81	−15	289	80

3. A monopolist's output is set where $MC = MR$ (where the MC and MR curves intersect). Extend a line vertically; it sets price where that line intersects the demand curve, here at $P*$. Profit is determined by dropping a vertical line from the price the monopolist charges to the ATC curve and multiplying by $Q*$. This is the shaded region in the graph below. (292-294; especially the "A Reminder" box on page 294)

4. Welfare loss from monopoly is shown as the shaded region on the graph below. (295)

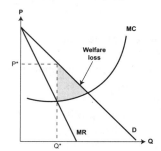

5. If a monopolist can (1) identify groups of customers who have different elasticities of demand, (2) separate them in some way, and (3) limit their ability to re-sell its product between groups, it can price discriminate. A price discriminating monopolist earns more profit than a normal monopolist because it can increase output without reducing the price it charged for previous units. It can charge a higher price to those with less elastic demands and a lower price to those with more elastic demands. Price discrimination increases profits. (296-297)

6. Without barriers to entry there would be no monopoly because profit-maximizing firms would always enter to compete away monopoly profits. (297-301)

7. The equilibrium of a monopolistic competitor is shown in the graph below. A monopolistic competitor earns no economic profit in the long run, so the price equals ATC. (304-305)

8. In the long run in both perfect and monopolistic competition, new firms can easily enter the market, so there is zero long-run economic profit. Monopolistic competitors face a downward-sloping demand curve and produce at a level where MR=MC<ATC in long-run equilibrium. On the other hand, perfect competitors face a perfectly elastic demand curve and produce at a level where MC=P=ATC in long-run equilibrium. (305-306)

━━━━ **ANSWERS** ━━━━

MATCHING

1-e; 2-d; 3-b; 4-a; 5-c.

━━━━ **ANSWERS** ━━━━

PROBLEMS AND APPLICATIONS

1. Your local cable television, water, gas, and electric companies are a few examples. In some small towns the only grocery store in town will behave as a monopoly. Note that it may be helpful to think in terms of regional markets, and in terms of the number of suitable substitutes available for the good or service. The smaller the number of suitable substitutes the greater the monopoly power. (288-289)

2. **a.** The monopolist will produce Q* and charge price P*. Because $P < ATC$ the monopoly is incurring an economic loss shown as the shaded area in the graph below. (290-295)

   b. Economic profits always attract other businesses. However, because the barriers to entry in a monopoly are so strong,

potential competitors will find it very difficult to enter this market. Therefore, economic profits are likely to persist for some time. If losses are incurred by a monopolist, like any other firm, the monopolist will shut down if $P < AVC$ in the short run. No firm can sustain losses in the long run. (293-295)

3. **a.** See the graph below. The monopoly would produce Q_m and charge price P_m. (290-292)
   b. See the graph below. The competitive outcome would be Q_c and P_c. (As you would expect, the monopolist charges a higher price and produces less than if the market were competitive.) (290-292 and especially Figure 14-1)
   c. The shaded area in the graph below illustrates welfare loss. Welfare loss is the amount by which the marginal benefits to society (measured by the prices people are willing to pay along the demand curve) exceed the marginal costs to society (measured by points along the marginal cost curve) for those units that would be produced in a competitive market but are not produced in a non-competitive market. (295-296)

4. To answer the following questions, first calculate *MC*, *MR,* and *AVC*. MC is the change in *TC*, *AVC* is *VC/Q*, and *MR* is the change in *TR*, where *TR* is $P \times Q$. This is shown below. (Marginal cost refers to the marginal cost of increasing to that row, e.g., the marginal cost of going from 0 to 1 is 5. The same goes for marginal revenue.) (289-290 and Table 14-1 on page 290)

Q	Price	TC	MC	TR	MR	AVC
0	—	60	—	0	—	0
1	46	65	5	46	46	5
2	42	81	16	84	38	10.5
3	38	111	30	114	30	17.00
4	34	145	34	136	22	21.25
5	30	189	44	150	14	25.8
6	24	249	60	144	–6	31.5

a. Monopolists maximize profits where *MR* = *MC*. *MR* = *MC* at 3 units. Corning will charge a price of $38. (289-290)

b. Profit = total revenue minus total costs = $3. (289-290)

c. If the market were competitive, then the firm would produce where *MC* = *P*. So *Q* is 4 units and *P* = $34. Profit = total revenue − total costs = −$9. The firm will still stay in business in the short run since *P* > *AVC*. (289-290)

5. a. The graph below shows a typical marginal cost curve for a firm. The profit-maximizing level of output for a monopolist is where *MC* = *MR*. It will set price by extending the quantity line to the demand curve and extending a horizontal line to the price axis. This is the price a monopolistically competitive firm would charge. All this is labeled as *Q** and *P** respectively. The profit-maximizing price and output procedure for a monopolistically competitive firm is the same as for a monopolist. (290-292, 304-306)

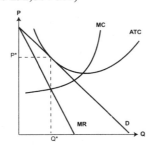

b. The average total cost curve consistent with long-run equilibrium in a market characterized by monopolistic competition is drawn on the graph above. It is tangent to the demand curve at the profit-maximizing price and quantity combination. Economic profit is zero. It is drawn this way because competition implies zero economic profit in the long run. (290-292, 304-306)

6. a. This graph depicts perfect competition because the demand curve facing the firm is horizontal and zero economic profit is earned. (305-306; especially Figure 14-9)

b. This graph depicts a monopolist because it faces a downward-sloping demand curve and it is earning economic profit. (305-306)

c. This graph depicts a monopolistic competitor because it faces a downward-sloping demand curve and its economic profit is zero. (It could also depict a monopolist if it so happens that the *ATC* curve is drawn as given.) (305-306)

A1. a. Rewriting the marginal cost equation with quantity supplied on the left gives: $Q_s = 2P - 6$. Setting this equal to quantity demanded gives equilibrium price at 4 and quantity at 2. (313-314)

b. Specifying the demand curve in terms of quantity demanded gives: $P = 5 − Q/2$. Multiplying this by Q gives total revenue $TR = 5Q − Q^2/2$. The marginal revenue is the first derivative of this. Thus, $MR = 5 − Q$. By setting MR = MC and solving for Q we get the quantity that would be produced if the chocolate market were a monopoly. (313-314)

$$5 − Q = Q/2 + 3$$
$$3/2Q = 2$$
$$Q = 4/3, \text{ or } 1.33.$$

The monopolist charges the price that consumers are willing to pay for that quantity. Substituting Q = 4/3 into the demand equation gives P = 13/3, or 4.33. You can see that if there is a monopoly in the market, the price charged is higher than the competitive market price; also, the quantity produced is lower. (313-314)

━━━━━ **ANSWERS** ━━━━━

MULTIPLE CHOICE

1. a   Monopoly means one firm; that firm may or may not make a supernormal profit. See pages 288-289.

2. b   Both monopolies and competitive firms produce where MR = MC. Recall that P = MR for a competitive firm. So, the profit-maximizing rule for a competitive firm is sometimes written: Produce where P = MC. See pages 291-292.

3. b   A monopolist produces where MR = MC. Since MR is below the demand curve, this means the monopolist produces where P > MC. If MR > MC, it will *increase* production. If MR < MC, it will *decrease* production. See pages 291-292.

4. c The marginal revenue curve equals the demand curve at the vertical axis and bisects the distance between the origin and the point where the demand curve intersects the horizontal axis. See page 291, "Added Dimension."

5. a Output is determined where marginal revenue equals marginal cost. This is shown where the MR and MC curves intersect. See pages 290-292, especially Figure 14-1.

6. a Output is determined where marginal revenue equals marginal cost. Profit is determined by the rectangle created by the relevant price and average cost at that output. See page 293, especially Figure 14-3, and "A Reminder" on page 294.

7. c A monopolist produces where MC = MR and charges a price determined by the demand curve. Since P = ATC, the monopolist is earning no profit. See Figure 14-4(a) on page 295.

8. c A monopolist produces where MC = MR and charges a price determined by the demand curve. This results in a price of P_3 and output Q_1. The profit per unit is P_3 minus P_2. A perfectly competitive market produces where MC intersects the market demand curve. See pages 290-293 and Figure 14-1 on page 290.

9. c A monopolist produces where MC = MR and charges a price determined by the demand curve. A perfectly competitive market produces where MC intersects the market demand curve. Welfare loss is lost consumer and producer surplus due to the decline in output. This is the triangle above the MC curve, below the demand curve and between Q_1 and Q_2. See pages 295-296, especially Figure 14-5.

10. d The monopolist produces where MC = MR, or 100, and charges a price determined by

the demand curve, or $11. Because ATC = $14, the monopolist is losing $3 per unit. $3 x 100 = $300 loss. See pages 290-292 and Figure 14-3 on page 294.

11. c A monopolist produces where MC = MR and charges a price determined by the demand curve. A perfectly competitive market produces where MC intersects the market demand curve. Welfare loss is lost consumer and producer surplus due to the decline in output. This is the triangle above the MC curve, below the demand curve and between the two levels of output. See pages 295-296, especially Figure 14-5.

12. a By segmenting the market into groups of customers with different elasticities of demand, a price-discriminating monopolist can increase profits by charging higher (lower) prices to consumers with a more inelastic (elastic) demand. See pages 296-297.

13. d By segmenting the market into groups of customers with different elasticities of demand, a price-discriminating monopolist can increase profits by charging higher (lower) prices to consumers with a more inelastic (elastic) demand. This requires all the options listed. See pages 296-297.

14. a If large fixed (setup) costs create barriers to entry for an industry and average total costs decline as output rises, it is more efficient for there to be only one producer. This industry is known as a natural monopoly. See pages 299-301.

15. d The firm would be making a loss of DCIE because price=I, quantity=F, and ATC=C. See pages 299-300.

16. a If there were no barriers to entry, competitors would enter the market and drive down price until only normal profits were earned. See page 297.

17. d The equilibrium output is determined where marginal costs equal marginal revenue. At that output average total costs equal price, but that price does not equal either marginal cost or marginal revenue. See pages 304-305 and Figure 14-8.

18. a   The equilibrium output is determined where marginal cost equals marginal revenue. See pages 304-305 and Figure 14-8.

19. b   In long-run equilibrium, a monopolistically competitive firm must make zero profit (a normal profit), so that no entry is induced. See pages 304-305.

20. b   If a firm makes a profit in the long run, it is a monopolist. Neither perfect or monopolistic competitors make a profit. See pages 305-306.

21. d   All profit-maximizing firms produce where MR=MC. See pages 291-292, 304.

22. c   If a firm sells a differentiated product and faces no barriers to entry in the long-run, it is a monopolistic competitor. Monopolistic competitors do not face barriers to entry and perfect competitors sell identical products. See pages 297-306.

A1. c   Specifying the demand curve in terms of quantity produced gives: $P = 5 - Q/4$. Multiplying this by Q gives total revenue $TR = 5Q - Q^2/4$. The marginal revenue is the first derivative of this. Thus, $MR = 5 - Q/2$. By setting $MR = MC$ and solving for Q we get the quantity produced: $5 - Q/2 = Q/2 + 1$; $Q = 4$. The monopolist charges the price that consumers are willing to pay for that quantity. Substituting $Q = 4$ into the demand equation gives $P = 4$. Thus, d is the correct answer. See pages 313-314.

━━━━ **ANSWERS** ━━━━

POTENTIAL ESSAY QUESTIONS

The following are annotated answers. They indicate the general idea behind the answer.

1. The objective of price discrimination is to increase profits. In order to price discriminate, a firm must be able to segment its markets or customers. It must also be able to determine which markets or customers have the more inelastic demand for the good or service, and then charge those people the higher price. Finally, the product cannot be easily resold.

2. The "monopolistic" element is the ability to charge a higher-than-competitive price that is directly related to the success the firm has in differentiating its product from its competitors. The "competitive" element is that there are many sellers who are able to earn only a zero economic profit in the long run because of the weak barriers to entry into the market (the only real barrier to entry is the ability to differentiate the product from competitors).

OLIGOPOLY AND ANTITRUST POLICY

15

CHAPTER AT A GLANCE

1. The central element of oligopoly is that there are a small number of firms in an industry, so that in any decision it makes, each firm must take into account the expected reaction of other firms. (315-316)

    Oligopolistic firms are mutually interdependent and can be collusive or non-collusive. If they collude and form a cartel, they can increase their collective profits. Although there is a tendency for collusion (getting together to avoid competing), holding firms to an agreement is difficult because each firm has a tendency to cheat.

    An oligopolist's price will be somewhere between the competitive price and monopolistic price.

2. No single general model of oligopoly exists because oligopolists have many strategies. (316-320)

    Two models of oligopoly behavior:

    *   *Cartel model: Firms set a monopoly price.*
    *   *Contestable market model: An oligopoly with no barriers sets a competitive price.*

        Most real-world oligopolies are between these extremes.

3. To measure industry structure, economists use one of two methods: the concentration ratio or a Herfindahl index. (320-323)

    A concentration ratio is the value of sales by the top firms of an industry stated as a percentage of total industry sales.

    A Herfindahl Index is a method used by economists (and the Department of Justice) to classify how competitive an industry is. A Herfindahl Index has 2 advantages over a concentration ratio: (1) it takes into account all firms in an industry, and (2) it gives extra weight to firms with especially large shares of the market.

4. Antitrust policy is the government's policy toward the competitive process. (324-325)

    Judgment by performance is the view that competitiveness of a market should be judged by the behavior of firms in that market.

    Judgment by structure is the view that competitiveness of a market should be judged by the structure of the market.

    Both criteria have their problems. There are no definitive criteria for judging whether a firm has violated antitrust statutes. However, since 1945, most court decisions have relied on judgment by structure for the reason of practicality.

    Two recent antitrust cases are (1) Microsoft and (2) AT&T.

    ✓ *Be prepared to discuss these cases.*

● SHORT-ANSWER QUESTIONS

1. State the central element of oligopoly and the two basic models of oligopolies.

2. Major oil producers in the world have formed a tight cartel, OPEC. At times, the cartel has fallen apart. What are the reasons the major oil producers have a powerful desire to keep OPEC strong?

3. How does the contestable market theory lead to determining competitiveness by performance rather than structure?

4. What is the 4-firm concentration ratio for an industry in which 10 firms all have 10% of the market?

5. What is a Herfindahl index for an industry in which 10 firms all have 10% of the market?

6. How does judging competition by structure differ from judging competition by performance?

7. What was the resolution of the AT&T antitrust case?

8. What was the resolution of the Microsoft antitrust case?

MATCHING THE TERMS
Match the terms to their definitions

___ 1.	antitrust policy	**a.** Judging the competitiveness of markets by the number of firms in the market and market shares.
___ 2.	cartel	**b.** A market structure with a few interdependent firms.
___ 3.	cartel model of oligopoly	**c.** A combination of firms that acts like a single firm.
___ 4.	concentration ratio	**d.** A model that bases pricing and output decisions on entry and exit conditions, not on market structure.
___ 5.	contestable market model	**e.** An index of market concentration calculated by adding the squared values of the individual market shares of all firms in the industry.
___ 6.	Herfindahl Index	
___ 7.	implicit collusion	**f.** An industry classification that categorizes firms by type of economic activity and groups firms with like production processes.
___ 8.	judgment by performance	
___ 9.	judgment by structure	**g.** Multiple firms making the same pricing decisions even though they have not consulted with one another.
___ 10.	North American Industry Classification System (NAICS)	**h.** A model that assumes that oligopolies act as if they were a monopolist that has assigned output quotas to individual member firms of the oligopoly so that total output is consistent with joint profit maximization.
___ 11.	oligopoly	**i.** Taking explicit account of a rival's expected response to a decision you are making.
___ 12.	strategic decision making	**j.** The value of sales by the top firms of an industry stated as a percentage of total industry sales.
		k. Government's policy toward the competitive process.
		l. Judging the competitiveness of markets by the behavior of firms in that market.

PROBLEMS AND APPLICATIONS

1. Fill in the following table, which captures the central differences among various market structures.

	Monopoly	Oligopoly	Monopolistic Competition	Perfect Competition
Number of Firms				
Pricing Decisions				
Output Decisions				
Profit				

2. Indicate whether the following statements reflect the cartel or contestable market model of oligopoly.

    a. The airline industry is oligopolistic because it is costly for new firms to enter the market due to limited gates at airports.

    b. The local plumbing industry is an oligopoly because social forces keep plumbers from setting prices that are different from one another.

    c. Oil producing countries could engage in a price war.

3. For each of the following calculate the four-firm concentration ratio and the Herfindahl index.

    a. 20 firms in the market each having equal shares.

    b. 10 firms are in the market. One firm has 91% of market share. The remaining 9 firms share the remaining market equally.

    c. The industry's top firm has 31% of the market and the next three have 2% apiece. There are 63 remaining firms, each with a 1% share.

    d. Four firms equally share the market.

    e. Rank each of these markets by how competitive they are: from the most to least competitive, first using the concentration ratio and then the Herfindahl index. Do they differ? Why or why not?

● MULTIPLE CHOICE

Circle the one best answer for each of the following questions:

1. In the cartel model of oligopoly, the firms would decide how much to produce where:
    a. marginal cost equals marginal revenue.
    b. marginal cost equals price.
    c. marginal cost equals average total cost.
    d. the kink in the demand curve is.

2. According to the kinked demand curve theory of sticky prices, in an oligopolistic market:
    a. a price decrease by one firm will not be followed by the other firms.
    b. a price increase by one firm will be followed by the other firms.
    c. the kinked demand curve is inelastic in the upper portion and elastic in the lower portion of the curve.
    d. the kinked demand curve is elastic in the upper portion and inelastic in the lower portion of the curve.

3. In a contestable market model of oligopoly, prices are determined by:
    a. costs and barriers to exit.
    b. costs and barriers to entry.
    c. costs, barriers to entry, and barriers to exit.
    d. costs alone.

4. There is only one firm in the market. The economist analyzing that market has said she would expect the price to equal the firm's average total costs.
    a. She must be analyzing this market using a contestable market model.
    b. She must be analyzing this market using a game theory model.
    c. She must be analyzing this market using a cartel model.
    d. She must not be an economist, because that answer is clearly wrong.

5. In the NAICS classification system, the
    broadest classification would be:
    a. a two-digit industry.
    b. a three-digit industry.
    c. a four-digit industry.
    d. a five-digit industry.

6. The top four firms in the industry have 10
    percent, 8 percent, 8 percent, and 6 percent
    of the market. The four-firm concentration
    ratio of this market is:
    a. 8.
    b. 32.
    c. 66.
    d. 264.

7. The top four firms in the industry have 10
    percent, 8 percent, 8 percent, and 6 percent
    of the market. The Herfindahl index of this
    market is closest to which of the following?
    a. 8.
    b. 32.
    c. 66.
    d. 264.

8. A market has the following characteristics:
    There is strategic decision making, output is
    somewhat restricted, there are few firms, and
    some long-run economic profits are possible.
    This market is:
    a. a monopoly.
    b. an oligopoly.
    c. monopolistically competitive.
    d. perfectly competitive.

9. In a market there are many firms selling
    differentiated products. This market is:
    a. a competitive market.
    b. a monopolistically competitive market.
    c. an oligopolistic market.
    d. a monopoly.

10. Several firms are operating in a market where
    they take the other firms' response to their
    actions into account. This market is:
    a. a competitive market.
    b. a monopolistically competitive market.
    c. an oligopolistic market.
    d. a monopoly.

11. Strategic decision making is most important in:
    a. competitive markets.
    b. monopolistically competitive markets.

    c. oligopolistic markets.
    d. monopolistic markets.

12. When judging the competitiveness of markets
    by the behavior of firms in that market, one is
    using the:
    a. "judgment by performance" criteria.
    b. "judgment by structure" criteria.
    c. "judgment by merger" criteria.
    d. "judgment by antitrust" criteria.

13. When judging the competitiveness of markets
    by the size and number of firms in that
    market, one is using the:
    a. "judgment by performance" criteria.
    b. "judgment by structure" criteria.
    c. "judgment by merger" criteria.
    d. "judgment by antitrust" criteria.

14. An important law in the U.S. regulation of
    markets is the:
    a. Standard Oil Antitrust Act of 1890.
    b. Sherman Antitrust Act of 1890.
    c. Alcoa Antitrust Act of 1890.
    d. Lincoln Antitrust Act of 1890.

15. In the Standard Oil and American Tobacco
    Company antitrust cases in 1911, the Court
    ruled that:
    a. the two companies had a monopolistic
    structure and therefore should be broken up.
    b. the two companies were guilty of unfair
    business practices and therefore should be
    broken up.
    c. the Sherman Antitrust Act did not apply.
    d. the two companies had to be disbanded.

16. In the ALCOA antitrust case in 1945, the Court
    ruled that the:
    a. company had a monopolistic structure and
    therefore should be broken up.
    b. company was guilty of unfair business
    practices and therefore should be broken up.
    c. Sherman Antitrust Act did not apply.
    d. two companies had to be disbanded.

17. The resolution of the AT&T antitrust case of
    the 1980s was:
    a. AT&T agreed to split up into three operating
    divisions.
    b. AT&T agreed to split up and allow the Baby
    Bells to be independent.

    c. AT&T was combined with MCI and Sprint.
    d. MCI and Sprint were broken off from AT&T and developed as competitors to AT&T.

18. In the Microsoft antitrust case:
    a. the government ruled that Microsoft was a monopoly and was involved in anti-competitive practices.
    b. the government divided Microsoft into two companies.
    c. Microsoft agreed to government regulation of its prices.
    d. Microsoft was forced to get out of the Internet business.

● POTENTIAL ESSAY QUESTIONS

You may also see essay questions similar to the "Problems & Applications" exercises.

1. What is the difference between the contestable market model and the cartel model of oligopoly? How are they related?

2. Why has there been a more lenient approach in the United States to the enforcement of antitrust laws in recent years?

■■■■ **ANSWERS** ■■■■

SHORT-ANSWER QUESTIONS

1. The central element of oligopoly is that there are a small number of firms in an industry so that, in any decision it makes, each firm must take into account the expected reaction of other firms. Oligopolistic firms are mutually interdependent and can be collusive or non-collusive. Two basic models are the cartel and contestable market models. (315-320)

2. Since there are only a few large oil-producing nations, together they are an oligopoly. Oil-producing nations have a powerful desire to keep OPEC strong because as a cartel it can increase the profits going to the combination of oil-producing nations by reducing output. (316-318)

3. In the contestable market theory, pricing decisions are based on the threat of new entrants into the market, not market share. Thus, even if the industry has only one firm, it could still price competitively. (318-320)

4. A concentration ratio is the value of sales by the top firms of an industry stated as a percentage of total industry sales. A 4-firm concentration ratio is calculated by adding together the market shares of the four firms with the largest market shares. In the case given, the 4-firm concentration ratio is 40. (322)

5. A Herfindahl index is a method used by economists to classify how competitive an industry is. It is calculated by summing the squares of the market shares of all the firms in the industry. In this case the Herfindahl index is $10 \times 10^2 = 1000$. (322)

6. Judging competition by structure is the view that competitiveness of a market should be judged by the number of firms in the market and their market shares. Judging competition by performance is the view that competitiveness of a market should be judged by the behavior of firms in that market. (324)

7. The AT&T case was settled by AT&T agreeing to be split up into regional companies handling local service and AT&T itself competing in the long-distance market. (329)

8. Whether one sees Microsoft as a monopolist depends on whether one views it in a static or dynamic framework, but the court did find Microsoft guilty. However, Microsoft may have still won by ending up only having to promise to not behave monopolistically in the future. (327-328)

■■■■ **ANSWERS** ■■■■

MATCHING

1-k; 2-c; 3-h; 4-j; 5-d; 6-e; 7-g; 8-l; 9-a; 10-f; 11-b, 12-i.

■■■■ **ANSWERS** ■■■■

PROBLEMS AND APPLICATIONS

1. See the following table. (321)

	Monopoly	**Oligopoly**	**Monopolistic Competition**	**Perfect Competition**
Number of Firms	One	Few	Many	Almost Infinite
Pricing Decisions	MC=MR	Strategic pricing	MC=MR	MC=MR=P
Output Decisions	Most output restricted	Output somewhat restricted	Output restricted relatively little by product differentiation	No output restriction
Profit	Possibility of long-run economic profit	Some long-run economic profit	No long-run economic profit possible	No long-run economic profit possible

2. a. Contestable. (318-319)
    b. Cartel. (318-319)
    c. Both cartel and contestable markets have price wars. (318-319)

3. A four-firm concentration ratio is the percent of total industry sales accounted for by the top four firms. It is calculated by adding together the top four firms' market shares. The Herfindahl index is calculated by adding the squared value of the market shares of *all* the firms in the industry. (322-323)
    a. Four-firm concentration ratio $= 5+5+5+5 = 20$. Herfindahl index is $20 \times 5^2 = 500$.
    b. Four-firm concentration ratio $= 91+1+1+1 = 94$. Herfindahl index is $91^2+1^2+1^2+1^2+1^2+1^2+1^2+1^2+1^2+1^2 = 8,290$.
    c. Four-firm concentration ratio $= 31+2+2+2 = 37$. Herfindahl index is $31^2+2^2+2^2+2^2+63 \times 1^2 = 1,036$.
    d. Four-firm concentration ratio $= 25+25+25+25 = 100$. Herfindahl index is $25^2+25^2+25^2+25^2 = 2,500$.
    e. A higher concentration ratio and Herfindahl index indicates that the market is less competitive. The ranking using the four-firm concentration ratio is a (20), c (37), b (94), d (100). Using the Herfindahl index, the ranking is a (500), c (1036), d (2500), b (8290). They differ because the Herfindahl index takes into account *all* the firms in the market and gives extra weight to a single firm with an especially large share of the market (this accounts for the difference in the ranking of b).

■■■ **ANSWERS** ■■■

MULTIPLE CHOICE

1. a   The cartel model has the oligopoly acting like a monopolist. See pages 316-317.

2. d   Because a price increase is not followed by other firms and sales plummet, the demand curve is elastic in the upper portion. However, a price decrease is followed by others and revenues fall.

Thus, demand is inelastic in the lower portion of the curve. See pages 317-318.

3. c   Costs determine reference price, and barriers to both entry and exit determine the degree to which price deviates from cost. See pages 318-320.

4. a   In a contestable market model, exit and entry conditions determine the firm's price and output decisions. Thus, if there are no barriers to entry and exit, even if there is only one firm in the industry, the firm will produce where price equals the firm's average total costs. See pages 316-320.

5. a   In the North American Industry Classification System (NAICS), the more numbers, the greater the particular subdivisions, so the answer is a two-digit sector. See pages 320-321.

6. b   The concentration ratio is calculated by summing the market shares of the top four firms. See page 322 .

7. d   The Herfindahl index sums the squares of the market shares of all firms in the industry. Squaring these market shares and adding them gives 264, so the Herfindahl index exceeds 264 if there are more than four firms. See page 322.

8. b   An oligopoly is a market in which a few firms operate, each taking into consideration other firms' behavior when making decisions. Because output is somewhat restricted, some long-run profit is possible. See page 321.

9. b   A monopolistically competitive market has many firms selling differentiated products. See page 321.

10. c   An oligopoly is a market in which a few firms engage in strategic decision making. See page 321.

11. c   It is within oligopolies that firms explicitly take other firms' expected reactions into account, so it is oligopoly where strategic decision making is most important. See page 321.

12. a "Judgment by performance" is judging the competitiveness of markets by the performance (behavior) of firms in that market. See pages 324-325.

13. b "Judgment by structure" is judging the competitiveness of markets by their structure (the relative size and number of competitors in that market). See pages 324-325.

14. b The Sherman Antitrust Act of 1890 was an early law passed to regulate the competitive process. See page 325.

15. b The court interpreted the Act as needing the firm to engage in unfair practices along with control of the market. It determined that Standard Oil engaged in unfair practices. See page 325.

16. a In the ALCOA case, the Court applied the monopolistic structure (or judgment by structure) standard. See page 325.

17. b AT&T split up into the Baby Bells. These Baby Bells then consolidated in the 1990s. See page 329.

18. a The court ruled that Microsoft was a monopoly and that it had engaged in anti-competitive practices. Essentially, Microsoft just promised not to behave monopolistically in the future. See pages 327-328.

◼ ANSWERS ◼

POTENTIAL ESSAY QUESTIONS

The following are annotated answers. They indicate the general idea behind the answer.

1. The cartel model argues that oligopolists will come together to behave as a monopoly in terms of their pricing and output decisions because it is in their self-interest to do so— they'll make more money. (However, there is always a tendency for a firm to want to "cheat" and the mere rumor of cheating can cause a breakdown of the collusion.) The contestable market model argues that an industry that looks like an oligopoly (because there are a few dominant firms in the industry) could set highly competitive prices and produce a competitive output level. What is important in pricing and output decisions, according to the contestable market model, is not the number of firms in the industry, but the strength of the barriers to entry that exist in the market. If there are few, if any, barriers to entry, then a competitive price and output level will be observed. These two models are related in that the stronger the barriers to entry, usually the fewer the number of firms, and therefore the greater the probability for collusion.

2. In recent years antitrust law has been lenient. There are three main reasons: First, because of a change in American ideology, "big business" is no longer viewed as necessarily bad. Second, the market structure in the U.S. has become less relevant as the United States has become more integrated into the global economy where there is generally more competition. Third, as technologies have become more complicated, the issues in antitrust enforcement also have become more complicated for the courts to handle.

REAL-WORLD COMPETITION AND TECHNOLOGY

CHAPTER AT A GLANCE

1. Firms consider more than profit maximization and they face problems with profit maximization. (335-340)

   - *Firms may forgo short-run profit to increase long-run profit.*
   - *Firms can face the monitoring problem.*
   - *Monopolists might not push hard for profits.*

2. The monitoring problem is that employees' incentives differ from the owner's incentives. By changing employees' incentives, the efficiency of the firm can sometimes be improved. (335-336)

   Self-interest-seeking managers are interested in maximizing firm profit only if the structure of the firm requires them to do so.

   An incentive-compatible contract is needed to match the goals of managers with owners.

3. Lazy monopolists don't push for efficiency. They suffer from X-inefficiency—operating far less efficiently than they could. (338-340)

   The threat of takeovers can limit X-inefficiency because takeovers might mean managers will lose their jobs.

4. When competitive pressures get strong, individuals often fight back through social and political pressures. Competition is a process— a fight between the forces of monopolization and the forces of competition. (340-344)

   Everyone generally likes competition, except for themselves.

   Competitive markets will exist if producers or consumers don't collude.

   The belief in competition as a process has led economists to support the deregulation of natural monopolies.

5. Actions firms take to break down monopoly include (1) lobbying government to change the law underpinning that monopoly if the monopoly is a legal monopoly and (2) making slight modifications to a monopolist's patent within the limits of the law. (341-346)

   Firms protect their monopolies by (1) advertising and lobbying government, (2) producing products as nearly unique as possible, and (3) charging low prices.

   Firms will spend money and time to obtain monopoly power until the marginal cost equals the marginal benefit.

6. Oligopoly tends to be most conducive to technological change. (346-348)

   Since the typical oligopolist realizes ongoing economic profit, it has the funds to carry out research and development. Moreover, the belief that its competitors are innovating also forces it to do so.

   Oligopolists are constantly searching for new ways to get an edge on competitors, so most technological advance takes place in oligopolistic industries.

7. Technology can determine market structure through network externalities, winner-take all industries, and technological lock-in. (348-349)

   Network externalities occur when greater use of a product increases the benefit of that product to everyone. These network externalities lead to pressures to establish product standards and to the adoption of inefficient standards.

● SHORT-ANSWER QUESTIONS

1. Is the high pay that top-level management receives an example of the monitoring problem?

2. What are the implications of the monitoring problem for economics?

3. How can corporate takeovers improve firms' efficiency?

4. What is meant by the phrase "Competition is a process, not a state."?

5. List two actions firms take to break down a monopoly.

6. List three ways in which firms protect their monopoly.

7. Explain how technology has changed competition.

8. Which market structure is most conducive to technological advance? Why?

MATCHING THE TERMS
Match the terms to their definitions

___ **1.** corporate takeover

___ **2.** dynamic efficiency

___ **3.** incentive-compatible contract

___ **4.** lazy monopolist

___ **5.** monitoring problem

___ **6.** network externality

___ **7.** reverse engineering

___ **8.** technological development

___ **9.** technological lock-in

___ **10.** X-inefficiency

a. The problem that employees' incentives differ from the owner's incentives.

b. An agreement in which the incentives and goals of both parties match as closely as possible.

c. A firm that does not push for efficiency, but merely enjoys the position it is already in.

d. Operating less efficiently than possible, which raises costs.

e. A firm or a group of individuals issues an offer to buy the stock of a company to gain control and install its own managers.

f. The ability to promote cost-reducing or product-enhancing technological change.

g. A firm buying up other firms' products, disassembling them, figuring out what's special about them, and then copying them within the limits of the law.

h. When greater use of a product increases the benefit of that product to everyone.

i. When prior use of a technology makes the adoption of subsequent technologies difficult.

j. The discovery of new or improved products or methods of production.

● PROBLEMS AND APPLICATIONS

1. College Retirement Equities Fund (CREF) is a pension fund designed for college teachers, which has billions of dollars invested in the stock market. A few years ago fund participants voted on a proposal that would have placed strict limits on the amount of compensation paid to CREF executives. Why do you think 75 percent of the participants voted against the proposal?

2. Demonstrate, using the graph below, the net gain to producers and the net loss to consumers if suppliers are able to restrict their output to Q_R. What is the net deadweight loss to society?

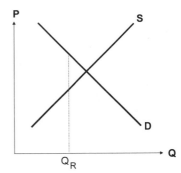

3. How can branding increase the monopoly position of a firm?

● MULTIPLE CHOICE

Circle the one best answer for each of the following questions:

1. The *best* definition of an incentive-compatible contract is:
  a. a contract with sympathetic incentives.
  b. a contract with compatible incentives.
  c. a contract in which the incentive structure makes the managers' goals correspond with the firm's goals as much as possible.
  d. a contract that pays bonuses.

2. A firm is making no profit. If there is X-inefficiency, what can we conclude?
  a. The firm is operating at least cost.
  b. The firm is operating using the fewest inputs possible.
  c. The firm is operating less efficiently than economically possible.
  d. We can say nothing about the efficiency of the firm.

3. The goals of managers are generally:
  a. identical to the goals of owners.
  b. identical to the goals of workers.
  c. totally inconsistent with the goals of owners.
  d. somewhat inconsistent with the goals of owners.

4. When there is little competitive pressure, large organizations have a tendency to make decisions that:
  a. benefit the consumer.
  b. benefit the managers.
  c. benefit the government.
  d. do not benefit anyone.

5. Economists would expect that generally:
  a. for-profit firms operate more efficiently than nonprofit firms.
  b. nonprofit firms operate more efficiently than for-profit firms.
  c. for-profit firms operate equally efficiently as nonprofit firms.
  d. nonprofit firms cannot exist because they operate so inefficiently.

6. Reverse engineering is:
  a. a firm or group of individuals that gains power from the outside by buying up all the stock of a company to gain control and install its own managers.
  b. when firms buy up other firms' products, disassemble them, figure out what's special about them, and then copy them within the limits of the law.
  c. when prior technology sets a firm back by making the adoption of subsequent technologies difficult.
  d. a method firms use to maintain their monopoly.

7. The inefficient design of the QWERTY keyboard, which was originally engineered to keep typewriter keys from sticking but is still used in today's computers, is an example of:
  a. technological development.
  b. reverse engineering.
  c. X-inefficiency.
  d. technological lock-in.

8. Refer to the graph below. If suppliers restrict output to L, what area represents the welfare loss to society?
  a. A + B.
  b. B + C.
  c. C + D.
  d. A + D.

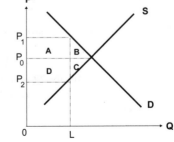

9. A patent is:
  a. a type of reverse engineering.
  b. a type of natural monopoly.
  c. a type of corporate takeover.
  d. a type of legal monopoly.

10. When regulated monopolies are allowed to pass on all cost increases to earn a normal profit, they:
    a. have a strong incentive to operate efficiently.
    b. have little incentive to operate efficiently.
    c. become a focal point of reverse engineering.
    d. will apply for a patent.

11. Ways in which firms try to protect their monopoly include all the following *except:*
    a. advertising and lobbying.
    b. charging low prices.
    c. making their product unique.
    d. reverse engineering.

12. Many economists consider competition today to be more intense than competition ten or twenty years ago because of:
    a. technological development.
    b. greater governmental regulation and more reverse engineering.
    c. more corporate takeovers and higher trade barriers.
    d. greater political tensions among governments and lower taxes.

13. Technological advance:
    a. decreases competition.
    b. decreases specialization.
    c. increases productivity.
    d. increases costs of production.

14. The market structure most conducive to technological advance is:
    a. perfect competition.
    b. monopolistic competition.
    c. oligopoly.
    d. monopoly.

15. Technological advances are most likely for markets that:
    a. earn economic profits.
    b. have one firm supplying all the output.
    c. are protected by government regulation.
    d. produce where MR = MC.

16. Network externalities:
    a. occur when greater use of a product increases the benefit of that product to everyone.
    b. inhibit the development of industry standards.
    c. make it more likely that the most efficient standards will be adopted.
    d. reduce the likelihood that an industry becomes a "winner takes all" industry.

● POTENTIAL ESSAY QUESTIONS

You may also see essay questions similar to the "Problems & Applications" exercises.

1. Describe two actions firms take to break down monopoly and three they take to protect their monopoly.

2. Explain how technology has changed competition.

━━━━━ ANSWERS ━━━━━

SHORT-ANSWER QUESTIONS

1. The monitoring problem is the problem of seeing that self-seeking individuals working for an organization follow the goals of the organization rather than their own goals. The high pay that top-level management receives might be pay for performance, or it might be an example of the monitoring problem. To determine which it is, one would need to consider the specific case and determine whether there are incentive-compatible contracts (such as low base pay and high optional bonuses based on performance) that make the managers' goals consistent with the goals of the firms' owners. (335-337)

2. Economics assumes that firms and the economy operate efficiently because firms maximize profits. The monitoring problem undermines that assumption since managers, to some degree, will follow their own goals rather than the profit-maximizing goal. Firms may become lazy monopolists and exhibit X-inefficiency. So the monitoring problem has significant implications. The degree to which firms become lazy monopolists will be limited, however, by competitive pressures. (335-339)

3. The answer to Question #2 above pointed out that when there is a monitoring problem a firm can exhibit X-inefficiency—it can have higher costs than necessary. When that happens, the firm's stock price will fall and it may be worthwhile for another firm to come in and take the inefficient firm over, eliminate the inefficiency, and develop better incentive-compatible contracts. Often, these takeovers are financed by large amounts of debt, which means that the resulting firm must make high interest payments. So even if the new firm does not establish incentive-compatible contracts, the high debt can force the firm to operate more efficiently. (338-339)

4. The basic idea of economics is that self-seeking individuals try to do the best they can for themselves—to make life as easy as possible for themselves. One of the important ways in which they can do that is to create a

monopoly for themselves. When they do that they create the possibility of profits for other individuals who come in and steal their market—thereby breaking down their monopoly. This process of monopolization and competition breaking down the resulting monopoly is pervasive in our economy and is what is meant by the phrase: "competition is a process, not a state." (340-343)

5. To acquire monopoly profits for themselves, firms will break down monopoly through political and economic means. If the monopoly is a legal monopoly, high profit will lead potential competitors to lobby to change the law underpinning that monopoly. If the law can't be changed—say, the monopolist has a patent—potential competitors will generally get around the obstacle by developing a slightly different product or by working on a new technology that avoids the monopoly but satisfies the relevant need. (341-342)

6. Three ways in which firms protect their monopoly are (1) advertising and lobbying; (2) producing products as nearly unique as possible; and (3) charging low prices that discourage entry. All these methods cost the firms money in the short run, but increase their monopoly rents (profits) in the long run. (344)

7. Technological advance is a result of specialization that allows producers to learn more about the particular aspects of production in which they specialize. As they learn more, they not only become more productive but are more likely to generate technological advances because they gain a deeper understanding of their speciality. Technology has changed competition because competitive success hinges on an ability to specialize. (346)

8. Oligopoly tends to be most conducive to technological change. Since the typical oligopolist realizes ongoing economic profit, it has the funds to carry out research and development. Moreover, the belief that its competitors are innovating also forces it to do so. Oligopolists are constantly searching for new ways to get an edge on competitors, so most technological advance takes place in oligopolistic industries. (346-348)

━━━━━ ANSWERS ━━━━━

MATCHING

1-e; 2-f; 3-b; 4-c; 5-a; 6-h; 7-g; 8-j; 9-i; 10-d.

━━━━━ ANSWERS ━━━━━

PROBLEMS AND APPLICATIONS

1. The fund participants are aware of incentive-compatible contracts. Structuring CREF executive pay based on the fund's performance in the stock market increases the chances that the interests of the owners and the managers of the fund are compatible. (335-336)

2. As shown on the graph below, if suppliers restrict supply to Q_R, they will be able to charge a price of P_R, which is higher than competitive price, P_C. This gives suppliers supplying Q_R additional income, labeled A. Some suppliers are excluded from the market $(Q_C - Q_R)$. They lose area C in producer surplus. Consumers who cannot now purchase as many goods lose consumer surplus represented by area B. Those who can afford the higher-priced good pay the higher price. Higher expenditures are represented by area A (the additional income to firms). Since A is transferred from consumers to producers, this is not a loss to society as a whole. However, areas B and C are lost by consumers and producers, respectively, but not transferred to anyone. Those areas, B and C, are the deadweight loss to society. (Figure 16-2 on page 341)

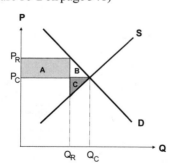

3. Branding is an important way in which firms try to differentiate their goods and services from real or potential competitors. If a firm is successful in distinguishing its product from

other producers and in associating that positive image with its brand name, then other firms will find it difficult to compete. Remember that differentiation (through branding and other means) acts as a barrier to entry, and the stronger the barriers, the greater the monopoly power. (See pages 344-345; "Real World Application")

━━━━━ ANSWERS ━━━━━

MULTIPLE CHOICE

1. c While incentive-compatible contracts could pay bonuses, they do not necessarily have to, which rules out this option. The contract with compatible incentives doesn't say what it is compatible with. See the definition of incentive-compatible contract on page 335.

2. c Whenever there is X-inefficiency, the firm is not operating at least cost. That is, it is not economically efficient. See page 338.

3. d Managers' goals are somewhat inconsistent with the goals of the owners. However, managers do not want to get fired and competitive pressures mean managers must make sufficient profits so they don't get fired. To that degree, their goals are consistent with the goals of the owners. See pages 335-337.

4. b When there are no competitive pressures, organizations tend to make decisions that benefit employees or the decision-makers within these organizations rather than consumers. See pages 335-337.

5. a While for-profit firms can exhibit inefficiency, the market limits that inefficiency. See pages 338-339.

6. b Reverse engineering is when firms buy up other firms' products, disassemble them, figure out what's special about them, and then copy them within the limits of the law. It is a method firms use to gather informa-

tion about competitive products and break down the monopolies firms may have on new products or technologies. See page 342.

7. d The QWERTY keyboard is an example of technological lock-in. Prior use of the QWERTY keyboard has made the adoption of newer, more efficient keyboards difficult. See page 349.

8. b The welfare loss is the triangle made up of areas *B* and *C*. This area represents the producer and consumer surplus lost but not gained by the other. The other areas represent transfers. See page 341 and Figure 16-2.

9. d A patent is the legal right to be the sole supplier of a product. It is a type of legal monopoly. See pages 341-342.

10. b When you can pass on cost increases, why try to hold costs down? See pages 338, 342-344.

11. d Reverse engineering is a method firms use to try to break down other firms' monopolies. See pages 341-342.

12. a Technological development increases competition by providing more specialized products. See page 346.

13. c Technological advance requires specialization. Specialization increases productivity and lowers costs of production. This results in more intense competition. See page 346.

14. c Oligopoly provides the best market structure for technological advance because firms have an incentive to innovate (they face competition) and they also have the profits to devote to research and development. See pages 346-348.

15. a Technological advance requires large amounts of investment. Only firms that earn economic profit can afford to invest in research and development. See page 346.

16. a Network externalities promote industry standards, although those standards may not be the most efficient. They also increase the likelihood that an industry becomes a "winner takes all" industry. See pages 348-349.

■■■■■ ANSWERS ■■■■■

POTENTIAL ESSAY QUESTIONS

The following are annotated answers. They indicate the general idea behind the answer.

1. Actions firms take to break down monopoly include (1) lobbying government to change the law underpinning that monopoly if the monopoly is a legal monopoly and (2) making slight modifications to a monopolist's patent within the limits of the law. Firms protect their monopolies by (1) advertising and lobbying government, (2) producing products as nearly unique as possible, and (3) charging low prices.

2. Technological advance requires specialization. Specialization increases productivity and lowers costs of production. This results in intense competition.

WORK AND THE LABOR MARKET

CHAPTER AT A GLANCE

1. The supply of labor reflects the choice between market and non-market activities. (355-358

   The higher the wages, the greater the labor supplied. This is the incentive effect.

   Higher marginal tax rates reduce the incentive to work.

2. Elasticity of market labor supply depends on: (358-359)
   - Individuals' opportunity cost of working.
   - The type of market being discussed.
   - The elasticity of individuals' supply curves.
   - Individuals entering and leaving the labor market.

   An elastic supply of labor means workers are quite responsive to a change in the wage rate.

3. Derived demand is the demand for factors of production by firms, which depends on consumers' demands. (359-360)

   For example, if the demand for automobiles increases, the demand for automotive workers increases. It simply takes more workers to produce more cars.

4. Four factors that influence the elasticity of demand for labor are: (360)
   - The elasticity of demand for the firm's good.
   - The relative importance of the factor in the production process.
   - The possibility of, and cost of, substitution in production.
   - The degree to which marginal productivity falls with an increase in the labor.

An elastic demand for labor means employers are quite responsive to a change in the wage rate. For example, an increase in the wage rate will result in a rather dramatic reduction in the number of workers employers wish to employ.

5. A monopsony is a market in which there is only one buyer. A bilateral monopoly is a market in which a single seller faces a single buyer. (364-365)

   A monopsony will hire fewer workers (Q_m) and pay a lower wage (W_m) compared to the competitive outcome.

   Unions have an incentive to act like a monopolist, restricting labor (Q_u) to raise the wages (W_u) of their members.

   Wages in a bilateral monopoly will be between what the monopolist and monopsonist push for.

6. To understand real-world labor markets one must broaden the analysis. (365-367)

   What we see in the real world is a consequence of the interaction of market, social, and political forces.

7. Three types of discrimination are discrimination based on: (367-369)

a. Individual characteristics that will affect job performance.
b. Correctly perceived statistical characteristics of the group.
c. Individual characteristics that don't affect job performance or are incorrectly perceived.

a is the hardest to eliminate.
c is the easiest to eliminate.

See also, Appendix A: "Derived Demand."

● SHORT-ANSWER QUESTIONS

1. Use the theory of rational choice and the concept of opportunity cost to explain why firms generally offer time-and-a-half for workers to work on Thanksgiving Day.

2. Suppose Congress passes an increase in the marginal income tax rate. What is the likely effect on work effort?

3. List four factors that influence the elasticity of labor supply.

4. Explain how the demand for labor is a derived demand.

5. What are four factors that influence the elasticity of labor demand?

6. Define the terms *monopsonist* and *bilateral monopoly*.

7. On average, women earn about 85 cents for every $1 earned by men. Discuss this phenomenon in terms of political forces, social forces, and market forces.

8. What are three types of demand-side discrimination?

MATCHING THE TERMS
Match the terms to their definitions

___ 1. bilateral monopoly

___ 2. closed shop

___ 3. comparable worth laws

___ 4. derived demand

___ 5. efficiency wages

___ 6. entrepreneurship

___ 7. incentive effect

___ 8. labor market

___ 9. marginal factor cost

___ 10. monopsony

___ 11. union shop

a. A market in which only a single firm hires labor.

b. A firm in which all workers must join the union.

c. A market with only a single seller and a single buyer.

d. A firm in which the union controls hiring.

e. Wage that is above the going market wage; paid to keep workers happy and productive.

f. Factor market in which individuals supply labor services for wages to other individuals and to firms that demand labor services.

g. Labor services that involve high degrees of organizational skills, concern, oversight, responsibility, and creativity.

h. How much a person will change his or her hours worked in response to a change in the wage rate.

i. Laws mandating comparable pay for comparable work.

j. The additional cost to a firm of hiring another worker.

k. The demand for factors of production by firms, which depends on consumers' demands.

● PROBLEMS AND APPLICATIONS

1. Use the graph below to answer the following questions.

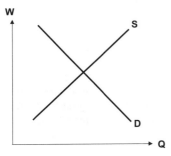

a. Label the equilibrium wage and number of workers.

b. If wages were set by the government above the equilibrium wage, what happens to the quantity supplied and the quantity demanded for labor? How do they differ?

c. Show how a technological innovation that leads to a higher demand for labor affects equilibrium wage and quantity of labor.

2. Consider again demand and supply in a labor market. For each of the following situations determine whether there would be an increase or a decrease in demand or supply of labor. Furthermore, determine the impact on the equilibrium wage rate (W) and the equilibrium quantity (Q) of labor. (You may want to use a graph of demand and supply curves for labor to help you.)

a. The demand for the product workers are producing increases.

b. It is Christmas Day, and workers value their leisure time more highly.

c. The other factory in town is now offering a higher wage rate.

d. The fringe (nonmonetary) benefits of this job have increased substantially. For example, workers are offered more lucrative health and dental coverage, better retirement programs, paid vacations, and company cars.

e. The price of a machine, which is a substitute for this labor, is now less expensive and its productivity has increased substantially due to an increase in technology. Note: the new technology does not affect worker productivity.

f. The firms in this industry have successfully convinced government to impose stricter tariffs and import quotas on a foreign good that is a substitute for the good produced by these workers.

g. The government has just adopted an "open-door" immigration policy.

h. Workers are now more productive.

3. Answer the following questions using the graph below.

a. Label the equilibrium wage and number of workers on the graph if the market is competitive.

b. Label the equilibrium wage and number of workers on the graph under a monopsonist. Compare this with the competitive outcome.

c. If there is a worker's union as well as a monopsonist, what would be the equilibrium wage and level of employment?

A1. Complete the table below for a perfectly competitive firm that produces halogen light bulbs. Each light bulb sells for $1. (Marginal values refers to the marginal change of increasing to that row, i.e., the marginal physical product of going from 23 to 24 workers is 9. The same goes for marginal revenue product.)

	No. of Workers	Total Product per hour	Marginal Physical Product per hour	Average Product per hour	Marginal Revenue Product per hour
	20	200		—	
A	21	—	—	—	15
B	22	228	—	—	—
C	23	—	—	10.39	—
D	24	—	9	—	—
E	25	—	—	10.20	—
F	26	260	—	—	—

a. Draw the corresponding labor demand curve, from the values in the table.

b. Suppose the price of halogen light bulbs falls to $.50 per bulb. How does this change labor demand?

c. If halogen light bulbs sold for $1 per bulb as in part *a*, how many workers would the firm hire if wages were $7 per hour? How many workers would the firm hire if wages were $11 per hour?

● MULTIPLE CHOICE

Circle the one best answer for each of the following questions:

1. Generally, economists believe the higher the wage:
   a. the higher the quantity of labor supplied.
   b. the greater the supply of labor.
   c. the lesser the supply of labor.
   d. the lower the quantity of labor supplied.

2. As the wage rate increases the opportunity cost of leisure:
   a. increases.
   b. decreases.
   c. remains the same.
   d. cannot be determined given the information provided.

3. An increase in the marginal tax rate will:
   a. increase the quantity of labor supplied.
   b. increase the supply of labor.
   c. decrease the supply of labor.
   d. decrease the quantity of labor supplied.

4. The irony of any need-based program is that it:
   a. increases the number of needy.
   b. decreases the number of needy.
   c. creates other needs.
   d. destroys needs.

5. Which of the following is *not* a factor influencing the elasticity of market labor supply?
   a. Individuals' opportunity cost of working.
   b. The elasticity of individuals' supply curves.
   c. The elasticity of market labor demand.
   d. Individuals entering and leaving the labor market.

6. Which of the following is *not* a reason why the labor supply for heads of households (primary workers) is more inelastic than that for secondary workers?
   a. Institutional factors, such as hours of work, are only slightly flexible.
   b. There are many more new secondary workers who can enter the market than there are primary workers.
   c. Heads of households have responsibility for seeing that there's food and shelter for the household family members.
   d. There are more secondary workers than primary workers.

7. The term "derived demand" refers to:
   a. demand by consumers for advertised products.
   b. the demand for luxury goods that is derived from cultural phenomena such as fashion.
   c. the demand for factors of production by firms.
   d. the demand for derivatives.

8. The more elastic the demand for a firm's good:
   a. the more elastic the firm's derived demand for factors.
   b. the less elastic the firm's derived demand for factors.
   c. The elasticity of demand for a firm's good has nothing to do with the firm's derived demand.
   d. The elasticity of demand could cause the elasticity of the derived demand to be either higher or lower.

9. As a factor becomes more important in the production process, the:
   a. firm's derived demand for the factor becomes less elastic.
   b. firm's derived demand for the factor becomes more elastic.
   c. firm's derived demand will not be affected.
   d. elasticity of the derived demand could become either higher or lower.

10. Economists distinguish entrepreneurship from labor because:
    a. entrepreneurship is more like capital.
    b. entrepreneurship has nothing to do with labor.
    c. entrepreneurship is such an important part of labor that it needs a specific discussion.
    d. entrepreneurs receive only profit.

11. A firm has just changed from being a competitive firm to being a monopolist. Its derived demand for labor:
    a. will increase.
    b. will decrease.
    c. might increase or might decrease.
    d. is unaffected because whether the firm is a competitive firm or a monopolist has no effect on the firm's derived demand for labor.

12. A monopsony in a labor market has:
    a. only a single seller and a single buyer of labor.
    b. only a single seller of labor.
    c. only a single buyer of labor.
    d. one seller and two buyers.

13. Compared to a competitive labor market, a monopsonist hires:
    a. fewer workers and pays them a higher wage.
    b. fewer workers and pays them a lower wage.
    c. more workers and pays them a higher wage.
    d. more workers and pays them a lower wage.

14. Which of the following cases of discrimination is likely to be most easily eliminated with market forces?
    a. A warehousing firm turns down an applicant because she is physically unable to lift boxes of the weight required by the job.
    b. An Internet firm begins a younger worker at a lower pay because younger workers are more likely to leave the job shortly after being trained.
    c. A manufacturing firm decides against hiring an individual who is black (even though the candidate is the most qualified) because the person doing the hiring is white.
    d. A retail store decides against hiring an individual who is black (even though the candidate is the most qualified) because they believe their customers will be less likely to buy from blacks.

15. Discrimination that is likely the most difficult to eliminate is discrimination that has:
    a. a social motivation.
    b. a cultural motivation.
    c. a political motivation.
    d. an economic motivation.

A1. The graph below shows the marginal revenue product of workers. If the wage is $10, approximately how many workers should it hire?

a. 4.
b. 8.
c. 12.
d. 16.

A2. The marginal product of input A is 20. The marginal product of input B is 40. The price of input A is 2. The price of input B is 3. Which of the following would be the best recommendation you could give based on this information? The firm should

a. hire more A and less B.
b. hire more B and less A.
c. hire more of both A and B.
d. not change its hiring of A and B.

POTENTIAL ESSAY QUESTIONS

You may also see essay questions similar to the "Problems & Applications" exercises.

1. What is a monopsony and how does a monopsony determine the quantity of workers employed and the wage it pays? How does this compare with the competitive labor market outcome? What is a bilateral monopoly? Could a bilateral monopoly result in a competitive labor market outcome?

2. How do market, social, and political forces interact in determining the equilibrium wage and quantity of workers employed in any real-world labor market?

ANSWERS

SHORT-ANSWER QUESTIONS

1. Work involves opportunity cost. By working one more hour, you have one less hour to devote to nonmarket activities. The theory of rational choice in the case of work means that you will supply work as long as the opportunity cost of working is less than the wage received. Since the opportunity cost of working on a holiday is greater than on other days, firms must offer workers higher wages to work on Thanksgiving Day. This demonstrates that the supply curve for labor is upward sloping: the higher the wage, the higher the quantity of labor supplied. (355-358)

2. An increase in the marginal tax rate is likely to reduce the quantity of labor supplied because it reduces the net wage of individuals and lowers the opportunity cost of not working. (355-358)

3. Factors that affect the elasticity of labor supply include (1) the individuals' opportunity costs of working, (2) the type of labor market, (3) the elasticity of the individuals' labor supplied, and (4) the individuals entering and leaving the market. (358-359)

4. Derived demand is the demand for factors of production by firms, which depends on consumers' demands. For example, if the demand for medical care increases, the demand for nurses increases. It simply takes more nurses to deliver more medical care. (359-360)

5. Factors that influence the elasticity of labor demand are (1) the elasticity of demand for the firm's good, (2) the relative importance of labor to production, (3) the possibility of, and costs of, substitution in production, and (4) the degree to which marginal productivity falls with an increase in labor. (360)

6. A *monopsonist* is the only buyer in a market. A *bilateral monopoly* is a market in which a single seller faces a single buyer. (364-365)

7. Real-world labor markets are complicated and must be explained through the interaction of political, social, and market forces. For example, the fact that women earn about 85 percent of men's earnings must be explained by these forces. Here are some of the many ways in which these forces can explain this phenomenon: It is argued that employers discriminate against women, paying them less for the same job, because they have a distaste for hiring women. This is an example of social forces at play and would result in lower wages.

   Women's lower pay may also result from social forces that discourage mothers from working outside the home so that women will supply labor intermittently, lowering their wage. This is an example of social forces and market forces. Comparable worth laws, anti-discrimination laws, and affirmative action laws have been passed in an effort to counteract this pay inequality. These are examples of social, political and legal forces at play in real-world labor markets. (367-370)

8. Three types of discrimination are (1) discrimination based on individual characteristics that affect job performance, (2) discrimination based on correctly perceived statistical characteristics of the group; and (3) discrimination based on individual characteristics that do not affect job performance or that are incorrectly perceived. (367-369)

ANSWERS

MATCHING

1-c; 2-d; 3-i; 4-k; 5-e; 6-g; 7-h; 8-f; 9-j; 10-a; 11-b.

ANSWERS

PROBLEMS AND APPLICATIONS

1. a. Equilibrium wage and number of workers with demand, D_0, and supply, S, are shown on the graph on the next page as W_E and Q_E. At this point, the quantity of labor demanded equals the quantity of labor supplied. At a wage above W_E, there will be pressure for wages to fall because the quantity of labor supplied exceeds the quantity of labor demanded. At a wage below W_E, there will be pressure for wages to rise because the quantity of labor

demanded exceeds the quantity of labor supplied. (Figure 17-2 on page 363)

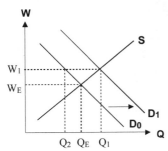

b. If wages were set by the government at W_1, the quantity of labor supplied would rise to Q_1 and the quantity of labor demanded would fall to Q_2. Quantity supplied would exceed quantity demanded. This is shown in the graph above. (Figure 17-2 and 361-364)

c. A technological innovation that leads to a higher demand for labor will lead to a higher equilibrium wage and higher quantity of labor employed as the demand curve shifts to the right from D_0 to D_1. Equilibrium wage will rise to W_1 and equilibrium quantity of labor will rise to Q_1. (361-364 and Figure 17-2 on page 363)

2. a. The demand for labor would increase, increasing W and Q. (Applying concepts introduced in the appendix to this chapter, notice that the increase in the demand for the product increases the price of the product. The higher price for the product increases workers' marginal revenue product—MRP = MPP × P—which is the competitive firms' demand for labor.) (359-363, 378-383)

b. The supply of labor would decrease on Christmas Day, which would increase W and decrease Q. (356-364 and Figure 17-3 on page 363)

c. Supply would decrease, increasing W and decreasing Q. (356-364)

d. Supply would increase, decreasing W and increasing Q. (356-364)

e. Demand would decrease, decreasing W and Q. (356-364)

f. Demand would increase, increasing W and Q. (356-364)

g. Supply would increase, decreasing W and increasing Q. (356-364)

h. Demand would increase (according to the appendix: workers' MRP would be greater), increasing W and Q. (356-364)

3. a. If the market is competitive, the wage and employment level will be where the demand and supply curves for labor intersect. This is at W_c and Q_c respectively on the graph below. (Figure 17-3 on page 364)

b. The monopsonist will hire workers where the marginal factor cost of labor intersects the demand for labor. A monopsonist would hire Q_m workers, less than the competitive level, and pay a wage W_m, lower than the competitive wage. (Figure 17-3 on page 364)

c. Unions would push for higher wages than a firm in a competitive market or a monopsonist would be willing to pay. The wage would be somewhere between W_u and W_m and would depend on negotiating skills and other noneconomic forces. The number of workers hired would then be somewhere between Q_u and Q_m depending on the negotiated wage. (Figure 17-3 on page 364)

A1. Below is the completed table for a perfectly competitive firm which produces halogen light bulbs.

No. of Workers	Total Product per hour	Marginal Physical Product per hour	Average Product per hour	Marginal Revenue Product per hour
20	200		10	
A 21	215	15	10.24	15
B 22	228	13	10.36	13
C 23	239	11	10.39	11
D 24	248	9	10.33	9
E 25	255	7	10.2	7
F 26	260	5	10	5

We use the following relationships to fill in the table: Marginal physical product equals the change in the total product. Average product is the total product divided by the number of workers. Marginal revenue product equals marginal physical product times the price of the product. (378-383, especially Figure A17-1)

a. The corresponding labor demand curve is shown on the graph below. The demand curve shows the marginal revenue product at each quantity of labor. Labor demand is a derived demand. A firm is willing to pay a wage up to the marginal revenue product of the additional worker to hire that additional worker. That is, keep hiring workers for as long as MRP >W and stop hiring when MRP = W. (378-383, especially Figure A17-1)

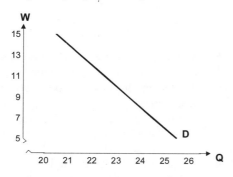

b. If the price of halogen light bulbs fell to $.50 per bulb, the marginal revenue product would be halved and the demand curve for labor would shift in as shown on the accompanying graph and table. (378-383)

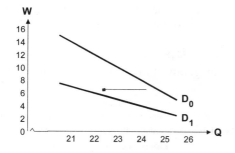

No. of Workers	Total Product per hour	Marginal Physical Product per hour	Average Product per hour	($0.50) Marginal Revenue Product per hour
	20	200		10	
A	21	215	15	10.24	7.5
B	22	228	13	10.36	6.5
C	23	239	11	10.39	5.5
D	24	248	9	10.33	4.5
E	25	255	7	10.2	3.5
F	26	260	5	10	2.5

c. A firm in a competitive industry will hire up to the point where the wage equals *MRP* (*MPP* times *P*). So at $1 per bulb and wages of $7 per hour, the firm would hire up to 25 workers; At $1 per bulb and a minimum wage of $11 per hour the firm would hire up to 23 workers. (378-383)

ANSWERS

MULTIPLE CHOICE

1. a   The supply curve of labor is generally considered to be upward sloping. When there is a movement along the supply curve caused by an increase in the wage, the movement is called an increase in the quantity supplied, not an increase in supply. See pages 355-356.

2. a   The opportunity cost of not working increases as the wage rate rises and that is why the labor supply curve slopes upward. See page 356.

3. d   An increase in the marginal tax rate will reduce the quantity of labor supplied because it reduces the net wage of individuals and hence, through individuals' incentive effect, causes them to work less. See pages 357-358.

4. a   A need-based program reduces people's incentives to prevent themselves from becoming needy, and thus a need-based program increases the number of needy. See pages 357-358.

5.   c   The elasticity of demand has no impact on the elasticity of supply. See page 358-359.

6.   d   The number of primary workers compared to the number of secondary workers has nothing to do with elasticity. See pages 358-359.

7.   c   Derived demand refers to the fact that the demand for factors of production is derived from the demand for a firm's goods. Because consumers demand a firm's goods, the firm demands factors of production to produce those goods. See pages 359-360.

8.   a   When a rise in price will cause significant loss of revenue (which it does when demand for the good is elastic), the firm takes that into account in its decision of what to pay workers and how many workers to hire. See page 360.

9.   a   As the importance of a factor to the production process rises, the less elastic is demand. This is because a more important factor has fewer substitutes. See page 360.

10.   c   Entrepreneurship is a type of creative labor that is very important and needs a separate discussion. Entrepreneurs can receive more than merely profit. See page 360.

11.   b   The monopolist uses marginal revenue, which is lower than the price that the competitive firm uses. Therefore, the monopolist's derived demand for labor is lower. See page 360.

12.   c   While a monopoly is a market with a single seller, a monopsony is a market with a single buyer. See page 364.

13.   b   A profit-maximizing monopsonist will pay a lower wage and hire fewer workers than if that labor market were competitive. See pages 364-365.

14.   c   Differential treatment based upon individual characteristics that do not affect job performance is costly to firms. Market forces will work toward eliminating this type of discrimination. The warehousing firm is turning down an applicant who cannot fulfill the duties of the job. The Internet firm is basing its decision on characteristics of the group to which the individual belongs. Although the particular individual may not quit the job, such statistical discrimination, using such rules of thumb does have a basis in keeping costs of a firm down. The final option is also costly to the firm. The easiest discrimination to eliminate is when economic incentives are working to eliminate it. See pages 367-369.

15.   d   Discrimination that is economically motivated out of individuals pursuing their self-interest is most difficult to eliminate. People are least motivated to adopt change they believe it may personally hurt them. See pages 367-369.

A1.   b   The firm should hire workers until the wage equals the marginal revenue product. See pages 378-383.

A2.   b   The marginal revenue per dollar is higher for input B so the firm should hire more of B and less of A. The other answers do not meet the cost minimization condition. See pages 378-383.

ANSWERS

POTENTIAL ESSAY QUESTIONS

The following are annotated answers. They indicate the general idea behind the answer.

1.   A monopsony is a market in which a single firm is the only buyer. The monopsonist's demand for labor is the market demand for labor. The monopsony also faces the market supply curve. The profit maximizing monopsony will hire fewer workers and pay a lower wage than the competitive outcome.

   A bilateral monopoly is a monopsony employing unionized workers. It's a bilateral monopoly because there is monopoly power on both sides of the labor market. It's possible that the monopoly power of the two sides will cancel out, giving rise to a competitive wage and quantity of labor employed.

WHO GETS WHAT?
THE DISTRIBUTION OF INCOME

18

CHAPTER AT A GLANCE

1. A Lorenz curve is a geometric representation of the share distribution of income among families in a given country at a given time. (387-388)

   It shows the relative equality of the distribution of income. The farther away from the diagonal line, the more <u>un</u>equal the distribution of income.

2. Poverty is defined by the U.S. government as earning income equal to or less than three times an average family's minimum food expenditures as calculated by the U.S. Department of Agriculture. The official poverty measure is an absolute measure because it is based on the minimum food budget for a family. It is a relative measure because it is adjusted for average inflation. (390)

   The poverty income threshold level is approximately $23,000 for a family of four. Poverty figures, like all statistics, should be used with care.

3. The United States has less income inequality than most developing countries but more income inequality than many developed countries. (392-394)

   Worldwide, income inequality is enormous. Therefore, the Lorenz curve of world income would show much more inequality than the Lorenz curve for a particular country.

4. In the United States wealth is significantly more unequally distributed than is income. (394-396)

   The bottom fifth have virtually no net wealth while the top fifth have more than 80 percent of the wealth.

5. Two alternative ways to describe income distribution are income distribution according to socioeconomic characteristics and distribution by class. (396-399)

   Most Americans are in the middle class. However, income differs substantially by class and by other socioeconomic characteristics such as age, race, and gender.

   Globalization has contributed to increased income inequality.

6. Three problems in determining whether an equal income distribution is fair are:
   (1) people don't start from equivalent positions; (2) people's needs differ; and (3) people's efforts differ. (399-401)

   When most people talk about believing in equality of income, they usually mean an equality of opportunity to earn income.

   Fairness is a philosophical question. People must judge a program's fairness for themselves.

7. Side effects of income redistribution are:
   a. the labor/leisure incentive effect;
   b. the avoidance and evasion incentive effects;
   c. the incentive effect to look more needy than you are. (402-407)

   Income is difficult to redistribute because of incentive effects of taxes, avoidance and evasion effects of taxes, and incentive effects of redistribution programs.

8. Expenditure programs have been more successful than taxes in redistributing income. (403-407)

   On the whole, the U.S. tax system is roughly proportional, so it is not very effective as a means of redistributing income.

● SHORT-ANSWER QUESTIONS

1. What does a Lorenz curve show?

2. What is the U.S. official definition of *poverty*?

3. How is the poverty definition both an absolute and a relative measure?

4. How does income inequality in the United States compare with other countries?

5. How does the Lorenz curve for household wealth compare with the Lorenz curve for family income in the United States?

6. What are two alternative ways to describe income distribution?

7. You and your friends are having a lunchtime discussion about fairness. A friend offers a statement that since income distribution has become more unequal in the past few decades, income distribution in the United States has become less and less fair. Assume you are a contrarian. How do you respond?

8. "Nevertheless," your friend says, "I believe the current distribution is not fair. The government should do something to make the income distribution more equal." You agree to some extent, but warn that there are side effects of redistributing income. State your argument.

9. Which has been more successful in the United States in redistributing income: expenditure or taxation programs? Why?

10. What are five expenditure programs that redistribute income?

MATCHING THE TERMS

Match the terms to their definitions

____ 1. income
____ 2. Lorenz curve
____ 3. Medicare
____ 4. poverty threshold
____ 5. progressive tax
____ 6. proportional tax
____ 7. public assistance
____ 8. regressive tax
____ 9. Social Security system
____ 10. Supplemental Security Income
____ 11. unemployment compensation
____ 12. wealth

a. A geometric representation of the share distribution of income among families in a given country at a given time.
b. The income below which a family is considered to live in poverty.
c. Payments received plus or minus changes in value of a person's assets in a specific time period.
d. The value of the things individuals own less the value of what they owe.
e. An average tax rate that increases with income.
f. A social insurance program that provides financial benefits to the elderly and disabled and to their dependents and/or survivors.
g. Means-tested social programs targeted to the poor and providing financial, nutritional, medical, and housing assistance.
h. An average tax rate that is constant regardless of income.
i. A multibillion-dollar medical insurance system.
j. Short-term financial assistance, regardless of need, to eligible individuals who are temporarily out of work.
k. An average tax rate that decreases with income.
l. A federal program that pays benefits, based on need, to the elderly, blind, and disabled.

● PROBLEMS AND APPLICATIONS

1. Use the Lorenz curve below to answer the following questions.

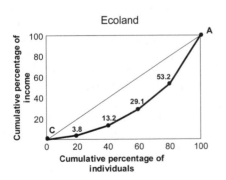

a. What percentage of total income do the top 20 percent of individuals in Ecoland receive?

b. What percentage of total income do the top 40 percent of individuals in Ecoland receive?

c. Which value, the one in part *a* or the one in part *b*, is greater? Why?

d   What does the straight line in the diagram represent? Describe points A and C. Why is the Lorenz curve always anchored at those points?

2. Use the following table to answer the questions.

Income quintile	% of Total Family Income		
	Eco-land	Fantasy-land	Text-land
Lowest 20%	5%	7%	2%
Second quintile	8	10	6
Third quintile	10	25	9
Fourth quintile	20	25	19
Highest 20%	57	33	64

a. Draw a Lorenz curve for each country.

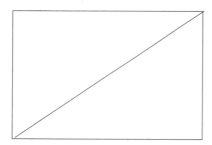

b   Rank the countries from most equal income distribution to least equal income distribution.

3. For each of the following state whether the tax is most likely proportional, regressive, or progressive with income.

a. 5 cent per gallon tax on gasoline.

b   School taxes based on assessed value of a home.

c. Sales tax of 6 percent.

d   Medical insurance taxes of 1.45% on all income.

⬤ MULTIPLE CHOICE

Circle the one best answer for each of the following questions:

1. The Lorenz curve is:
    a. a type of supply curve.
    b a type of demand curve.
    c. a geometric representation of the share distribution of income.
    d a geometric representation of the socioeconomic distribution of income.

2. Refer to the graph below. Which of the four Lorenz curves demonstrates the most income inequality?
    a. A.
    b B.
    c. C.
    d D.

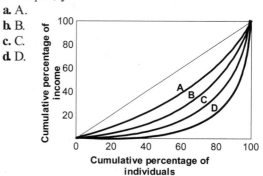

3. A family is in poverty if its income is:
    a. above the poverty income threshold level.
    b. less than $14,280.
    c. less than three times the average food budget for that family size.
    d. less than one-fifth the national average household income level for that family size.

4. The official definition of poverty is:
    a. an absolute measure of poverty since it is based upon a minimum food budget determined in the 1960s.
    b. a relative measure of poverty since the poverty line is defined as the income level that exceeds the income of 15 percent of all households in the United States.
    c. both a relative and absolute measure of poverty since the minimum food budget is adjusted each year for average inflation in the economy.
    d. neither an absolute nor relative measure of poverty since the poverty threshold changes each year.

5. If the government increases the amount of food stamps and housing assistance it gives out, the level of poverty in the United States, as officially defined:
    a. will be reduced.
    b. will be increased.
    c. will remain unchanged.
    d. cannot be determined from the information.

6. Recent studies show that income mobility in the United States is:
    a. unmeasurable no matter what country.
    b. lower than in European countries.
    c. higher than in European countries.
    d. about the same as in European countries.

7. A Lorenz curve for the entire world would show:
    a. more income inequality than in the United States.
    b. less income inequality than in the United States.
    c. approximately the same level of income inequality as in the United States.
    d. no income inequality.

8. In a Lorenz curve for the United States, household wealth would:

a. show the same amount of inequality as does family income.
b. show more inequality than does family income.
c. show less inequality than does family income.
d. would show no wealth inequality at all.

9. Refer to the graph below. The Gini coefficient is shown by which area?
    a. A/B.
    b. A/(A + B).
    c. B/A.
    d. B/(A + B).

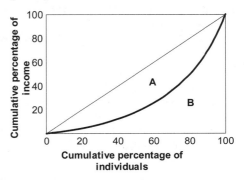

10. The U.S. class system is *best* represented by which shape?
    a. A diamond.
    b. A right-side-up pyramid with upper class on the top.
    c. A pentagon.
    d. A square.

11. One reason why the size of the lower class has expanded recently is:
    a. rising consumer prices.
    b. increased globalization.
    c. bankruptcy of Social Security.
    d. lower government spending.

12. Imposing a tax of 40 percent on high income workers in order to give the revenue to low income workers may not be especially effective in redistributing income if the tax:
    a. has large incentive effects.
    b. has no incentive effects.
    c. is seen as a sin tax.
    d. is not seen as a sin tax.

13. The largest government program to redistribute income is the:
   a. Social Security system.
   b. Medicaid program.
   c. Supplemental Nutritional Assistance Program (SNAP)
   d. Supplemental Security Income (SSI) program.

14. On the whole, the U.S. tax system is:
   a. unfair.
   b. roughly progressive.
   c. roughly proportional.
   d. roughly regressive.

15. In the United States, government spending programs:
   a. are less effective than tax policies in redistributing income.
   b. are more effective than tax policies in redistributing income.
   c. and tax policies are equally effective in redistributing income.
   d. and tax policies have had no measurable impact in redistributing income.

16. The U.S. federal program that pays benefits, based on need, to the elderly, blind, and disabled is called:
   a. Medicare.
   b. Medicaid.
   c. Temporary Assistance to Needy Families (TANF).
   d. Supplemental Security Income (SSI).

● POTENTIAL ESSAY QUESTIONS

You may also see essay questions similar to the "Problems & Applications" exercises.

1. Explain three problems in determining whether an equal income distribution is fair. When people talk about believing in the equality of income, what do they usually mean?

2. What are two direct methods through which government redistributes income? Which has generally been more successful and why?

━━━━ ANSWERS ━━━━

SHORT-ANSWER QUESTIONS

1. A Lorenz curve is a geometric representation of the share distribution of income among families in a given country at a given time. (387-388)

2. The official definition of *poverty* is an income equal to or less than three times an average family's minimum food expenditures as calculated by the U.S. Department of Agriculture. (390)

3. The official poverty measure is an absolute measure because it is based on the minimum food budget for a family. It is a relative measure because it is adjusted for average inflation. (390-391)

4. The United States has less income inequality than most developing countries but more income inequality than many developed countries. (392-394)

5. The Lorenz curve for household wealth is more bowed than the Lorenz curve for family income. This means that household wealth is less equally distributed than family income. (394-395 and Figure 18-5)

6. Two alternative ways to describe income distribution are income distribution according to socioeconomic characteristics and income distribution according to class. (396-399)

7. Determining whether an equal income distribution is fair is problematic. You tell your friend that, first of all, people do not start from equivalent positions and income depends upon those initial positions. Second, people's needs differ; some people are happy with less income, while others seem to need a higher income. Lastly, people's efforts differ; some people are willing to work harder than others. Shouldn't that effort be rewarded with higher income? Equality is not synonymous with fairness. (399-401)

8. Although some might agree that a more equal distribution is desirable, there are side effects of redistributing income. They are: (1) A tax to redistribute income may result in a switch from labor to leisure and, consequently, less production and less total income. (2) An increase in taxes to redistribute income might lead to attempts to avoid or evade taxes, leading to a decrease in measured income. (3) Government programs to redistribute money may cause people to make themselves look poorer than they really are. (402)

9. In the United States, expenditure programs have been more successful than tax programs for redistributing income. This is because, on the whole, the U.S. tax system is roughly proportional, so it is not very effective as a means of redistributing income. (406-407)

10. Five expenditure programs to redistribute income are (1) Social Security, (2) public assistance, (3) Supplemental Security Income, (4) unemployment compensation, and (5) housing programs. (404-406)

━━━━ ANSWERS ━━━━

MATCHING

1-c; 2-a; 3-i; 4-b; 5-e; 6-h; 7-g; 8-k; 9-f; 10-l; 11-j; 12-d.

━━━━ ANSWERS ━━━━

PROBLEMS AND APPLICATIONS

1. a. 46.8%. The top 20 percent of individuals earn 46.8 percent of the income. Calculate this by starting at 80% on the horizontal axis. Draw a vertical line to the Lorenz curve. Look at the value on the vertical axis where this line intersects the Lorenz curve. This is the percent of income that the bottom 80% of individuals earn. To get the amount that the top 20% earn, subtract this number, 53.2, from 100. (387-388)

   b. 70.9%. Going through the same exercise as in part 1a but starting at 60%, we find that the bottom 60% earn 29.1% of total income. Subtracting this from 100, we get 70.9%, the percent of total income earned by the top 40%. (387-388)

c. Part *b* is greater than part *a*. This has to be true, because the vertical axis is the *cumulative* percentage of income. If the top 20% earn a certain percentage of the total, the top 40% includes that top 20% plus more. (387-388)

d. The straight line represents the Lorenz curve if income were equally distributed. Point A says that 100% of individuals earn 100% of the income. This is true by definition. Point C says that 0% of individuals earn 0% of the income. The Lorenz curve is anchored at those points by definition. (387-388)

2. a. First we want to calculate the cumulative percentage of income for each country. We do this below by cumulatively adding together consecutive percentages.

Income quintile	Cumulative % of Income		
	Eco-land	Fantasy-land	Text-land
Lowest 20%	5%	7%	2%
Second quintile	13	17	8
Third quintile	23	42	17
Fourth quintile	43	67	36
Highest 20%	100	100	100

The Lorenz curve is the graph of these values connected. This is shown in the graph below. (387-388)

b. Fantasyland; Ecoland; Textland. The country most bowed out to the right of the diagonal line has the least equal income distribution. This is Textland. The country bowed out the least has the most equal income distribution. This is Fantasyland. Ecoland is in the middle. (387-388)

3. a. 5 cent per gallon tax on gasoline is a sales tax and sales taxes tend to be slightly regressive since poor people often spend a higher percentage of their incomes on gasoline than do rich people. (403)

b. School taxes based on assessed value of a home are considered to be roughly proportional since the value of a person's home is related to income. (403)

c. A sales tax is regressive since poor people often consume a higher percentage of their incomes than do rich people. (403)

d. Medical insurance taxes are proportional since the rate is 1.45% on all income, no matter how high or low. (403)

ANSWERS

MULTIPLE CHOICE

1. c A Lorenz curve describes how income is distributed in a country. It has proportion of the population on the horizontal axis and proportion of income on the vertical axis. See pages 387-388.

2. d A Lorenz curve describes how income is distributed in a country. It has proportion of the population on the horizontal axis and proportion of income on the vertical axis. The further the Lorenz curve is from the diagonal, the more unequally income is distributed. See pages 387-388.

3. c A family is in poverty if its income is equal to or less than three times an average family's minimum food expenditures as calculated by the U.S. Department of Agriculture. See page 390.

4. c The poverty threshold equals three times the minimum food budget. Thus, it is in part an absolute measure. But since it is adjusted for average inflation and not just inflation on food, and since food prices have risen more slowly than average inflation, it is a relative measure. See pages 390-391.

5. c These aspects of income are not taken into account in determining U.S. poverty figures. See pages 390-391.

6. b While in the 1960s and 70s studies showed that U.S. income mobility was high, recent studies show that it has declined and is now lower than in Europe. See pages 391-392.

7. a Since world income is more unequally divided among countries, the world Lorenz curve would have to show more income inequality. See pages 392-394.

8. b In the United States wealth is considerably less equally distributed than income. See pages 394-395.

9. b The Gini coefficient describes the degree of income inequality. It is the area between the diagonal and the Lorenz curve divided by the total area below the diagonal. See "Added Dimension" box on page 393.

10. c The U.S. class system is best seen as a pentagon. There is a relatively small upper class, a large middle class, and a smaller but still relatively large lower class. See pages 396-399, especially Figure 18-6.

11. b Increased globalization has held down wages in the lower-skilled manufacturing sector, increasing the size of the lower class. While rising consumer prices would affect the poverty threshold, they haven't risen sufficiently to account for the expansion of the lower class. See pages 397-399.

12. a Incentive effects can undermine attempts to redistribute income. See page 402.

13. a As stated in the text, the Social Security system is by far the largest expenditure program to supplement income. See pages 403-404.

14. c The overall U.S. tax system is roughly proportional. This can be deduced from the observation that the U.S. tax system does little to redistribute income. Whether it is fair or not is a matter of opinion. See page 404.

15. b In the United States, government spending programs are more effective than tax policies in redistributing income. See pages 406-407

16. d Medicare is a multibillion-dollar medical assistance insurance system for the elderly. Medicaid is medical assistance to the poor. TANF provides assistance to needy families with children under age 19. See pages 404-406.

ANSWERS

POTENTIAL ESSAY QUESTIONS

The following are annotated answers. They indicate the general idea behind the answer.

1. Three problems in determining whether an equal income distribution is fair are (1) people don't start from equal positions, (2) people's needs differ, and (3) people's efforts differ.

    When people talk about believing in equality of income, they usually mean they believe in equality of opportunity for comparably endowed individuals to earn income. If equal opportunity of equals leads to inequality of income, that inequality in income is fair. Unfortunately, there's enormous latitude for debate on what constitutes equal opportunity of equals.

2. The two methods are taxation (policies that tax the rich more than the poor) and expenditures (programs that help the poor more than the rich). Most government redistribution of income works through expenditure programs (public assistance; social programs), not through taxes. This is because on the whole, the U.S. tax system is roughly proportional, so it is not very effective as a means of redistributing income.

Pretest
Chapters 13 - 18

Take this test in test conditions, giving yourself a limited amount of time to complete the questions. Ideally, check with your professor to see how much time he or she allows for an average multiple choice question and multiply this by 30. This is the time limit you should set for yourself for this pretest. If you do not know how much time your teacher would allow, we suggest 1 minute per question, or 30 minutes.

1. In a perfectly competitive market:
   a. firms sell a differentiated product where one firm's output can be distinguished from another firm's output.
   b. there are so many firms selling output in the market that no one individual firm has the ability to control the market price.
   c. economic profits can be earned in the long run.
   d. there are very strong barriers to entry that can prevent potential competitors from entering the market.

2. Refer to the graph below. A competitive firm is producing at output A.

   a. It could increase profits by increasing output.
   b. It could increase profits by decreasing output.
   c. It cannot increase profits.
   d. One can say nothing about profits from the diagram.

3. In order to maximize profits (or minimize losses) a firm should produce at that output level at which:
   a. total revenue is maximized.
   b. average total costs are minimized.
   c. marginal revenue equals marginal cost.
   d. marginal revenue exceeds marginal cost by the greatest amount.

4. Refer to the graph below. The firm's profit in this case will be measured by:

   a. the rectangle ABEF.
   b. the rectangle ACDF.
   c. the rectangle ABHG.
   d. the rectangle BCDE.

5. Normal profits are:
   a. approximately 6 percent of costs.
   b. approximately 8 percent of costs.
   c. returns to the owners of business for the opportunity cost of their implicit inputs.
   d. generally larger than accounting profits.

6. Monopoly is the market structure in which:
   a. one firm makes up the entire market.
   b. two firms make up the entire market.
   c. the market is made up of a few big firms.
   d. firms make a supernormal profit.

7. A profit-maximizing monopolist will:
   a. produce an output level at which MR > MC.
   b. produce an output level at which P > MC.
   c. always earn an economic profit in the short run.
   d. increase production when MR < MC.

8. Refer to the graph below. The monopolist represented is:

a. making a profit.
b. making a loss.
c. making zero profit.
d. unable to determine what kind of profit it is making.

9. Refer to the graph below. Which area represents the welfare loss due to a monopolist?

a. A.
b. A + B.
c. B + C.
d. A + B + C.

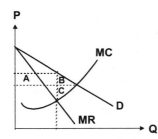

10. If the government forced a natural monopolist to charge consumers the price that a perfect competitor would charge, the monopolist would make a loss represented by rectangle:

a. ABGH.
b. DCFH.
c. IEFH.
d. None of the above.

11. Refer to the graph below. Which of the following is the output chosen by the monopolistically competitive firm?

a. Q_1.
b. Q_2.
c. Q_3.
d. Output cannot be determined.

12. A firm makes a profit in the long run. It is a:
a. perfect competitor.
b. monopolist.
c. monopolistic competitor.
d. This is true for all above.

13. In a contestable market model of oligopoly, prices are determined by:
a. costs and barriers to exit.
b. costs and barriers to entry.
c. costs, barriers to entry, and barriers to exit.
d. costs alone.

14. The top four firms in the industry have 10 percent, 8 percent, 8 percent, and 6 percent of the market. The four-firm concentration ratio of this market is:
a. 8.
b. 32.
c. 66.
d. 264.

15. A market has the following characteristics: There is strategic decision making, output is somewhat restricted, there are few firms, and some long-run economic profits are possible. This market is:
a. a monopoly.
b. an oligopoly.
c. monopolistically competitive.
d. perfectly competitive.

16. When judging the competitiveness of markets by the behavior of firms in that market, one is using the:
a. "judgment by performance" criteria.
b. "judgment by structure" criteria.
c. "judgment by merger" criteria.
d. "judgment by antitrust" criteria.

17. In the ALCOA antitrust case in 1945, the Court ruled that the:
    a. company had a monopolistic structure and therefore should be broken up.
    b. company was guilty of unfair business practices and therefore should be broken up.
    c. Sherman Antitrust Act did not apply.
    d. two companies had to be disbanded.

18. A firm is making no profit. If there is X-inefficiency, what can we conclude?
    a. The firm is operating at least cost.
    b. The firm is operating using the fewest inputs possible.
    c. The firm is operating less efficiently than economically possible.
    d. We can say nothing about the efficiency of the firm.

19. Refer to the graph below. If suppliers restrict output to L, what area represents the welfare loss to society?
    a. A + B.
    b. B + C.
    c. C + D.
    d. A + D.

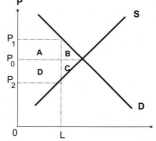

20. When regulated monopolies are allowed to pass on all cost increases to earn a normal profit, they:
    a. have a strong incentive to operate efficiently.
    b. have little incentive to operate efficiently.
    c. become a focal point of reverse engineering.
    d. will apply for a patent.

21. Technological advances are most likely for markets that:
    a. earn economic profits.
    b. have one firm supplying all the output.
    c. are protected by government regulation.
    d. produce where MR = MC.

22. The irony of any need-based program is that it:
    a. increases the number of needy.
    b. decreases the number of needy.
    c. creates other needs.
    d. destroys needs.

23. The term "derived demand" refers to:
    a. demand by consumers for advertised products.
    b. the demand for luxury goods that is derived from cultural phenomena such as fashion.
    c. the demand for factors of production by firms.
    d. the demand for derivatives.

24. As a factor becomes more important in the production process, the:
    a. firm's derived demand for the factor becomes less elastic.
    b. firm's derived demand for the factor becomes more elastic.
    c. firm's derived demand will not be affected.
    d. elasticity of the derived demand could become either higher or lower.

25. A firm has just changed from being a competitive firm to being a monopolist. Its derived demand for labor:
    a. will increase.
    b. will decrease.
    c. might increase or might decrease.
    d. is unaffected because whether the firm is a competitive firm or a monopolist has no effect on the firm's derived demand for labor.

26. Discrimination that is likely the most difficult to eliminate is discrimination that has:
    a. a social motivation.
    b. a cultural motivation.
    c. a political motivation.
    d. an economic motivation.

27. The Lorenz curve is:
    a. a type of supply curve.
    b. a type of demand curve.
    c. a geometric representation of the share distribution of income.
    d. a geometric representation of the socioeconomic distribution of income.

28. If the government increases the amount of food stamps and housing assistance it gives out, the level of poverty in the United States, as officially defined:
    a. will be reduced.
    b. will be increased.
    c. will remain unchanged.
    d. cannot be determined from the information.

29. One reason why the size of the lower class has
expanded recently is:
a. rising consumer prices.
b. increased globalization.
c. bankruptcy of Social Security.
d. lower government spending.

30. Imposing a tax of 40 percent on high income
workers in order to give the revenue to low
income workers may not be especially
effective in redistributing income if the tax:
a. has large incentive effects.
b. has no incentive effects.
c. is seen as a sin tax.
d. is not seen as a sin tax.

━━━━━ ANSWERS ━━━━━

1.	b	(13:2)	**16.**	a	(15:12)
2.	a	(13:6)	**17.**	a	(15:16)
3.	c	(13:9)	**18.**	a	(16:2)
4.	b	(13:13)	**19.**	b	(16:8)
5.	c	(13:19)	**20.**	b	(16:10)
6.	a	(14:1)	**21.**	a	(16:15)
7.	b	(14:3)	**22.**	a	(17:4)
8.	c	(14:7)	**23.**	c	(17:7)
9.	c	(14:11)	**24.**	a	(17:9)
10.	d	(14:15)	**25.**	b	(17:11)
11.	a	(14:18)	**26.**	d	(17:15)
12.	b	(14:20)	**27.**	c	(18:1)
13.	c	(15:3)	**28.**	c	(18:5)
14.	b	(15:6)	**29.**	b	(18:11)
15.	b	(15:8)	**30.**	a	(18:12)

*Key: The figures in parentheses refer to multiple
choice question and chapter numbers. For example
(1:2) is multiple choice question 2 from chapter 1.*

THE LOGIC OF INDIVIDUAL CHOICE: THE FOUNDATION OF SUPPLY AND DEMAND

CHAPTER AT A GLANCE

1. The principle of diminishing marginal utility states that after some point, the marginal utility received from each additional unit of a good decreases with each unit consumed, other things equal. (412-414)

   Marginal means "extra."
   Utility means "satisfaction."

2. The principle of rational choice tells us to spend our money on those goods that give us the most marginal utility per dollar. (415-416)

   If $MU_x/P_x > MU_y/P_y$, choose to consume an additional unit of good x;

   If $MU_x/P_x < MU_y/P_y$, choose to consume an additional unit of good y;

   If $MU_x/P_x = MU_y/P_y$, you are maximizing utility; you cannot increase your utility by adjusting your choices.

   $MU_x/P_x = MU_y/P_y$ means the extra satisfaction per last dollar spent on x equals that for y.

3. When the ratios of the marginal utility to the price of goods are equal, you're maximizing utility; that is the utility maximizing rule. (416-418)

   The equality: $MU_x/P_x = MU_y/P_y$ implies a combination of quantities of goods x and y consumed that will maximize your satisfaction given your budget, preferences, and the prices of x and y. No other combination of goods x and y will satisfy you as much.

4a. According to the principle of rational choice, if there is diminishing marginal utility and the price of a good goes up, we consume less of that good. Hence, the principle of rational choice leads to the law of demand. (419-421)

   If $MU_x/P_x = MU_y/P_y$ and then P_x increases, we get $MU_x/P_x < MU_y/P_y$ and we buy more of y and buy less of x.

   The law of demand tells us that less will be purchased at higher prices. There are two effects that account for this – the income effect and the substitution effect.

4b. According to the principle of rational choice, if there is diminishing marginal utility and the price of supplying a good goes up, you supply more of that good. (421-422)

   Consider labor. As the wage rate goes up, you will be willing to work more hours. Note that the law of supply can be derived from the principle of rational choice.

5. Three assumptions of the theory of choice are: decision making is costless, tastes are given, and individuals' maximize utility. (422-426)

   We must understand that these three assumptions don't always hold. The ultimatum game suggests that people care about fairness as well as maximizing their total utility. The status quo bias suggests that actions are based on perceived norms.

6. Behavioral economists look at choices in ways other than utility maximization. (422-426)

   Behavioral economists build upon traditional economics by conducting experiments to reveal how people make decisions.

   See also, Appendix A: "Indifference Curve Analysis."

● SHORT-ANSWER QUESTIONS

1. What is marginal utility?

5. Explain why you're maximizing utility when the ratios of the marginal utility to the price of goods are equal.

2. Suppose you and your friend are studying hard for an economics exam. You have a craving for double cheese pizza. You order a large. Your mouth is watering as you sink your teeth into the first slice. Oh, the pleasure! You eagerly reach for the second slice. The additional pleasure that you get from this slice is less than that from the first. The third and fourth slice each give you even less pleasure. What principle does this describe? State the principle in general terms.

6. Suppose you are maximizing utility by consuming two Big Macs at $2 apiece and three ice cream cones at $1 apiece. What happens to the number of Big Macs and ice cream cones consumed if the price of an ice cream cone rises to $2? How does this change in consumption account for the law of demand?

7. Why can economists believe there are many explanations of individual choice, but nonetheless focus on self-interest?

3. Suppose you had $8 to spend. You like going to see Ben Affeck movies a lot, but you like to see John Turturro movies even more. If these were your only choices to spend the $8 on, which movie would you go to see? Show how your choice follows the principle of rational choice.

8. Describe the ultimatum game. What have economists learned about people's tastes from the ultimatum game? What are the implications for the theory of rational choice?

4. What are the formulas that embody the principle of rational choice?

MATCHING THE TERMS

Match the terms to their definitions

___ **1.** conspicuous consumption	**a.** As you consume more of a good, at some point, consuming another unit of the good will yield less additional pleasure compared to the preceding unit.
___ **2.** income effect	**b.** A rule stating that one should consume that combination of goods where the ratios of their marginal utilities to their prices are equal.
___ **3.** marginal utility	
___ **4.** principle of diminishing marginal utility	**c.** A measure of the pleasure or satisfaction one gets from consuming a good or service.
___ **5.** principle of rational choice	**d.** Spend your money on those goods that give you the most marginal utility per dollar.
___ **6.** status quo bias	**e.** The satisfaction one gets from consuming one additional unit of a product above and beyond what has already been consumed up to that point.
___ **7.** substitution effect	
___ **8.** total utility	**f.** The total satisfaction one gets from a product.
___ **9.** ultimatum game	**g.** Consumption of goods not for one's direct pleasure, but simply to show off.
___ **10.** utility	
___ **11.** utility maximizing rule	**h.** Individuals' actions are influenced by the current situation even when that situation is not important to the decision.
	i. An exercise that demonstrates people care about fairness as well as personal total utility.
	j. The reduction in quantity demanded because the price increase has made us poorer.
	k. The reduction in quantity demanded because the relative price has risen.

● PROBLEMS AND APPLICATIONS

1. a. Fill in the blanks for the following table that shows how marginal utility and total utility change as more and more chocolate chip cookies are consumed. (Marginal utility refers to the marginal utility of increasing to that row; e.g., the marginal utility of going from 0 to 1 is 20.)

Number of choc. chip cookies	Total utility	Marginal utility
1	___	20
2	37	___
3	51	___
4	___	11
5	___	8
6	___	5
7	77	___
8	___	−1

b. On the axes below, graph the total utility curve of the table above.

c. Graph the marginal utility curve on the axes for b.

d. Is the principle of diminishing marginal utility operative in this case? Explain your answer.

e. At what point does the principle of diminishing marginal utility take effect? At what point does marginal utility become zero?

2. Using the principle of rational choice, choose the best option in each case:

a. A $2 slice of pizza giving you 80 units of utility and a $2 hero sandwich giving you 60 units of utility.

b. A $40,000 BMW giving you 200,000 units of utility and a $20,000 Toyota giving you 120,000 units of utility.

c. Taking an economics course that meets 3 times a week for ten weeks giving 900 units of utility or taking a history course that meets 2 times a week for ten weeks giving 800 units of utility. Both class periods last 50 minutes. There is no homework or studying.

d. Taking Tory out for a date at the Four Seasons restaurant in New York City at a cost of $120 which gives you 600 units of utility and taking Sam out at the corner pizza place at a cost of $15 which gives you 60 units of utility. (Tory is short for Victoria or Torrence and Sam is short for Samantha or Samuel — you choose which.)

3. Suppose you are taking courses from two different colleges, both on a part-time basis. One college offers only science courses. The other offers only humanities courses. Each class meets for the same amount of time and

you have an unlimited number of hours you can devote to course work, but only $10,500 to devote to tuition. Science courses cost $1,500 a course and humanities courses cost $3,000 a course. You are taking the courses for enjoyment and you have estimated the utility from the consumption of these courses as presented in the following table:

Number of courses	Science Total utility	Humanities Total utility
0	0	0
1	4,500	7,500
2	7,500	12,000
3	9,750	15,750
4	11,250	18,750
5	11,750	21,000
6	12,000	22,500

a. How many science courses and how many humanities courses should you take (assuming you follow the principle of rational choice)?

b. Suppose the price of humanities courses falls to $1,000 a course, how would your answer to part *a* change?

A1. Suppose you have a budget constraint of $10 to spend on pens and notebooks. Pens are 50 cents apiece and notebooks are $1 apiece. Draw the budget constraint, putting pens on the vertical axis and notebooks on the horizontal axis.

a. What is the slope of the line?

b. What happens to the budget constraint if your income available to spend falls to $8? What is the slope of the new curve? Show this graphically on the graph for part *a*.

c. Given the new $8 budget constraint, now suppose the price of notebooks rises to $2 apiece. What happens to the budget constraint? Show this graphically using the same axes as in the graph for parts *a* and *b*.

A2. Suppose the following table depicts your indifference between combinations of pens and notebooks:

	Notebooks	Pens
A	12	6
B	8	7
C	6	8
D	5	10
E	4	14

a. Graph the indifference curve on the axes below, with pens on the vertical axis and notebooks on the horizontal axis.

b. What is the marginal rate of substitution between combinations C and D?

c. Combine the indifference curve from question A2 with the $10 budget constraint from question A1 on the graph above. What is the combination of goods you will choose using the principle of rational choice?

● MULTIPLE CHOICE

Circle the one best answer for each of the following questions:

1. The principle of diminishing marginal utility says that after some point the marginal utility received from each additional unit of a good:
   a. remains constant with each good consumed.
   b. increases with each unit consumed.
   c. decreases with each unit consumed.
   d. approaches infinity with each good consumed.

2. The utility gained from eating one slice of pizza is 30 and the utility gained from eating a second slice of pizza is 20. From this we know:
   a. the marginal utility of the second slice of pizza is 50.
   b. the total utility of the second slice of pizza is 50.
   c. the marginal utility of the second slice of pizza is 20.
   d. there is not enough information to compute the marginal utility.

3. With regard to utility, it is true that
   a. the total satisfaction one gets from one's consumption of a product is called marginal utility.
   b. if you buy one Big Mac that gives you marginal utility of 400 and a second one that gives you marginal utility of 250, total utility of eating two Big Macs is 650.
   c. according to the law of diminishing marginal utility, the more we consume of something, the smaller the total satisfaction received from that good.
   d. when choosing between two goods, a rational consumer will choose that product that gives the greatest total utility per dollar.

4. Doug's utility from catching his first baseball is 700 units. His utility from catching his second baseball is 500 units. Doug's:
   a. marginal utility of catching his first baseball is 200 units.
   b. total utility after catching the second baseball is 500 units.
   c. total utility decreased after catching the second baseball.
   d. marginal utility of catching the second baseball is 500.

5. When the marginal utility curve is:
   a. zero, the total utility is at its maximum.
   b. decreasing, the total utility curve is increasing.
   c. zero, the total utility curve is at its minimum.
   d. decreasing, the total utility curve is decreasing.

6. The principle of rational choice specifically states that you choose how to spend additional income based on what gives you:
   a. the most total utility for that dollar.
   b. the most marginal utility for that dollar.
   c. the most average utility for that dollar.
   d. the least total utility for that dollar.

7. The price of good A is $1; the price of good B is $2. The marginal utility you get from good A is 40; the marginal utility you get from good B is 60. Assuming you can make marginal changes, you should:
   a. consume more of good A and less of good B.
   b. consume more of good B and less of good A.
   c. keep consuming equal amounts of both goods.
   d. realize that you don't have enough information to answer the question.

8. The price of good A is $2; the price of good B is $2. The marginal utility you get from good A is 40; the marginal utility you get from good B is 60. Assuming you can make marginal changes, you should:
   a. consume more of good A and less of good B.
   b. consume more of good B and less of good A.
   c. keep consuming equal amounts of both goods.
   d. realize that you don't have enough information to answer the question.

9. The price of good A is $1; the price of good B is $2. The marginal utility you get from good A is 40; the marginal utility you get from good B is 80. Assuming you can make marginal changes, you should:
   a. consume more of good A and less of good B.
   b. consume more of good B and less of good A.
   c. keep consuming the amount of both goods that you are currently consuming.
   d. realize that you don't have enough information to answer the question.

10. Dennis is deciding where to spend his spring break. If he goes to Vail, Colorado, the trip will give him 10,000 units of utility (satisfaction) and will cost him $500. If, instead, he travels to Padre Island, Texas, the trip will give him 6,000 units of pleasure and will cost him $400. Dennis should go to:
    a. Vail because his total pleasure will be greater.
    b. Padre Island because it is cheaper.
    c. Vail because his pleasure per dollar spent will be greater.
    d. Padre Island because his pleasure per dollar spent will be greater.

11. Economists assume that consumers will choose to purchase and consume:
    a. those goods that cost the least.
    b. those goods with the highest total utility.
    c. that combination of goods at which marginal utilities per dollar spent are equal.
    d. that combination of goods for which total utilities per dollar spent are equal.

12. The rational consumer will buy more of good X when:
    a. $MU_X/P_X < MU_Y/P_Y$.
    b. $MU_X/P_X > MU_Y/P_Y$.
    c. $MU_X/P_X = MU_Y/P_Y$.
    d. the price of good X increases.

13. If $MU_X/P_X = MU_Y/P_Y$ and the price of Y decreases, then the rational consumer will:
    a. continue consuming the same combination of X and Y.
    b. buy more of Y.
    c. buy more of X.
    d. buy less of X and Y.

14. The income effect generally:
    a. contributes to the law of demand.
    b. is based on the substitution effect.
    c. is based on the change in relative prices on quantity demanded.
    d. determines whether a good is a complement.

15. If your marginal utility of additional income is 60 units of utility, your opportunity cost of working is $5.00 per hour, and you are currently working 10 hours per week at $6.00 per hour, what is the minimum wage that you will require to work another hour?

a. 60 units of utility.

b. $5.00.

c. $6.00.

d. Insufficient information has been given to answer this question.

16. The theory of bounded rationality suggests that:

   a. all goods will be normal goods.

   b. all goods will be substitutes.

   c. many of our decisions are based on rules of thumb.

   d. individual tastes will be bounded and hence there will be diminishing marginal utility.

17. A focal point equilibrium is an equilibrium in which a set of goods is consumed:

   a. because the goods are subjectively preferred to all other goods.

   b. because the goods are objectively preferred to all other goods.

   c. not because the goods are necessarily preferred to all other goods, but simply because through luck, or advertising, they have become the goods to which people gravitate.

   d. through luck, or advertising, they have become focal points to which people gravitate despite the fact that other goods are definitely preferred.

18. Economists' theory of choice assumes:

   a. decision making has costs.

   b. peoples' preferences are given, and are not shaped by society.

   c. people do not always make decisions that are rational.

   d. people maximize many things, one of which is utility.

19. Behavioral economists find that people:

   a. always give the same answer regardless of how questions are posed.

   b. care only about maximizing their own utility, not fairness.

   c. tend to make choices consistent with the perceived norm.

   d. can handle decisions with 2 choices just as easily as decisions with 5 choices.

20. The ultimatum game suggests people:

   a. ultimately care only about income.

   b. choose based on their own self-interest no matter what.

c. care about fairness as well as income.

d. behave rationally when it comes to income.

A1. Refer to the graph below. The budget constraint reflects a relative price of chocolate (in terms of soda) of:

   a. one-fourth.

   b. one-half.

   c. one.

   d. two.

A2. Refer to the graph below on the left. If the price of chocolate falls, the budget constraint will:

   a. rotate out and become flatter.

   b. rotate in but keep the same slope.

   c. rotate in and become steeper.

   d. rotate out and become steeper.

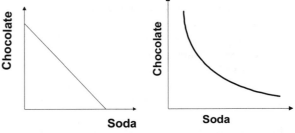

A3. Refer to the graph above on the right. The absolute value of the slope of the indifference curve represents:

   a. the marginal utility of chocolate divided by the marginal utility of soda.

   b. the marginal utility of soda divided by the marginal utility of chocolate.

   c. the marginal utility of soda times the marginal utility of chocolate.

   d. the marginal utility of chocolate divided by the price of chocolate.

A4. Refer to the graph below. The equilibrium in the indifference curve model is at point:

   a. A.

   b. B.

   c. C.

   d. D.

● POTENTIAL ESSAY QUESTIONS

You may also see essay questions similar to the "Problems & Applications" exercises.

1.   Discuss the principle of diminishing marginal utility. How is this related to the principle of rational choice and the law of demand?

2.   Distinguish between the income and substitution effects.

ANSWERS

SHORT-ANSWER QUESTIONS

1. Marginal utility refers to the satisfaction one gets from the consumption of an incremental or additional product above and beyond what has already been consumed up to that point. (412-414)

2. The fact that you enjoy each subsequent slice less and less follows the principle of diminishing marginal utility. It states that after some point, the marginal utility received from each additional unit of a good decreases with each unit consumed. (414)

3. You would choose to see the John Turturro movie because it would give more pleasure for the same amount of money. This decision follows the principle of rational choice which tells us to spend our money on those goods that give us the most marginal utility per dollar. (414-416)

4. The formulas that embody the principle of rational choice are:
   If $MU_x/P_x > MU_y/P_y$, choose to consume an additional unit of good x;
   If $MU_x/P_x < MU_y/P_y$, choose to consume an additional unit of good y;
   If $MU_x/P_x = MU_y/P_y$, you're maximizing utility. (416-418)

5. If the ratios of the marginal utility to the price of goods are equal, you cannot adjust your spending in any way to increase total utility. Changing your spending will result in additional total utility for that good you increased. But that additional utility is less than the decrease in utility for that good that you have given up. Thus, the marginal utilities per dollar are no longer equal and overall total utility has fallen. Total utility is maximized where the ratios of the marginal utility to the price of goods are equal. (416-418)

6. If you were initially maximizing utility, it must be that $MU_{Macs}/\$2 = MU_{i.c.}/\$1$. If the price of ice cream cones rises, then you are no longer maximizing utility because $MU_{Macs}/\$2 > MU_{i.c.}/\$2$.

To once again maximize utility, you would raise the marginal utility of ice cream cones and lower the marginal utility of Big Macs by choosing to consume more Big Macs and fewer ice cream cones because the marginal utility per dollar spent on Big Macs is greater than that for ice cream cones. You would adjust your consumption to the point where the marginal utilities per dollar were once again equal. The price of ice cream cones *relative to Big Macs* rose and the quantity demanded fell; and the price of Big Macs *relative to ice creams* fell and the quantity demanded rose. This is the law of demand in action. (419-422)

7. Economists believe there are many explanations of individual choice, but nonetheless they focus on self-interest because their simple self-interest theory cuts through many complications and in doing so often captures a part of reality other approaches miss. (422-426)

8. The ultimatum game is a game in which one person is given a sum of money that they can then share with another person. The person with the money can offer the other person any amount of that sum. If the offer is accepted, both people keep the money as negotiated. If the offer is rejected, all money must be returned. While economic theory suggests any offer would be accepted, offers that aren't close to half the sum are generally rejected. This suggests that people care about fairness as well as maximizing their total utility. The implications are that the assumptions of the theory of rational choice do not always hold true in reality. (425)

ANSWERS

MATCHING

1-g; 2-j; 3-e; 4-a; 5-d; 6-h; 7-k; 8-f; 9-i; 10-c; 11-b.

ANSWERS

PROBLEMS AND APPLICATIONS

1. **a.** This question tests the concepts of marginal utility, total utility, and the principle of diminishing marginal utility. Marginal utility is the satisfaction one gets from the consumption of an *incremental* product. Total utility is the total satisfaction from all units consumed up to that point of consumption; it is the sum of all marginal utilities from consumption. (412-414)

Number of choc. chip cookies	Total utility	Marginal utility
1	20	20
2	37	17
3	51	14
4	62	11
5	70	8
6	75	5
7	77	2
8	76	−1

    b. The total utility curve is shown below. It is bowed downward because the marginal utility diminishes as more cookies are consumed.(412-414, especially Figure 19-1)

    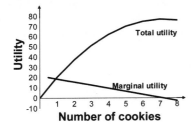

    c. The marginal utility curve is shown above. Its slope is always negative because the marginal utility of each additional cookie is always declining. (412-414, especially Figure 19-1)

    d. The principle of diminishing marginal utility is operative in this case. It states that as more of a good is consumed, beyond some point the additional units of consumption will yield fewer units of utility than the previous units. This is shown in the table by the third column. Its values are always declining. (412-414)

    e. The principle of diminishing marginal utility

operates from the second cookie on. The second cookie gave less pleasure than the first cookie. This is true throughout, from 2 through 8. Marginal utility becomes zero between 7 and 8 cookies. The marginal utility of the 7th cookie is 2, but the marginal utility of the 8th is −1. (414)

2. The principle of rational choice, discussed on page 416, states: Spend your money on those goods that give you the most marginal utility (MU) per dollar. (416-419)

    a. Choose the $2 slice of pizza. Marginal utility per dollar of the slice of pizza is 80 units of utility/$2 = 40 units of utility per dollar. Marginal utility per dollar of a hero sandwich is 60/ $2 = 30 units of utility per dollar. 40>30.

    b. Choose the $20,000 Toyota. Marginal utility per dollar for the Toyota is 120,000 units of utility/$20,000 = 6 units of utility per dollar. Marginal utility per dollar for the BMW is 200,000/$40,000 = 5 units of utility per dollar. 6>5.

    c. Choose the history course. Here the two alternatives have a cost in time, not money. The analysis is the same. Just calculate the marginal utility per minute and choose the one with the higher marginal utility per minute. Marginal utility per minute for the economics course is 900 units of utility/1500 minutes = 0.6 units of utility per minute. Marginal utility per minute for the history course is 800 units of utility/ 1000 minutes = 0.8 units of utility per minute. 0.8 > 0.6.

    d. Take Tory out on a date to the Four Seasons. Marginal utility per dollar for taking Tory out is 600 units of utility/ $120 = 5 units of utility per dollar. Marginal utility per dollar for taking Sam out is 60 units of utility/ $15 = 4 units of utility per dollar. 5 > 4.

3. This tests your understanding of the principle of rational choice, which states that a rational individual will adjust consumption of all goods until the marginal utilities per dollar are equal. (416-419)

    a. You should take 3 science courses and 2 humanities courses, given your budget constraint of $10,500. To determine this, first you must calculate the marginal utilities, and then the marginal utilities per dollar when you are spending all your money. We show the calculations to arrive at the answer in the table below. Following the principle of rational choice, select that combination where the marginal utilities per dollar are equal. Looking only at those combinations where you are spending all your money, this is at the combination of 3 science courses and 2 humanities courses. We reached this conclusion by figuring out different combinations of courses beginning with 6 science courses, calculating how many humanities courses could be purchased with the remaining funds, and comparing marginal utilities per dollar. If the marginal utility per dollar of science courses is lower than that for humanities course, choose one less science course and repeat the calculation. Keep doing this until the marginal utilities per dollar are the same for both.

SCIENCE COURSES

Number of Courses	Total utility	Marginal utility	MU per $
0	0	0	0
1	4,500	4,500	3
2	7,500	3,000	2
3	9,750	2,250	1.5
4	11,250	1,500	1
5	11,750	500	0.33
6	12,000	250	0.17

HUMANITIES COURSES

Number of Courses	Total utility	Marginal utility	MU per $
0	0	0	0
1	7,500	7,500	2.5
2	12,000	4,500	1.5
3	15,750	3,750	1.25
4	18,750	3,000	1
5	21,000	2,250	0.75
6	22,500	1,500	0.5

b. Now you should take 3 science courses and 6 humanities courses, given your budget constraint of $10,500. First you must calculate the marginal utilities and then the marginal utilities per dollar. This is shown in the accompanying table. Next, following the principle of rational choice,

select that combination where the marginal utilities per dollar are equal and you cannot buy any more courses. This is at the combination of 3 science courses and 6 humanities courses.

SCIENCE COURSES

Number of Courses	Total utility	Marginal utility	MU per $
0	0	0	0
1	4,500	4,500	3
2	7,500	3,000	2
3	9,750	2,250	1.5
4	11,250	1,500	1
5	11,750	500	0.33
6	12,000	250	0.17

HUMANITIES COURSES

Number of Courses	Total utility	Marginal utility	MU per $
0	0	0	0
1	7,500	7,500	7.5
2	12,000	4,500	4.5
3	15,750	3,750	3.75
4	18,750	3,000	3
5	21,000	2,250	2.25
6	22,500	1,500	1.5

A1. The budget constraint is drawn below. It was constructed by first finding out the y-intercept —how many pens could be bought with the entire $10: 20 pens—and then finding out the x-intercept—how many notebooks could be bought with the entire $10: 10 notebooks. Connect these points to get the budget constraint. (431)

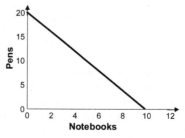

a. The slope of the budget constraint is $-P_{notebooks}/P_{pens} = -\$1/0.50 = -2$.

b. The budget constraint shifts in, intersecting the pen axis at 16 and the notebook axis at 8. To find this, use the process described above to find the initial budget constraint. Since relative prices did not change, the slope is still -2. This is shown below.

c. Since relative prices changed, the budget constraint rotates. To find the new budget constraint, find first how many notebooks can be bought at their new price: 4. The y-intercept remains at 16 since the price of pens did not change. The budget constraint rotates in along the notebook axis and intersects it at 4 notebooks. Since notebooks became more expensive, the slope became steeper. The slope of the line is $-P_{notebooks} / P_{pens} = -\$2/0.50 = -4$. This is shown below.

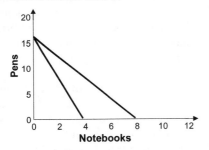

A2. a. To graph the indifference curve, plot each set of points which give the same utility. This is done below. (432-433)

b. The marginal rate of substitution between the combinations C and D is equal to the slope between C and D, $MU_{notebooks} / MU_{pens} = -2$. (432)

c. To find where you maximize utility given the budget constraint, find that point where the slope of the budget constraint equals the marginal rate of substitution between pens and notebooks. This is at points between C and D shown in the graph below. At points between C and D, the slope of the budget constraint is equal to the marginal rate of substitution: $MU_{ntbks} / MU_{pens} = -2 = -P_{ntbks} / P_{pens}$. The budget constraint is tangent to the indifference curve at points between C and D. This implies that any other indifference curve that intersects the budget constraint line gives you less total utility than does the current indifference curve. A rational choice maximizes your own utility. Hence, you should choose combinations represented by points between C and D. (433)

ANSWERS

MULTIPLE CHOICE

1. c The principle of diminishing marginal utility says that after some point, the additional satisfaction one gets from consuming additional units declines. See page 414.

2. c When we say that the utility of the second slice of pizza is 20, we mean we are getting an additional 20 units of utility, so the marginal utility of the second slice is 20. See pages 412-413.

3. b Options a, c, and d would be true statements if "total" was changed to "marginal." See pages 412-413, especially the table in Figure 19-1.

4. d Doug's marginal utility for catching the second baseball—the utility obtained from catching one additional baseball—is 500 units. His total utility is still increasing and is equal to 1200 units after catching the second baseball even though his marginal utility is decreasing. See pages 412-414.

5. a   When the marginal utility curve is zero, the total utility curve is at its maximum. When you can obtain zero additional units of utility from a specific activity or object, you are maximizing utility. The total utility curve can be either increasing or decreasing when the marginal utility is falling. What matters is when the marginal utility is negative. When marginal utility is negative total utility is falling. See pages 412-414.

6. b   You are better off by choosing to spend an additional sum of money on the good that provides you the greatest marginal utility per dollar. See pages 414-418.

7. a   Applying the rational choice rule, you divide the MU by the price. Increase consumption of the good that gives the greater marginal utility per dollar. Since 40/1 is greater than 60/2 then increase consumption of A and decrease consumption of B. See pages 414-418.

8. b   Increase the consumption of that good that provides the greatest MU/P. Since 40/2 is less than 60/2 you consume more of good B. See pages 414-418.

9. c   Increase the consumption of that good that provides the greatest MU/P. Since 40/1 equals 80/2 you continue to consume the same amounts of both goods you are currently consuming. See pages 414-418.

10. c   The trip to Vail will give Dennis the greatest marginal utility per dollar spent. See pages 414-418.

11. c   This is the rational choice. See page 416.

12. b   When $MU_X/P_X > MU_Y/P_Y$ the marginal utility for the money spent on good X exceeds that for good Y. You are getting more satisfaction for the last dollar spent on good X. Therefore, buy more of good X. See page 416.

13. b   A decrease in the price of Y will cause $MU_X/P_X < MU_Y/P_Y$. Therefore, one should buy more of good Y (and less of good X). See pages 419-420.

14. a   The income effect says that quantity demanded will fall when prices rise because the price increase makes the person poorer. It is different than the substitution effect, which is based on changes in relative prices. See pages 420-421.

15. b   Only the opportunity cost is needed to determine what would be required to get you to work another hour. See pages 421-422.

16. c   The theory of bounded rationality suggests that many of our decisions are based on rules of thumb rather than on the principle of rational choice. See page 422.

17. c   A focal point equilibrium may be the preferred equilibrium but it does not necessarily have to be the preferred equilibrium if individuals had better information. See page 423.

18. b   Economists' theory of choice assumes that decision making is costless, people's preferences are given (and are not shaped by society), and individuals are rational and attempt to maximize utility. See pages 423-424.

19. c   Behavioral economists have found that people tend to make decisions consistent with the perceived norm. This is the status quo bias. They also find that decisions are not costless. The greater the number of choices, the more costly the decision. Also people care about fairness as well as maximizing utility. See page 426.

20. c   The ultimatum game suggests people care about fairness as well as total income. If individuals always behaved rationally and maximized the total income, the second individual would accept any amount given to him or her by the first individual and the first individual would always give a small amount. This is not the case; the first

individual generally shares the money 50/50 and when he or she does not the scanty offer is almost always rejected, showing that individuals value fairness as well as total income. See page 425.

A1. d   Divide the intercept on the soda axis by the intercept on the chocolate axis to find the price of chocolate in terms of soda. One can buy either 6 sodas or 3 chocolates, or, 2 sodas or 1 chocolate. See page 431.

A2. d   A fall in the price of chocolate means that the same amount of soda will give more pieces of chocolate, so the budget constraint rotates up from the intersection of the soda axis, becoming steeper. See page 431.

A3. b   A movement down the curve represents the soda needed to compensate the individual—i.e., keep her utility constant—for giving up some chocolate. See pages 431-432.

A4. c   The equilibrium is where the indifference curve is tangent to the budget constraint. See page 432.

■■■■■ ANSWERS ■■■■■

POTENTIAL ESSAY QUESTIONS

The following are annotated answers. They indicate the general idea behind the answer.

1. As we consume more of any good or service the marginal utility declines. We consume combinations of goods and services for which their marginal utilities in relation to their prices are equal. If the price for good X falls, the marginal utility of good X in relation to its price will be greater than for other goods and services. We are simply getting more satisfaction for the money spent on the last unit of good X consumed. Therefore, we buy more of good X. So as the price of good X falls we find it rational to buy more of good X. This is the law of demand.

2. When the price of a good rises, the quantity demanded generally will fall. There are two forces that lead to this. First, because the price of the good relative to other goods has increased, consumers will substitute other goods whose prices have not risen for the good whose price has risen. This is called the substitution effect. The rise in the price of the good has also reduced the purchasing power of the income of consumers. Consumers just cannot buy as much as before because the price increase has made them poorer. The decline in quantity demanded because the price increase has made consumers poorer is called the income effect.

GAME THEORY, STRATEGIC DECISION MAKING, AND BEHAVIORAL ECONOMICS

20

● CHAPTER AT A GLANCE

1. Game theory can be structured to reflect the assumptions of a variety of models, making it more flexible than economists' traditional models of market behavior. (436-437)

    Game theory looks at strategic interaction among individuals and firms.

2. A prisoner's dilemma game is a game where the decision of one player affects the outcome for both players. The two players must make simultaneous decisions. (438)

    The prisoner's dilemma can be illustrated with a pay-off matrix. See page 439 in the textbook for an example. Players are assumed to make the best choice for themselves given the expected decision of the other player.

3. A Nash equilibrium is the set of strategies for each player in a game where no one can improve his or her payoff by changing strategy unilaterally. (440)

    A Nash equilibrium assumes players do not collude.

4. A dominant strategy is preferred regardless of one's opponent's move. A mixed strategy is choosing randomly. (443-440)

    The best strategy for rock, paper, scissors is a mixed strategy. It keeps your opponent guessing. The classic prisoner's dilemma game has a dominant strategy of each prisoner confessing.

5. Endowment and framing effects are examples of findings in behavioral economics that challenge the assumptions of the standard model. (449)

    Once people acquire something, they tend to want to keep it. This is the endowment effect.

    The way a question is framed affects the decision, even if the outcomes are the same. This is framing effects.

6. It only takes a few individuals to act as the model assumes (that is, rationally) for the predictions of the traditional model to hold. (451-452)

    Those individuals who are rational will be able to take advantage of the irrationality of others.

    See also, Appendix A: "Game Theory and Oligopoly."

SHORT-ANSWER QUESTIONS

1. There are two roommates. Both want to have a television for the apartment that costs $300, although neither has revealed that information to the other. Each values TV watching at $325. If only one roommate expresses the desire to have a TV, he will pay the entire cost. If both express a desire to have a TV, they will split the cost. If neither expresses a desire to have a TV, they don't get one. Draw a payoff matrix showing the gain of each roommate that reflects the situation and explain the strategic decision for each individual. How would their answer differ if they could cooperate?

2. Does the prisoner's dilemma game have a Nash equilibrium? Why or why not?

3. How would you expect the results of a single play ultimatum game to differ from a repeated play ultimatum game?

4. If a game arrives at a Nash equilibrium, is that Nash equilibrium to be preferred to a cooperative equilibrium?

5. In the 2/3rds game what is the Nash equilibrium? Would you expect it to be reached?

6. Is it true that in a Vickrey auction since the winner only pays the second-highest bid, winners can be expected to do better than in normal "highest bidder" auctions? Why?

7. In showing houses real estate agents sometimes show either expensive or run-down houses first, and then bring the client to the house they believe is best for them. Why?

8. Professor of Law Cass Sunstein asked two different groups of law students the following questions:

    Group 1: Under existing regulation of arsenic in drinking water, you face an annual cancer risk of 1 in 500,000. The government is proposing to tighten the regulation, in a way that would decrease the risk to 1 in 600,000. How much would you be willing to pay each year, in increased water bills, to favor the government's proposal? Choose one (a-f).

    a. $25; b. $50; c. $100; d. $200; e. $400; f. over $400.

    Group 2: Under existing regulation of arsenic in drinking water, you face an annual cancer risk of 1 in 600,000. The national government is proposing to loosen the regulation, in a way that would increase the risk to 1 in 500,000. How much would you have to be paid each year, in reduced water bills, to favor the government's proposal? Choose one (a-f).

    a. $25; b. $50; c. $100; d. $200; e. $400; f. over $400.

    While the value of each proposal was identical in terms of the probabilistic loss of life, the first group's median answer was $25 while the second group's median answer was $100. How would you explain the difference?

9. When an economist says that he doesn't care whether most people are rational or not, but only cares that "no money is left on the table," what does he or she mean?

MATCHING THE TERMS
Match the terms to their definitions

___ 1. backward induction	a. The tendency of people to base their choices on how the choice is presented.
___ 2. cheap talk	b. A sealed-bid auction where the highest bidder wins but pays the price bid by the next-highest bidder.
___ 3. cooperative game	c. A strategy of choosing randomly among moves.
___ 4. dominant strategy	d. You begin with a desired outcome and then determine the decisions that could have led you to that outcome.
___ 5. framing effect	e. A game in which each player is out for him or herself and agreements are either not possible or not enforceable.
___ 6. game theory	f. A game in which players can form coalitions and enforce the will of the coalition on its members.
___ 7. mixed strategy	g. A question structured in a way to extract strategic information about the person answering.
___ 8. Nash equilibrium	h. A game where players make their decisions at the same time as other players without knowing what choice the other players have made.
___ 9. noncooperative game	i. A game where players make decisions one after another; one player responds to the known decisions of other players.
___ 10. payoff matrix	j. A set of strategies for each player in the game in which no player can improve the payoff by changing his or her strategy unilaterally.
___ 11. prisoner's dilemma	k. A strategy that is desired by a player regardless of the opponent's move.
___ 12. screening question	l. Communication that occurs before the game is played that carries no cost and is backed up only by trust, and not any enforceable agreement.
___ 13. sequential game	m. A table that shows the outcome of every choice by every player, given the possible choices of all other players.
___ 14. simultaneous move game	n. A well-known two-person game that demonstrates the difficulty of cooperative behavior in certain circumstances.
___ 15. Vickrey auction	o. Formal economic reasoning applied to situations in which decisions are interdependent.

● PROBLEMS AND APPLICATIONS

1. A famous game developed by O. Hayword is called the Battle of Bismarck Sea. In the game, a Japanese admiral has to transport troops to New Guinea. He can take the rainy northern route or the sunny southern route. The United States knows the convoy will sail, and wants to attack it, but does not know which route the Japanese will take. The Americans have only enough reconnaissance planes to check out one route. If they explore the southern route and find the Japanese took that route, they will likely get three days of bombing in, but only one day of bombing in if the Japanese take the northern route. If the United States explores the northern route and find the Japanese, they will only get two days of bombing in because one of the days will have weather too bad to bomb. If instead the Japanese took the Southern route, they get in 2 days of bombing.

   a. Construct a payoff matrix with days of bombing as the positive payoff for the United States and the negative payoff for the Japanese.

b. What is the United States's dominant strategy?

c. What is the Japanese dominant strategy?

d. If the Japanese have a dominant strategy what does it make sense for the United States to do?

2. To show their bravery some boys have played a game of chicken in which they drive cars headed directly towards each other, to see who is the first one to swerve off, which means you are a chicken and you lose face. Assume that if you are chicken you get a payoff of one and the other gets 3; if you both swerve at the last minute, you each get a payoff of 2, and if you both go straight, you die which is denoted by a payoff of zero.

a. Draw the relevant payoff matrix.

b. What is the Nash equilibrium in the game?

c. If you have a reputation for being crazy, can that affect the outcome of the game?

d. How would your play differ if the other driver made it clear that they would decide whether to swerve or not by flipping a coin, and would not make a rational choice?

3. Consider the following pay-off matrixes:

a.

	H	T
H	+1, −1	0, 0
T	0, 0	−1, +1

b.

	H	T
H	+1, −1	+1, −1
T	−1, +1	−1, +1

c.

	H	T
H	+2, −1	+1, −1
T	−1, +1	−1, +2

d.

	H	T
H	3, 3	0, 2
T	2, 0	1, 1

a. For each of the payoff matrices listed, is there a dominant strategy for Player A (whose options are the rows and whose payoffs are specified by the first value in each square). If so, what is it?

b. If you were playing the game specified by payoff matrix *a* 100 times, what percentage of the time should you call heads (H)?

A1. Suppose there are two ice-cream stands on opposite sides of the road, Ben's stand and Jerry's stand. Each has identical costs of 25 cents a cone. Each has the option of charging $1 a cone or $1.50 a cone. If Ben and Jerry collude and charge $1.50 a cone each will sell 50 cones a day. Ben thinks that he would sell more cones if he sells his at $1 a cone. If he does this, he will sell 80 cones and Jerry will sell 20. Jerry is considering the same strategy. If they both charge $1, each will sell 50 cones day.

a. Construct a payoff matrix for Ben and Jerry.

b. If the stand is to be in business only one day, what would you advise Ben?

c. If the stands are to be in business all summer long, what would you advise Ben?

● MULTIPLE CHOICE

Circle the one best answer for each of the following questions:

1. Game theory is best described as:
   a. formal economic reasoning applied to situations in which decisions are independent.
   b. formal economic reasoning applied to situations in which decisions are interdependent.
   c. the analysis of dilemmas facing prisoners.
   d. a recreational activity of economists.

2. Game theory is a tool:
   a. used only by economists to study strategic interaction where individuals' decisions are independent.
   b. used by economists and other social scientists to study strategic interaction where individuals' decisions are independent.
   c. used only by economists to study strategic interaction where individuals' decisions are interdependent.
   d. used by economists and other social scientists to study strategic interaction where individuals' decisions are interdependent.

3. The economic way of thinking is best described as:
   a. create a simple model, empirically test it, and use it to guide your analysis.
   b. translate a problem to a graph and solve for an equilibrium.
   c. analyze all aspects of a problem and use that analysis to guide your thinking about the problem.
   d. create a simple model and use it to guide your analysis.

4. A payoff matrix shows:
   a. the payoffs that one player must make to the other player.
   b the payoff for each choice of each player.
   c. the best choices for each player.
   d the best and worst choices for each player.

5. The Nash equilibrium solution for the following payoff matrix is:

	A	A
B	A: 1, B: 100	A: 0, B: 1
B	A: 2, B: 0	A: 5, B: 2

   a. 1, 100.
   b. 2, 0.
   c. 0, 1.
   d There is more than one equilibrium solution.

6. If individuals can cooperate and share the gains, which payoff is the most likely?

	A	A
B	A: 1, B: 100	A: 0, B: 1
B	A: 2, B: 0	A: 5, B: 2

   a. 1, 100.
   b. 2, 0.
   c. 0, 1.
   d 5, 2.

7. The prisoner's dilemma is a well-known game in which:
   a. cooperation is costless.
   b. independent action is not necessarily the best joint action, but is the best independent action.
   c. firms always cheat.
   d firms never cheat.

8. Cheap talk:
   a. is an enforceable agreement.
   b. occurs after the game.

c. is backed up only by trust.

d. is a paid agreement.

9. A player's dominant strategy:
   a. is one that achieves a Nash equilibrium.
   b. changes depending on the choice of the opponent.
   c. consists of choosing randomly among moves.
   d. is preferred regardless of the opponent's move.

10. Generally, a repeated game will have:
    a. the same solution as a single play game.
    b. the same solution as a simultaneous play game.
    c. a different solution than a single play game.
    d. a different solution than a simultaneous play game.

11. If play in a game consistently deviates from the predicted play, the most likely reason is:
    a. players must not be rational.
    b. players' decisions are not described by the assumptions of the game.
    c. the game is incorrectly structured.
    d. economic reasoning is wrong.

12. In the game rock/paper/scissors, you should:
    a. generally choose rock because it breaks scissors.
    b. generally choose paper because it covers rock.
    c. generally choose scissors because it cuts paper.
    d. look for a pattern in your opponent's play and choose accordingly.

13. If a person chooses rock, paper, or scissors randomly, she is following:
    a. a mixed strategy.
    b. a dominant strategy.
    c. a sequential strategy.
    d. a consecutive strategy.

14. Making the standard assumptions, in a single play ultimatum game, the first player's best strategy is to:
    a. split the money evenly with a bit more going to yourself.
    b. give most money to the opponent.
    c. give most money to yourself.
    d. take all the money for yourself.

15. Making the traditional assumptions, in an infinitely long repeated play ultimatum game, the first player's best strategy is most likely to:
    a. split the money evenly with a bit more going to yourself.
    b. give the most money to the opponent.
    c. give the most money to yourself.
    d. take all the money for yourself.

16. In the 2/3rds game, in which you are to choose a number that is 2/3rds of the average chosen by the group, the Nash equilibrium is:
    a. zero.
    b. 11.
    c. 22.
    d. 33.

17. In a Vickrey auction:
    a. since the bidder pays only the next highest bid, he gets a better price than in a standard auction.
    b. even though the bidder pays only the next highest bid, he does not get a better price than in a standard auction.
    c. since the bidder pays the highest price, he pays a higher price than in a standard auction.
    d. even though the bidder pays the highest price, he does not get a better price than in a standard auction.

18. In the "trust game" a player is given money, which he can either keep, or give to someone else. If he gives the money to someone else, that money is tripled, and the second person can return some portion to the first player. The Nash equilibrium in this game is:
    a. for the first player to keep the entire sum.
    b. for the first player to keep half the money and give the other half to the second player.
    c. for the first player to give the entire sum to the other player.
    d. There is no Nash equilibrium for this game.

19. The fact that restaurants offer early-bird specials instead of peak-time surcharges is an example of:
    a. the endowment effect.
    b. framing effects.
    c. non-zero sum game.
    d. irrational behavior.

20. If most people don't conform to the assumptions of the standard model:
    a. the outcome of the model could not be true.
    b. the outcome of the model could still be true.
    c. society will have to better educate its people.
    d. the assumptions have to be revised.

A1. Strategic decision making is most important in:
    a. competitive markets.
    b. monopolistically competitive markets.
    c. oligopolistic markets.
    d. monopolistic markets.

A2. If a firm promises to match the price of its competitors, the customer:
    a. will be better off because the policy lowers prices of goods.
    b. will be better off because the policy is costless.
    c. may be worse off because the guarantee will push other firms out of business.
    d. may be worse off because it will discourage price competition by other firms.

● POTENTIAL ESSAY QUESTIONS

You may also see essay questions similar to the "Problems & Applications" exercises.

1. You are thinking of buying some shares of stock, and you know that people will be retiring soon and selling their stock to finance their retirement. Thus, the stock market can be expected to fall, and you would be best off if you sold your stock now. If the assumptions of this question are correct, is the reasoning correct?

2. Martin Shubik, a famous game theorist, has designed the following game called the dollar auction. In it, a dollar bill is auctioned according to two rules.
    a. The dollar bill goes to the highest bidder.
    b. The second highest bidder also has to pay the amount of his higher bid but he gets nothing in return.
    What would be your strategy in this game? Is it possible for the bidding to exceed $1.00?

3. Can a policy of a pre-emptive war be justified on game theoretic grounds?

ANSWERS

SHORT-ANSWER QUESTIONS

1.

	A wants TV	A doesn't want TV
B wants TV	175,175	325,25
B doesn't want TV	25,325	0,0

If player A states he wants the TV, then player B's best strategy is to state that he doesn't want it. If player A states that he doesn't want the TV then player B's best strategy is to state that he wants it. The reverse is true for Player B. There are no dominant strategies, but two Nash equilibria. If the players could cooperate, there would likely be a push for both saying they wanted the TV, and they would split the costs. (438-440)

2. The prisoner's dilemma game has a Nash equilibrium because there is an outcome (both confess) if each player follows his best strategy and assumes that the other player follows his or her best strategy, and no player can do better by changing strategy unilaterally. (438-440)

3. I would expect more money to be shared in a repeated play ultimatum game since it would allow for signals of willingness to share to be sent by the first player, and for the second player to punish the first player if he does not share. (444)

4. No, cooperative equilibria can lead to better outcomes for both players. The Nash equilibrium is best only for those games in which no cooperation is allowed or possible. (438-440)

5. The Nash equilibrium in the 2/3rds game is zero. It would probably not be reached regardless of how many times the game is played, because all individuals would not be expected to be following the "best" strategy. (444-445)

6. No, it is not true. The reason is that the bidder's strategy changes, so that each bidder now has an incentive to bid his true reservation price rather than simply the price that beats the next highest bidder. This happens only if the auction is a sealed-bid auction. (449)

7. This is probably because they are trying to take advantage of framing effects. By showing expensive or run-down houses first, the agent changes the frame of reference for the client and makes them more likely to see the final house as a good buy. (450-451)

8. I would explain the results in terms of the endowment effect. Since people already had safer drinking water, they were less likely to give it up (require a higher payment) to lose that safety than they were willing to pay to gain that increased safety. What people are more likely to keep is what they have (safe water or money). (450-451)

9. For the predictions of economic theory to hold true, only a portion of the population has to exhibit "rational" behavior. The "rational" ones will devise schemes to take advantage of other people's irrationality and transfer money that the irrational ones leave on the table to themselves. This makes the system operate as if all people were rational. (450-451)

ANSWERS

MATCHING

1-d; 2-l; 3-f; 4-k; 5-a; 6-o; 7-c; 8-j; 9-e; 10-m; 11-n; 12-g; 13-i; 14-h; 15-b.

ANSWERS

PROBLEMS AND APPLICATIONS

1. **a.**(438-440)

	Japan Northern route	Japan Southern route
U.S. Northern route	2, −2	2, −2
U.S. Southern route	1, −1	3, −3

b. The United States does not have a dominant strategy. They do better by choosing north if the Japanese choose north, but better by choosing south if the Japanese choose south. (438-440)

c. The Japanese have a dominant strategy since they come out better off if they go north. If they go south and the United States chooses south, they are bombed for three days. (438-440)

d. Since the Japanese have a dominant strategy, it makes sense for the United States to do the reconnaissance on the Northern Route. (438-440)

2. a. The game of "chicken" can be described by the following payoff matrix. (438-441)

	Swerve	Go straight
Swerve	2, 2	1, 3
Go straight	3, 1	0, 0

b. There are two Nash equilibria in this game—the upper right and lower left payoffs. If the other person is swerving, which is the best option, then it is in your interest to go straight. But the same reasoning holds for the other player, which is why it is called a game of chicken. (438-441)

c. Yes, if you are known as crazy, you are expected to go straight, and this changes the other player's dominant strategy to become one of swerving. (438-441)

d. This again changes the strategy for the other player, since there is now a 50% chance that you are going to swerve. It will make him more likely to swerve. (438-441)

3. a. In a, b, and c, Player A's dominant strategy is heads. Player A has no dominant strategy for d. (438-440)

b. Because there is a benefit to predicting the other person's choice, you should have a mixed strategy. You should play heads or tails randomly with equal probability. (438-440, 443)

A1. a. The payoff matrix follows on the next column. Ben's strategies are listed vertically. Jerry's strategies are listed horizontally. The first number in each cell is Ben's profits calculated as quantity times profit per unit. The second number is Jerry's profit calculated in the same way. (458-459, Figure A20-3)

		Jerry's Price	
		$1.50	$1.00
Ben's Price	$1.50	$62.50/$62.50	$25/$60
	$1.00	$60/$25	$37.50/$37.50

b. If the stand is to be in business only one day I would tell Ben that his profit-maximizing strategy is to charge $1. Expected profit of charging $1.50 is $43.75 ((62.5+25)/2), assuming it is equally likely that Jerry will charge $1.50 or $1.00. Expected profit of charging $1.00 is $48.75 ((60+37.5)/2), assuming it is equally likely that Jerry will charge $1.50 or $1.00. He should charge $1.00. (458-459)

c. If they were going to sell ice cream all summer long, I would recommend that Ben and Jerry develop some level of trust between themselves and collude to charge $1.50 each. This way they maximize joint profits. (458-459)

ANSWERS

MULTIPLE CHOICE

1. b The best description is b. "c" and "d" are too narrow, and "a" is incorrect since the strategic element of game theory emphasizes agent interdependence. See page 437.

2. d Since game theory is used by all social scientists, the answer must be b or d, and since game theory studies interdependent decisions, the answer must be d. See pages 436-437.

3. a As the Solow quote emphasizes in the text, the economic approach involves modeling and empirically testing that model. See page 437.

4. b The payoff matrix is a table showing the outcome of every choice of every player, so b is the best answer. See page 439.

5. d There are two Nash equilibria. Assuming that the individuals can expect the other player to choose the outcome that maximizes his payoff, the best that the players can do is to follow this same strategy. See pages 439-440 and Figure 20-1 on page 439.

6. a   I would expect that a is the most likely since it has the higher combined payoff, and I would expect that some sharing arrangement would be made. See page 440 and Figure 20-1.

7. b   In the prisoner's dilemma game, cooperation is beneficial for both prisoners, but difficult to achieve. Firms do not always get together. There may or may not be cheating, but firms expect others to cheat. See Figure 20-1 on page 438.

8. c   Cheap talk is communication that occurs before the game is played that carries no cost and is backed up only by trust, and not any enforceable agreement. See page 440.

9. d   A player's dominant strategy always is a strategy that is preferred by a player regardless of the opponent's move. It doesn't always lead to a Nash equilbrium. See page 440.

10. c   Simultaneous play games could be repeated or single play games so b and d are not possibilities. Since repeated games offer more possibilities for implicit cooperation than single-play games do, a repeated game generally will have a different solution than a single play game. See pages 441 and 444.

11. b   Games require strict assumptions, which are often not met in real life, which is the most likely reason why games deviate from predicted play. See pages 449-451.

12. d   In games, you should use backward induction to determine your play. Backward induction requires you to look for a pattern and take advantage of it. See pages 442-444.

13. a   A mixed strategy is a strategy of choosing randomly among moves. It is used in many simultaneous games that don't have a single dominate strategy as well as in many sequential games where rollback strategy is impossible. See page 443.

14. c   Since the game is played only once, the other person should accept any offer that gives him more than zero, so c is the best answer. See pages 444.

15. a   Since the game is being played again and again, the other person will likely punish you if you give most of the money to yourself and thus a is most likely the best strategy. See page 444.

16. a   The Nash equilibrium is zero since choosing 2/3rds of an average always drives the average down, and through backward induction approaches zero. See pages 442-445

17. b   In a Vickrey auction, the bidder pays the second-highest price, so the answer must be a or b. It is b because the bidders' strategies change, since they now have an incentive to bid the full value of the good, rather than to make a bid that just beats the next highest bidder. See page 449.

18. a   Since the second player will be assumed to keep all the money he is given and not return any to the first player, the Nash equilibrium is for the first player to keep all the money. See page 450.

19. b   The effect of charging peak-time eaters more is the same as charging non-peak time eaters less. Restaurants advertise that they discount off-peak dinners as a way to frame the practice as a discount rather than a surcharge to peak eaters. See pages 449-451.

20. b   Even if most people don't conform to the standard model, if at least some do, they will take advantage of those who do not, which may result in the identical aggregate outcome. See pages 451-452.

A1. c   Only oligopolies make strategic decisions. Monopolies have no competitors and perfect competitors have too many competitors. Monopolistic competitors act independently of one another. See pages 456-457.

A2. d   The best answer here is d. This is an example of implicit collusion to raise the market price. See pages 457-458.

━━━━━ ANSWERS ━━━━━

POTENTIAL ESSAY QUESTIONS

The following are annotated answers. They indicate the general idea behind the answer.

1. Other things equal, a greater number of retirees would mean that more people will be selling stocks and that stock prices will fall. But other things don't remain equal. Other stock market investors likely have already realized this same probability and have already sold their stocks. Thus, if people are rational, one would expect that the current price of stocks already reflects the effect of the greater number of retirees on future stock prices. When one thinks strategically, one realizes that other people who have just as much information as you do, are likely to have acted on it, and eliminated the possibility of gain from simple insights.

2. My strategy would be to not enter into the game since it is most likely that the dollar will go for more than $1.00, since the second highest bidder's best strategy is to bid one cent higher. Here's why. Say the highest bid is $0.99 and the next highest is $0.98. If the bidding ends there, the 2nd highest bidder pays $0.98 and gets nothing. If, instead, she bids $1.00, she becomes the highest bidder and cuts her $0.98 losses to zero. But wait. Now the person who bid $.99 is the second-highest bidder and is therefore out $.99. So, he, then has an incentive to bid $1.01 to win the $1 so that he loses only 0.01 instead of $.99. This bidding can go on forever. Since in this game, the best strategy once people have entered the bidding process is for the bidding to go on forever, the best strategy is not to enter the game, (or to make an agreement with the other bidders to collude and split the profits and losses).

3. One could argue that a policy of a pre-emptive war can be justified on game-theoretic grounds if one assumes that there is a first-mover advantage (striking pre-emptively gives one an advantage in a likely war) or if the cost of not striking pre-emptively is greater than a pre-emptive strike. Of course, that also holds for the other side, and cooperation and diplomacy are almost always the best joint strategy.

THINKING LIKE A MODERN ECONOMIST

21

CHAPTER AT A GLANCE

1. Traditional building-blocks are the assumptions that (1) people are completely rational and (2) are self-interested.

    Behavioral building-blocks are the assumptions that (1) people behave purposefully and (2) follow their enlightened self-interest. (463-468)

    Traditional → people are completely rational.
    Behavioral → people are predictably irrational.

2a. Heuristic models are models that are expressed informally in words. They are verbal rather than mathematical.

    Heuristic models are merely stepping stones to more formal models; they are not sufficiently precise to test scientifically. (462, 468-473)

    Heuristic = Informal = Non-mathematical = Verbal

2b. Traditional heuristic models are informal, verbal models that are based on the narrow assumptions of complete rationality and self-interest. (468-470)

    Behavioral heuristic models are informal, verbal models that are based on the broader assumptions of purposeful action and enlightened self-interest. (471-473)

3. Empirical models are based on statistical patterns in the data. They are created by first collecting and analyzing data and then formulating an hypothesis.
    Formal models begin with assumptions that are combined to formulate a hypothesis. The hypotheses are tested against the data. (473-482)

- *Empirical models: collect data then formulate hypotheses.*
- *Formal models: formulate hypotheses then test against the data.*

4. Modern economists use many types of formal models. Three are: butterfly effect models, game theory models, and ACE models. (477-479)

    Butterfly effect models are models in which a small change causes a large effect.

    Game theory models are models that focus on strategic interaction among individuals.

    An agent based computational economic (ACE) model is a culture dish approach to the study of economic phenomenon in which agents are allowed to interact in a computationally constructed environment and the researcher observes the results of that interaction. This approach is fundamentally different from standard modeling; it is computer-based and has no equations to be solved.

5. Traditional economists tend to have one framework from which they derive policy precepts. Modern economists allow for multiple frameworks and multiple policy precepts. (482-483)

    Traditional economics suggests that the market is likely to be the best way to deal with a problem, and that, left alone, the market will guide people toward doing the best they, and society, can, given the constraints.

    Modern economics in general is less sure that the market will solve every problem; while it accepts the useful functions of the market, it also recognizes the limitations of the market.

● SHORT-ANSWER QUESTIONS

1. How do traditional building-blocks differ from behavioral building-blocks?

2. Define the inductive approach and the deductive approach. Which of the reasoning approaches does traditional economics use? What about modern economics?

3. What is a model?

4. How do traditional heuristic models differ from behavioral heuristic models? Give an example of each.

5. How do empirical models differ from formal models? Give an example of each.

6. Describe the tradeoff between simplicity and complexity that exists for models.

7. List and define three types of formal models used by modern economists.

8. How and why do modern economics and traditional economics differ in their policy prescriptions? Give a specific example.

MATCHING THE TERMS
Match the terms to their definitions

____ **1.** agent-based computational economic (ACE) model

____ **2.** behavioral economics

____ **3.** butterfly effect model

____ **4.** coefficient of determination

____ **5.** deductive approach

____ **6.** econometrics

____ **7.** empirical model

____ **8.** endowment effect

____ **9.** enlightened self-interest

____ **10.** game theory model

____ **11.** inductive approach

____ **12.** heuristic model

____ **13.** model

____ **14.** modern economist

____ **15.** natural experiment

____ **16.** path-dependent model

____ **17.** precommitment strategy

____ **18.** purposeful behavior

____ **19.** regression model

____ **20.** self-confirming equilibrium

____ **21.** traditional economist

a. An economist who is willing to use a wider range of models than did earlier economists.

b. Behavior such as habits and rules of thumb that may be incompatible with the traditional economic understanding of rationality.

c. A model in which one analyzes the strategic interaction of individuals when they take into account the likely response of other people to their actions.

d. When people value something more just because they have it.

e. Microeconomic analysis that uses a broader set of building-blocks than rationality and self-interest used in traditional economics.

f. A model in which the path to equilibrium affects the equilibrium.

g. A simplified representation of the problem or question that captures the essential issues.

h. An economist who studies the logical implications of rationality and self-interest in relatively simple algebraic or graphical models, such as the supply and demand model.

i. Models that statistically discover a pattern in the data.

j. An equilibrium in a model in which people's beliefs become self-fulfilling.

k. An approach to understanding a problem or question in which understanding is developed empirically from statistically analyzing what is observed in the data.

l. A model that is expressed informally in words.

m. A model that uses a culture dish approach to the study of economic phenomena in which agents are allowed to interact in a computationally constructed environment and the researcher observes the results of that interaction.

n. An empirical model in which one statistically relates one set of variables to another.

o. A measure of the proportion of the variability in the data that is accounted for by the statistical model.

p. An event created by nature that can serve as an experiment.

q. When people can care about other people as well as themselves.

r. A model in which a small change causes a large effect.

s. A strategy in which people consciously place limitations on their future actions, thereby limiting their choices.

t. The statistical analysis of economic data.

u. An approach that begins with certain self-evident principles from which implications are logically determined.

PROBLEMS AND APPLICATIONS

1. You are the research assistant to Princeton economics professor Orley Ashenfelter. Together you have been working on a new regression model to determine the quality of wine grown in Spirits-land. After collecting and analyzing your data, you have come up with the relationship below.

    a. Use the equation to predict the quality of wine for each year. Write the values in the table.

    Wine quality $= 8 + 0.1$(winter rainfall) $+ 0.002$(average growing season temperature) $- 0.05$(harvest rainfall)

	Wine quality	Winter rainfall	Average growing season temperature	Harvest rainfall
2010		4	75	2
2011		4	75	2
2012		10	80	6
2013		7	60	15

    b. Is this an empirical or a formal model? Why?

2. Complete the following table.

	Earlier Economics	Modern Economics	
		Behavioral Economists	Traditional Economists
Assumptions	1.	1.	1.
	2.	2.	2.
Approach			
Types of models			

3. State for each of the following if it is an example of an empirical model or if it is an example of a formal model. And then explain why.

    a. An equation that is derived from last semester's data that summarizes the statistical relationship between the number of students and the average final grade in a particular professor's class.

    b. A model that uses production possibility curves for Portugal and Britain with regard to wheat and wine production to show how comparative advantage and specialization allow both countries to consume outside of their individual production possibility curves.

    c. A supply and demand model for the price of livestock.

    d. An equation that is derived from last year's data that summarizes the statistical relationship between the number of livestock sold and the average price of livestock.

    e. A model that uses equation $Qs = -5 + 2P$ for quantity supplied of livestock and the equation $Qd = 10 - P$ for quantity demanded of livestock.

● **MULTIPLE CHOICE**

Circle the one best answer for each of the following questions:

1. In modern economics supply and demand is
    considered:
    a. the holy grail of economics.
    b. an important stepping stone, but just a
    stepping stone.
    c. the glue that holds economics together.
    d. an empirical model.

2. What is the "glue" that holds economics
    together?
    a. Modeling.
    b. Supply and demand.
    c. Economic theories.
    d. Data analysis.

3. Traditional economists assume:
    a. complete rationality and enlightened self-
    interest.
    b. purposeful behavior and enlightened self-
    interest.
    c. complete rationality and self-interest.
    d. purposeful behavior and self-interest.

4. Behavioral economists assume:
    a. complete rationality and enlightened self-
    interest.
    b. complete rationality and self-interest.
    c. purposeful behavior and self-interest.
    d. purposeful behavior and enlightened self-
    interest.

5. Which of the choices below are examples of
    models?
    a. A small replica of a proposed house.
    b. A computer simulation that simulates the
    growth of bacteria.
    c. The online game Second Life.
    d. All of the above.

6. Behavioral economists argue:
    a. that the supply/demand model should be
    discarded.
    b. traditional building-blocks do not explain
    everything.
    c. models built on traditional building-blocks
    are irrelevant.
    d. All of the above.

7. What real-world behaviors do behavioral
    economists incorporate into their models?
    a. That people make choices based on rules of
    thumb.
    b. Endowment effects.
    c. Precommitment strategies.
    d. All of the above.

8. What type of economist is most likely to rely
    primarily on deductive reasoning?
    a. Behavioral economists.
    b. Modern economists.
    c. Traditional economists.
    d. Modern traditional economists.

9. Inductive reasoning:
    a. uses logic to find implications.
    b. uses observed data to develop understand-
    ing.
    c. does not use models to find implications.
    d. characterizes the work of traditional econo-
    mists.

10. Heuristic models are:
    a. informal and verbal simplified representa-
    tions that capture the essential issues of a
    problem.
    b. models based on the behavioral building-
    blocks of purposeful behavior and enlight-
    ened self-interest.
    c. models that statistically discover a pattern in
    the data.
    d. models that are based only on formal logical
    relationships.

11. A path-dependent model is a model:
    a. that is independent of history.
    b. in which decisions are independent of one
    another.
    c. in which how one gets to equilibrium affects
    equilibrium.
    d. in which small changes result in large
    changes in equilibrium.

12. Why are heuristic models limited?
    a. They are not sufficiently precise, making
    their validity difficult to test.
    b. Their traditional building-blocks make them
    too abstract to be of practical use.
    c. Their behavioral building-blocks make them
    too dependent on context.
    d. They are too mathematical and reliant on
    theory.

13. Which types of economists rely on empirical work?
    a. Traditional economists.
    b. Behavioral economists.
    c. Modern traditional economists.
    d. All modern economists.

14. An empirical economist uses:
    a. deductive reasoning only.
    b. econometrics and empirical models.
    c. ACE models only.
    d. inductive methods only.

15. Econometrics is:
    a. the statistical analysis of economic data.
    b. the measure of the proportion of the variability in data accounted for by the statistical model.
    c. the computationally constructed environment in an agent based computation economic model.
    d. the parameters of strange attractor models.

16. The supply/demand model is an example of:
    a. an empirical model.
    b. a regression model.
    c. a formal model.
    d. a heuristic model.

17. All of the following are formal models *except*:
    a. butterfly effect models.
    b. game theory models.
    c. supply and demand models.
    d. heuristic models.

18. With regard to policy, traditional economists generally are more likely than behavioral economists to suggest that:
    a. the market is likely to be the best way to deal with a problem.
    b. there are limitations of the market.
    c. because there are multiple frameworks within which a problem can be thought about, there is fundamental ambiguity about the appropriate policy.
    d. there is a potential role for government interventions and public policy in the economy even when there are no externalities.

19. With regard to policy, behavioral economists are more likely than traditional economists to suggest that:
    a. free market policy guarantees both liberty and prosperity.
    b. there is an important role for government intervention and public policy even when there are no externalities.
    c. the market is likely to be the best way to deal with a problem.
    d. there is no ambiguity about what policy should be.

● POTENTIAL ESSAY QUESTIONS

You may also see essay questions similar to the "Problems & Applications" exercises.

1. Respond to the following statement: "Formal models, as abstract simplifications (based on theories) of problems or issues, do a poor job of describing what goes on in the real world. Economists should 'bring the model to the data' and concentrate on empirical models instead."

2. When housing bubbles burst, people are sometimes unwilling to sell their house for less than they bought it. What assumptions or building-blocks does this call into question? Which perspective (traditional or behavioral) provides a better explanation for this phenomenon? Why?

3. Behavioral economists argue that people tend to make choices based on rules of thumb. How could traditional economists reconcile their assumption that people are rational with this use of rules of thumb?

ANSWERS

SHORT-ANSWER QUESTIONS

1. The traditional building-blocks are the assumptions that people are (1) completely rational and (2) self-interested. Behavioral building-blocks are the assumptions that people (1) behave purposefully and (2) follow their enlightened self-interest.

    Traditional building-blocks are narrower and more restrictive than behavioral building-blocks. As a result, models based on traditional building-blocks are more analytically powerful; they provide simplicity and insight by highlighting the relevant general issues. Models based on behavioral building-blocks provide less clear-cut results but capture how people actually behave. (463-464)

2. An inductive approach is an approach to understanding a problem or question in which understanding is developed empirically from statistically analyzing what is observed in the data. A deductive approach is an approach to understanding a problem or question that begins with certain self-evident principles from which implications are logically deduced. Traditional economics is typically characterized as a deductive approach and modern economics involves more use of induction. (462-463)

3. A model is a simplified representation of a problem or question that captures the essential issues. (461)

4. A heuristic model is a model that is expressed informally in words. Traditional heuristic models are informal, verbal models that are based on the narrow assumptions of complete rationality and self-interest. Behavioral heuristic models are informal, verbal models that are based on the broader assumptions of purposeful action and enlightened self-interest. The broader assumptions of behavioral heuristic models allow for a much wider range of models and sets of explanations, as well as a much wider range of policy interventions, compared to traditional heuristic models. Behavioral heuristic models take social dimensions of problems into account; traditional heuristic models don't.

    Economists Steven Landsburg's models *"How More Sex is Safer Sex"* and *"Why Car Insurance Costs More Some Places than Others"* are examples of traditional heuristic models. Economist Robert Frank's models *"Why are People More Likely to Return Cash than a Lampshade?"* and *"Why Don't More People Wear Velcro Shoes?"* are examples of behavioral heuristic models. (462, 468-473)

5. Empirical models begin with a pattern found in the data. (They are created by first collecting and analyzing data and then formulating a hypothesis.) Formal models are those derived by first formulating the hypothesis and then testing it with data.

    Empirical models, by "letting the data speak," quantifiably and scientifically support the implications and conclusions of heuristic models. Simple relationships derived from data help explain and sometimes predict outcomes in the real world. However, because of the impossibility of controlled experiments, "letting the data speak" will not necessarily provide definitive answers. Formal models rely on theoretical models to guide economists in interpreting data and drawing out policy implications from the models. But because of the almost infinite number of potential interrelationships, outcomes, and models, there is a formal theoretical model that can arrive at just about any possible conclusion. An example of an empirical model is the regression model. An example of a formal model is the butterfly effect model. (473-482)

6. Each new relationship added to a model involves an additional level of technical difficulty. The more complex the model, the harder it is to arrive at a conclusion. (477-478)

7. Modern economists use many types of formal models. Here are three: (1) Butterfly effect models – models in which a small change causes a large effect. In these models, because a small change could tip the economy into a low-growth, high-unemployment equilibrium that would be difficult to escape, there is a serious potential for economic depression. (2) Game theory models – models in which one analyzes the strategic interaction of individuals when they take into account the likely re-

sponse of other people to their actions. Game theory is the subject of most graduate micro-economic studies and courses. (3) Agent based computational economic (ACE) models – a culture dish approach to the study of economic phenomena in which agents (encapsulated collections of data and methods representing an entity residing in an environment on the computer) are allowed to interact in a computationally constructed environment and the researcher observes the results of that interaction. This approach is fundamentally different from standard modeling; it is computer-based and has no equations to be solved. (476-479)

8. Traditional economics and modern economics differ significantly in their policy prescriptions because they use different assumptions and methodologies. Traditional economics suggests that the market is likely to be the best way to deal with a problem, and that, left alone, the market will guide people toward doing the best they, and society, can, given the constraints. Modern economics in general is less sure that the market will solve every problem; while it accepts the useful functions of the market it also recognizes the limitations of the market. The difference in policy prescriptions occurs because of the different assumptions and viewpoints underlying the two perspectives. Traditional economics has more narrow assumptions. Modern economics has broad assumptions. Traditional economics tends to favor policies directed at achieving more growth. Behavioral economics is more likely to allow for the distribution of income to be taken into account. (482-483)

ANSWERS

MATCHING

1-m; 2-e; 3-r; 4-o; 5-u; 6-t; 7-i; 8-d; 9-q; 10-c; 11-k; 12-l; 13-g; 14-a; 15-p; 16-f; 17-s;18-b; 19-n; 20-j; 21-h.

ANSWERS

PROBLEMS AND APPLICATIONS

1. a. (475)

	Wine quality	Winter rainfall	Average growing season temperature	Harvest rainfall
2010	8.45	4	75	2
2011	8.45	4	75	2
2012	8.86	10	80	6
2013	8.07	7	60	15

   b. This is an empirical model. It statistically discovers a pattern in the data. In addition it is a regression model, that is, an empirical tool in which one statistically relates one set of variables to another.

2. ("A Reminder Box" on page 480.)

	Earlier Economics	Modern Economics	
		Behavioral Economists	Traditional Economists
Assumptions	Rationality	Purposeful behavior	Rationality
	Self-interest	Enlightened Self-interest	Self-interest
Approach	Primarily deduction	Induction and deduction; emphasis on experimental economics and empirical models	Induction and deduction; emphasis on empirical models
Types of models	Simple supply/demand models	All types including highly complex mathematical models and ACE models	All types including highly complex mathematical models and ACE models

3. a. This is an example of an empirical model, specifically a regression model. An empirical relationship is derived using the concept of goodness-of-fit that results in an algebraic representation of a pattern in the data. Because the model is derived from data and not based on theory, it is an empirical model. (473-482)

b. This is an example of a formal model. The model makes use of the theory of comparative advantage to highlight the important implications specialization and division of labor have for international trade. Because the model is based on a theory and not derived from data, it is a formal model. (473-482)

c. This is an example of a formal model. The model makes use of the invisible hand theorem. Because the model is carefully based on deductive reasoning, it is a formal model. (473-482)

d. This is an example of an empirical model. A mathematical relationship is derived using the concept of goodness-of-fit that results in an algebraic representation of a pattern in the data. Because the model is derived from data, it is an empirical model. (473-482)

e. This is an example of a formal model. While the model is expressed algebraically it is still not based on data analysis, but on the invisible hand theorem. Because the model is carefully based on deductive reasoning, it is a formal model. (473-482)

ANSWERS

MULTIPLE CHOICE

1. b As discussed on pages 461, the author states that his goal in including this chapter is to disabuse you of the idea that the supply and demand model is the holy grail of economics. He also points out that models are the glue that holds economics together. The supply and demand model is not an empirical model. He also says that supply and demand is just a stepping stone.

2. a As discussed on page 461, modeling is the glue that holds modern economics together.

3. c As discussed on page 463, traditional economists are economists who study the logical implications of rationality and self-interest.

4. d As discussed on page 463, behavioral economists are economists who use a broader set of building-blocks than rationality and self-interest. They believe rationality should be broadened to purposeful behavior and self-interest to enlightened self-interest.

5. d On pages 462-464 several different examples are given of what might be considered models. The proposed house, the computer simulation, and Second Life are all mentioned as possible examples.

6. b As discussed on pages 467-468, behavioral economists do not advocate discarding the supply/demand model. Behavioral economists recognize that traditional building-blocks do not explain everything.

7. d As discussed on pages 464-466, behavioral economists incorporate the idea that people will make choices based on rules of thumb into their models. Behavioral economists also incorporate endowment effects and precommitment strategies into their models.

8. c As discussed on pages 462-463, traditional economists use primarily deductive reasoning.

9. b As discussed on pages 462-463, inductive reasoning is an approach in which understanding is developed by analyzing what is observed in the data. It is a method used by both modern traditional and behavioral economists. Approaches that begin with certain self-evident principles from which implications are logically deduced is deductive reasoning.

10. a As discussed on page 462, a heuristic model is an informal or verbal model.

11. c As discussed on pages 469-470, a path-dependent model is a model in which the path to equilibrium affects the equilibrium. Options a and b are the opposite of a path-dependent model. Option d describes the butterfly effect model.

12. a   As discussed on pages 470-473, heuristic means verbal and informal. Heuristic models are limited because they are not sufficiently precise, making their validity difficult to test.

13. d   As discussed on pages 473-474, because economists try to understand the real world at some point, all rely on empirical work.

14. b   As discussed on pages 473-474, empirical economists can use traditional assumptions and deduction. What distinguishes them from other economists is their reliance on statistical techniques such as econometrics and models based on data (empirical models).

15. a   As discussed on page 473, econometrics is the statistical analysis of economic data.

16. c   As discussed on page 477, the supply/demand model is a formal deductive model based on traditional building blocks. It is not based on informal observations nor is it a statistical test.

17. d   As discussed on pages 477-479, butterfly effect models, game theory models, and supply/demand models are all formal models.

18. a   As discussed on pages 470, 482-483, traditional economists are likely to believe that markets are the best way to deal with a problem. The other options describe behavioral economists.

19. b   As discussed on pages 470, 482-483, behavioral economists are much more likely to support government intervention. Traditional economists are much more likely to support the market as the way to deal with a problem and see much less ambiguity.

━━━━━ ANSWERS ━━━━━

POTENTIAL ESSAY QUESTIONS

The following are annotated answers. They indicate the general idea behind the answer.

1.   It is true that "letting the data speak" and "bringing the model to the data" will ground theory in mathematics and science. What primarily distinguishes modern economists from other social scientists is economists' reliance on formal empirical methods. Modern economics is based on experiments that can be replicated, or on statistical analysis of real-world observations. With the amount of data and computing power available increasing exponentially, empirical analysis and statistics are likely to play an increasingly significant role in modern economics.

However, data by themselves have no meaning. Data must be interpreted and given meaning by economists. How a modern economist interprets the data depends on what model and building-blocks he or she is implicitly or explicitly using. Data must be organized by theories.

Economics is not a laboratory science. Moral and practical problems severely limit when controlled experiments can be utilized. Given this limited ability to conduct controlled experiments, letting the data speak will not necessarily provide the definitive answer. As a result, economists need theoretical models to guide them in interpreting data and drawing out policy implications from their work.

2.   I'll start with a humorous quote: "Economists tend to think people are crazy because they won't sell their homes for less than they paid for them—and people think economists are crazy for thinking things exactly like that" – Professor Christopher Mayer.

The loss-averse behavior of people who don't want to sell their homes for less than they bought them for is an example of predictably irrational behavior. This behavior is irrational because the market is the means for determining how much something is worth. In this situation, it is irrational to take into account the price you paid for your house. That's a sunk cost. This irrationality calls into question the traditional assumption that people are completely rational.

Behavioral economics, which says that people are not perfectly rational but instead are predictably irrational, provides an alternative explanation for this phenomenon. According to behavioral economics, people take things beside economic factors, such as social factors, into account when making a decision. People tend to avoid losses even when it doesn't make sense not to. Thus, they will refuse to lower the asking price on their house.

3. The traditional assumptions and building-blocks of economics, while narrow, can still be used to explain what seems to be irrational behavior. For example, people often make choices based on rules of thumb rather than using the economic decision rule and calculating the marginal costs and benefits.

A behavioral economist would describe this as predictably irrational behavior. People "do what they see others doing" without rationally weighing the costs and benefits of each decision. This fits nicely with the behavioral assumption of purposeful behavior. In this case, purposeful behavior reduces the costs of making decisions.

However, this behavior can also be construed as rational. Part of rationally weighing the costs and benefits of each decision involves the cost of calculating the opportunity cost. There is an opportunity cost, not only for the decision, but for the decision to weigh the costs and benefits. The opportunity cost of weighing the costs and benefits is the time it takes to calculate and compare the marginal cost with the marginal benefit. Because time is a scarce commodity, it is highly valued. If people were to rationally compare the marginal cost with the marginal benefit of every single decision in their lives then they would use up significant amounts of valuable time. It is also unnecessary. Therefore, it can be considered rational to forgo weighing the costs and benefits and instead make choices based on rules of thumb. That means, in some cases, it is rational to be irrational.

BEHAVIORAL ECONOMICS AND MODERN ECONOMIC POLICY

CHAPTER AT A GLANCE

1. Behavioral economics is the branch of modern economics that broadens the assumption about behavior from rationality and self-interest to purposeful behavior and enlightened self-interest. (488-491)

   Mechanism design is a coordination mechanisms based on the work of behavioral economist's explanations which account for people's predictable irrationalities.

   Shadow prices are an example of a coordination mechanism.

2a. Choice architecture is the context in which decisions are presented. (492-493)

   How choices are presented affects the choices people make.

2b. A nudge is the deliberate design of the choice architecture to alter people's behavior in predictably positive ways. (493)

   Nudges take into account people's predictable irrationalities.

3. A nudge policy is when government structures choices so that people are free to choose what they want, but are also more likely to choose what government believes is best for them. (493-494)

   Supporters argue that nudge policies meet the criterion of libertarian paternalism: they do not restrict an individual's free choice

   (libertarian), but they make people more likely to make a choice that is better for themselves in the long run (paternalistic).

4. Supporters of nudge policies argue that nudges can be useful when (1) benefits and costs are separated by time, (2) choices are complicated and have many dimensions, and (3) choices are infrequent. (494-495)

   - *Choices where Benefits and Costs Are Separated by Time People tend to make less-than-optimal choices when the benefits and costs of their choices are separated by time. Most people weight the immediate costs and benefits more, and future costs and benefits less. Examples include weight loss, saving money, and studying.*

   - *Complicated Choices with Many Dimensions People are not good at making complicated choices that involve many different variables. Choosing what type of loan to take out to pay for college is an example of such a complicated choice.*

   - *Infrequent Choices Infrequent decisions provide little opportunity to practice making choices, evaluate feedback, or explore one's preferences, so it is particularly difficult to make the best choice. Examples of such infrequent decisions include what college to attend and what type of mortgage to take out.*

5. Two types of nudge policies are (1) advantageous default option and (2) information and encouragement nudges. (495-496)

- *Advantageous default option nudges* People tend to select the default option. By taking advantage of that tendency economic policy makers can direct people to do what they think is better for them, while still leaving people free to choose. An example is making employees opt out of a health insurance plan.
- *Information and encouragement nudges* Government encourages people to make certain choices that the government has decided is good for them. An example is for the government to inform people about how their energy use compares to the average.

6. A push policy is a regulatory or tax policy to get firms or individuals to use "appropriate" nudges. (497-498).

   If government can institute the behavioral economic policy directly, or if a private firm chooses to implement a policy on its own, it's a nudge. Push policies restrict free choice by the firm for the greater good and therefore can no longer claim to satisfy the libertarian paternalism criterion.

7. Traditional economists highlight four concerns about nudge and push policies (499-501):

(1) Very few policies meet the criterion of libertarian paternalism.

   In reality, most government interventions are push policies that rely on regulation to tell firms what they can and can't do.

(2) Designing helpful policies is complicated.

   Nudge policies often require more information than government has.

(3) It isn't clear that government knows better.

   Even if economists could agree that people do not always act in their own self-interest, it isn't clear that government can determine what is in people's best interest either.

(4) Government policy may make the situation worse.

   Nudge policies substantially increase the potential for government failure.

● SHORT-ANSWER QUESTIONS

1. What process do modern economists follow to align people's incentives with desired ends?

2. In an effort to limit the amount of trash companies produce, Congress passes a regulation allowing each company to produce a maximum of 1,000 tons of trash per year. Is this likely an example of a mechanism designed by an economist? Why or why not? Can you suggest a potentially more efficient policy?

3. What is a nudge policy? Give an example.

4. Why would a behavioral economist argue that nudges are sometimes necessary?

5. Going through her contract, an employee sees that 5% of her yearly salary is withheld to pay for health insurance. She can check a box to not have the 5% withheld and go without health insurance, but she decides to leave the box unchecked. Might this be an example of nudge policy in action? Why or why not?

6. In the example above, why can the decision to encourage employees to opt into a health plan be described as libertarian? In what way is it paternalistic?

7. What are three types of choices where nudges can be useful? Give an example of each.

8. What are two types of nudge policies? Give an example of each.

9. What is it called when the government uses a regulatory or tax policy to get firms to use "appropriate" nudges?

10. Seeing the "smoking kills" warning on a box of cigarettes, a shopper decides to buy a pack of gum instead. Is this an example of nudge policy in action? Why or why not?

11. Why do traditional economists reject the argument that nudge policies should be implemented whenever possible? Provide four concerns they might offer.

—————————————   **MATCHING THE TERMS**   —————————————

Match the terms to their definitions

___ 1.	behavioral economic policy	a.	Any economic policy based upon models using behavioral economic building blocks that take into account people's predictable irrational behavior.
___ 2.	choice architecture		
___ 3.	coordination mechanism	b.	Economics devoted not only to studying markets, but also to designing markets and other coordinating mechanisms.
___ 4.	economic engineering		
___ 5.	incentive compatibility problem	c.	Methods of coordinating people's wants with other people's desires.
___ 6.	libertarian paternalistic policy	d.	Prices that aren't paid directly, but instead are paid in terms of opportunity costs borne by the demander, and thus determine his or her action indirectly.
___ 7.	mechanism design	e.	A problem in which the incentive facing the decision maker does not match the incentive needed for the mechanism to achieve its desired end.
___ 8.	nudge		
___ 9.	nudge policy		
___ 10.	push policy		
___ 11.	shadow price	f.	Identifying a goal and then designing a mechanism such as a market, social system or contract to achieve that end.
		g.	The context in which decisions are presented.
		h.	A deliberate design of the choice architecture that alters people's behavior in predictably positive ways.
		i.	A policy that leaves people free to choose what they want, but encourages them to make a choice that the government believes is in their interest.
		j.	A policy that leaves people free to choose, but nonetheless guides them toward a choice that a well-intentioned observer would see as good for them.
		k.	A regulatory or tax policy to get firms or individuals to use "appropriate" nudges.

● PROBLEMS AND APPLICATIONS

1. Indicate whether each of the following policies is libertarian, paternalistic, both, or neither.

    a. In order to encourage its students to eat a healthier lunch, a public high school eliminates french fries, pizza, and hamburgers from its menu and offers salads and sandwiches instead.

    b. A large grocery store positions its most profitable products in the front of the store and at eye level along the rows.

    c. If you choose to save 10% of your salary and access it only after you retire, your employer will supplement your savings by putting an additional 10% into your saving account. In order to opt out of this savings plan, you must check a box in your contract saying that you do not want to have any money withheld.

2. For each of the following cases, say whether or not a nudge might be helpful. Explain why or why not.

    a. Many overweight Americans want to lose weight, but they continue to eat unhealthfully and watch TV instead of exercising.

    b. A student who needs a loan for college looks on a website and sees that there are 8 different options. She has no idea which is the best for her, so she just chooses randomly.

    c. A group of friends is trying to decide whether to go see a movie or go play a round of miniature golf.

    d. A couple is trying to choose what type of mortgage to take out on their new house.

3. Classify the following nudges as either a "potentially advantageous default nudge," an "information and encouragement nudge," "a nudge, but not one of the two specific types," or "not a nudge" and give a brief explanation.

    a. A chocolate-chip cookie cereal advertises its product on TV during programming mostly watched by children.

    b. When purchasing an expensive new laptop, the contract is written so that you must explicitly choose to opt out of highly subsidized insurance for your computer.

    c. A college administration promotes a study in the campus newspaper showing that the average student has only one alcoholic drink per week.

    d. The government passes a new regulation requiring firms to put a label on their products if any animals were used to test the product.

4. Classify the following cases as a nudge, a push, or neither.

    a. The government passes a new regulation requiring cell phone companies to present your bill in a specific, simplified format so that you can see the source of all your costs.

    b. A variety of potato chips has the words "New, baked, not fried! Half as many calories" in big letters on its packaging.

    c. Seeing six different brands of ketchup on the supermarket shelf that all look identical, a customer just chooses one randomly.

    d. The government taxes pesticides in order to encourage organic food production.

5. For each of the following statements, indicate whether it was likely made by a behavioral economist or a traditional economist.

    a. "Having more stuff doesn't necessarily make people happier. Relative, not absolute, income is what matters."

    b. "Designing successful nudge policies is too complicated to make it worthwhile."

    c. "People are rational and know their own wants and desires better than the government."

    d. "People are predictably irrational and we need to take such irrationalities into consideration when designing policy."

    e. "Price incentives are the only thing that matters to consumers."

● MULTIPLE CHOICE

Circle the one best answer for each of the following questions:

1. Economic engineering:
    a. takes shadow prices into account in its designs.
    b. grew out of traditional economic models.
    c. tries to design mechanisms to better coordinate people's actions.
    d. all of the above.

2. Shadow prices are:
    a. extra fees that businesses such as cell phone companies hide from their customers.
    b. the cost to taxpayers of push policies put in place by the government.
    c. opportunity costs faced by the demander that indirectly influence his or her decisions.
    d. the price increase that firms use to cover the cost of advertising.

3. The cap-and-trade system designed by economists to limit the overall production of CO_2 emissions is an example of:
    a. mechanism design.
    b. an incentive compatibility problem.
    c. a shadow price.
    d. an "information and encouragement" nudge.

4. Who would agree with the statement, "Even assuming no externalities, voluntary trade might not necessarily make people better off."
    a. Traditional economists.
    b. Behavioral economists.
    c. Both.
    d. Neither.

5. Nudges:
    a. always make consumers better off.
    b. are often suggested by traditional economists as a way to guide individuals to make better choices than they would on their own.
    c. aren't controversial because they meet the libertarian paternalistic criterion.
    d. are sometimes used by firms to guide their customers to make choices that benefit the firm.

6. Structuring a health care program with a default option of automatic enrollment, is an example of:
    a. using choice architecture to influence people's choices.
    b. a policy that is neither libertarian nor paternalistic.
    c. a policy that will lead most people to not choose a health care plan.
    d. a policy that would likely be supported by traditional economists more than behavioral economists.

7. In which of the following cases would consumers be least likely to benefit from a nudge?
    a. Choices in which benefits and costs are separated by time.
    b. Complicated choices with many dimensions.
    c. Choices where the marginal costs and benefits are clear.
    d. Infrequent choices.

8. An advocacy group mailing out flyers with big pictures of melting ice and flooded areas, as well as a list of ways families can cut down on energy usage in order to help slow global warming is an example of:
    a. an advantageous default option nudge.
    b. an infrequent choice nudge.
    c. an information and encouragement nudge.
    d. a push policy.

9. When the government uses a regulatory or tax policy to get firms or individuals to use "appropriate" nudges, it is called a:
    a. nudge policy.
    b. traditional economic policy.
    c. push policy.
    d. default option policy.

10. According to some behavioral economists:
    a. conspicuous consumption goods lead to long-term increases in measured satisfaction.
    b. certain types of material goods don't matter much to our well being and often crowd out those goods that do matter.
    c. if people work more so they can buy more, society will be better off.
    d. the government should never try to change the way in which income is distributed.

11. Which of the following is *not* a misgiving expressed by traditional economists about behavioral economic policies?
    a. The only nudges that help society are those by private firms.
    b. Very few policies meet the criterion of libertarian paternalism.
    c. It isn't clear that government knows better than individuals in most cases.
    d. Government policies may make the situation worse, rather than better.

● POTENTIAL ESSAY QUESTIONS

You may also see essay questions similar to the "Problems & Applications" exercises.

1. Late pick-ups can be a big problem for daycare centers. To solve the problem some centers followed the traditional economic solution: They imposed a fine for parents who picked up the kids late. Use the concept of shadow prices to discuss why this policy made the problem of late pick-ups even worse.

2. Traditional economists assume that individuals are rational and pursue their self-interest at all times. How do the concepts of choice architecture and economic engineering challenge these assumptions? Does this mean that the traditional economic models need to be rethought?

3. In your opinion, should the government pursue nudge policies? What are the benefits and risks of such policy?

━━━━ ANSWERS ━━━━

SHORT-ANSWER QUESTIONS

1. Modern economists use their insights about incentive compatibility problems to design mechanisms that align incentives with desired ends. The process of mechanism design involves identifying a goal and then designing a mechanism such as a market, social system or contract, to achieve that goal. (488-490)

2. No, an economist would be highly unlikely to impose such rigid regulations that do not take incentives into account. A potentially more efficient policy (that uses economic reasoning) would be to give companies permits allowing them to produce 1,000 tons of trash and then allow companies to buy and sell permits. This solution (similar to the cap-and-trade program for CO_2 emissions) is an example of mechanism design because it creates a market to achieve the goal of trash reduction. (488-490)

3. In nudge policy, government structures choices facing people so that they are free to choose what they want, but also more likely to choose what is "best" for them. For example, employees having to check a box to opt out of a health insurance plan, rather than check a box to opt into the plan. (493-494)

4. According to behavioral economists, people are predictably irrational and sometimes make choices that are not in their own best interests in the long run. By influencing people's choices via specifically designed choice architecture, nudges can help people behave in predictably positive ways. In other words, nudges help people make choices that are better for themselves in the long run. (492-493)

5. Yes, this is an example of an advantageous default option nudge. Studies show that if the employee was faced with the choice of checking a box in order to opt into the health insurance plan, she would be more likely to end up choosing to not have the health insurance. (493-496)

6. Making employees opt out of health insurance (or savings) plans is libertarian because no one is making them take part in the plan. They are still free to opt out, but it requires them to take a specific action to do so. Such policies are paternalistic because they are designed to further what government sees as the employee's best long-run interest. (493-494)

7. Three types of choices where nudges can be useful are choices in which benefits and costs are separated by time, complicated choices with many dimensions, and infrequent choices. Whether to exercise or watch TV is a choice where benefits and costs are separated by time because the benefits of exercising are long-term. What type of student loan to take out is an example of a complicated choice with many dimensions. Choosing a mortgage is an infrequent and complicated decision. People could potentially be helped to make better choices if they were nudged in each of these examples. (494-495)

8. Two types of nudge policies are advantageous default option nudges and information and encouragement nudges. Making an employee check a box to opt out of a savings plan is an example of an advantageous default option nudge. Sending people information about how much energy they use, the effects of high energy use, and how to reduce their energy consumption is an example of an information and encouragement nudge. (495-496)

9. This is an example of a push policy. A push policy is any regulatory tax policy put in place by the government to get firms or individuals to use "appropriate" nudges. (496-497)

10. It depends. Viewed from the perspective of the government and the consumer, it is a type of nudge policy. But when one takes the cigarette company into account, it is a push policy rather than a nudge policy. Cigarette companies do not put such warnings on their boxes by free choice or for the good of the customer; government requires that cigarette companies put the health warnings on their products. This is a case of the government using regulation to get firms to use what it considers an appropriate nudge. (496-497)

11. Traditional economists have expressed serious misgivings about behavioral economic policies. First, they say that very few nudge policies meet the criterion of libertarian paternalism. Second, designing helpful policies is complicated. Third, they argue that it isn't clear that government knows better than individuals, even if individuals are sometimes irrational. Finally, they believe that government policies often make the situation worse because the policies may be inefficient and may have unintended consequences. (499-501)

■ ANSWERS ■

MATCHING

1-a; 2-g; 3-c; 4-b; 5-e; 6-j; 7-f; 8-h; 9-i; 10-k; 11-d.

■ ANSWERS ■

PROBLEMS AND APPLICATIONS

1. a. Paternalistic, but not libertarian. The school is trying to help students make healthier choices (paternalistic), but is doing so by restricting their freedom to choose what to eat (not libertarian). (493-494)

   b. Libertarian, but not paternalistic. Customers still have the freedom to purchase whatever they want (libertarian), but the grocery store has its own interests at heart, not the interests of its customers (not paternalistic). (493-494)

   c. Both libertarian and paternalistic. Employees have the freedom to save or to not save (libertarian), but the company uses a nudge to increase the likelihood that they will choose to save (paternalistic). (493-494)

2. a. Yes, a nudge could be useful in this scenario because the benefits and costs are separated by time. In other words, the benefits of exercising aren't enjoyed until well into the future. (494-495)

   b. Yes, a nudge could help in this scenario because the student faces a complicated choice with many dimensions. (494-495)

   c. No, this is not a scenario that could be resolved with a nudge. (494-495)

   d. Yes, a nudge could help in this scenario because the couple is faced with an infrequent and complicated decision. (495-496)

3. a. "A nudge but not one of the two specific types." Firms use advertising to nudge consumers, but this is not one of the types of nudge policies to help the consumer make a better long-run choice. (494-495)

   b. "A potentially advantageous default nudge." Consumers would be less likely to purchase this highly subsidized insurance if they had to opt into the insurance plan. If the subsidy is high enough, then the insurance could be potentially advantageous from the consumer's viewpoint, although from society's viewpoint it is unclear, since the money to provide the subsidy has to come from somewhere. (495-496)

   c. "An information encouragement nudge." By publishing the study, the college administration is seeking to nudge students to drink less by decreasing the pressure many students feel to drink in order to fit in. (495-496)

   d. "Not a nudge." This is a push policy because the government is using regulation to make firms put a label on their product. (495-496)

4. a. A push. Anytime the government enacts a regulatory policy to get firms or individuals to use "appropriate" nudges it is considered a push policy. (493, 496-497)

   b. A nudge. Advertising by firms is a type of nudge, even if the firm doesn't necessarily have the customer's best interests in mind. (493, 496-497)

   c. There is neither a nudge nor a push in this example. (493, 496-497)

   d. A push. Anytime the government enacts a tax policy to get firms or individuals to use "appropriate" nudges it is considered a push policy. (493, 496-497)

5. a. Behavioral economist. Traditional economists say that having more makes you happier. Behavioral economists, on the other hand, argue that people care about relative as well as absolute consumption and income. This proposition has potentially radical implications because it introduces the possibility that government can improve society's overall welfare by changing the way in which income is distributed. (498-499)

b. Traditional economist. This is one of the main criticisms traditional economists cite against the idea that government should use more nudge policies. (498-499)

c. Traditional economist. This is another criticism that traditional economists use against the implementation of push policies. (498-499)

d. Behavioral economist. Although many traditional economists recognize that individuals sometimes make irrational choices, they do not agree that such irrationality is predictable or should be used as the basis for government policies. (498-499)

e. Traditional economist. Traditional economists are likely to focus on prices as the main incentive that consumers consider and therefore base their theories on this assumption. (498-499)

ANSWERS

MULTIPLE CHOICE

1. **d** Economic engineering tries to design mechanisms to better coordinate people's actions. It can sometimes be based on shadow prices and is based on the work of behavioral economics. See pages 487-488.

2. **c** Shadow prices are not a money price on a good or service, but rather the often obscured opportunity costs that influence the demander indirectly. See page 488.

3. **a** The cap-and-trade system is an example of a market designed by economists in order to help achieve a goal as efficiently as possible. In this case the goal was to reduce CO_2 emissions. See pages 488-490.

4. **b** Behavioral economists would agree with this statement because they believe that

individuals can be irrational. An irrational individual does not necessarily make trades that will benefit themselves even if there are no externalities. See pages 487 and 492.

5. **d** Nudges are not only used by the government to help people make good choices. In fact, nudges have existed almost as long as firms have been in business. The difference is that firms use nudges for their own benefit, rather than for the benefit of their customers. See pages 492-494.

6. **a** This type of advantageous default option nudge works because individuals respond differently to different choice architectures. In this case, employees are more likely to participate in the health care plan. It is libertarian because people are free to choose. See pages 492-494.

7. **c** If the marginal costs and benefits are clear, there is less reason that individuals need a nudge. Individuals facing the other three choices could be helped by a nudge. See pages 494-495.

8. **c** Whenever the government or an advocacy group provides individuals with information about the effects of their choices and ways to alter those choices, it is called "an information and encouragement" nudge. See pages 495-496.

9. **c** Firms are often opposed to implementing nudges that will help customers because those nudges will lower the profit of the firm. When the government makes firms implement such nudges, it is called a push policy. See pages 496-497.

10. **b** Some behavioral economists believe that relative consumption and income must be taken into account along with absolute consumption and income. Some consumption is conspicuous consumption and does not increase society's welfare in the long run. The resources that go towards conspicuous consumption could be better used to help the poor or those who need health care. See pages 498-499.

11. a   Traditional economists focus their criticisms on the fact that it is difficult to implement true nudge policies and that the government often makes the situation worse because it does not know what is best for individuals. They do *not*, however, argue that nudges used by private firms are necessarily good for society. See pages 499-500.

ANSWERS

POTENTIAL ESSAY QUESTIONS

The following are annotated answers. They indicate the general idea behind the answer.

1.   Using traditional economic thinking, by increasing the cost of picking up the kids late the new policy should have led to a decrease in the number of late pick-ups. In reality, the number of late pick-ups increased because the new cost of picking kids up late, in the form of a fine, was smaller than the previous moral shadow cost of being late. In other words, when there was no fine, parents felt guilty about being late. This guilt was the shadow price that kept most parents from being late. Once a fine was imposed, the moral shadow price was eliminated. This example shows that people are social creatures and that more than simple price incentives must be considered when designing policies to accomplish a specific goal.

2.   Traditional economists base their theories on the assumptions that individuals are rational and always pursue their self-interest. Behavioral economists argue that choice architecture—the context in which decisions are presented—affects the choices that people make. This means that economists, by engineering the choice architecture people face, can encourage them to make a certain choice. For example, when a school lunch service places the healthier foods in easily visible, easy-to-reach locations, while putting the unhealthy foods mostly out of sight, students are more likely to choose a healthier lunch.

This shows that choice architecture can be a useful tool for encouraging students to eat more healthfully. If this is one of the goals of society, then designing choice architecture can be a useful tool for achieving its goals.

3.   This is an open-ended opinion question, but a good answer must consider the advantages and disadvantages of nudge policies. Behavioral economists believe that society can be made better off through the use of nudge policies. Without curtailing people's freedom, people can be encouraged to make better choices in the long run through simple changes in choice architecture and economic engineering (the libertarian paternalism criterion). When individuals face choices in which benefits and costs are separated by time, complicated choices with many dimensions, or infrequent choices, nudges can help them make better decisions than they otherwise might. Traditional economists, however, focus more on price and add that there are many risks to nudge policies. First of all, very few policies meet the libertarian paternalism criterion. Second, designing helpful nudge policies is complicated. Third, it isn't clear that government knows better than individuals what is good for those individuals. Finally, government policies often make the situation worse due to inefficiencies and unintended consequences.

MICROECONOMIC POLICY, ECONOMIC REASONING, AND BEYOND

23

CHAPTER AT A GLANCE

1. Economists' views on social policy differ widely because: (506-508)

    1. they have different underlying values,
    2. they interpret empirical evidence differently, and
    3. they use different underlying models.

    Analysis should be as objective as possible. Unfortunately, in practice, social goals are seldom neat—they're generally vaguely understood and vaguely expressed.

2. Liberal and conservative economists agree on many policy prescriptions because they use the same models. These models focus on incentives and individual choice. (508)

    There is more agreement among economists than most lay people realize because they all use cost/benefit analysis. Disagreement among economists usually arises because they assess the qualitative benefits and costs (those benefits and costs that cannot be easily measured) differently.

3. Cost/benefit analysis is analysis in which one assigns a cost and benefit to alternatives, and draws a conclusion on the basis of those costs and benefits. (508-513)

    Economists argue that government should keep regulating until the marginal benefits of regulation just equal the marginal costs. Unfortunately, many costs and benefits (especially social and political) cannot be easily quantified.

4. Three separate types of failure of market outcomes include: (513-518)

    1. failures due to distributional issues,
    2. failures due to rationality problems of individuals, and
    3. failures due to violations of inalienable, or at least partially inalienable, rights of individuals.

    Failure of market outcomes occurs when the market is not achieving society's goals even though it is functioning properly.

5. Government failure as well as market failure exists. For the government to correct a problem it must: (518-519)

    1. recognize the problem,
    2. have the will to deal with it, and
    3. have the ability to deal with it.

    Government can often not do all three of these well. Often the result is that government action is directed at the wrong problem at the wrong time. And sometimes the government fails to improve a situation (hence the term "government failure.")

    Economics provides the tools, not the rules, for policy. Economics involves the thoughtful use of economic insights and empirical evidence. An economist must carefully consider all views. Subjective moral value judgments can't be ignored.

● SHORT-ANSWER QUESTIONS

1. List three reasons why the statement "If you laid all economists end to end, they still wouldn't reach a conclusion" is partly true with regard to social policy.

2. Although the quotation in Question #1 has some validity, nevertheless liberal and conservative economists often agree in their views on social policy. What is the basis for their agreement?

3. What is cost/benefit analysis?

4. When it comes to the actions of politicians regulating our economy, most economists are cynics. Why?

5. What are three types of failure of market outcomes?

6. Why are many economists doubtful that the government can correct failure of market outcomes?

7. Your friend finds you tucked away in a cozy chair in the library studying for an economics exam on policy issues. Your friend says, "Why are you wasting your time? All you have to remember is *supply and demand* and you'll be able to answer any question in economics." How do you respond?

MATCHING THE TERMS
Match the terms to their definitions

___ 1. cost/benefit approach
___ 2. economic efficiency
___ 3. failure of market outcome
___ 4. Marxian (radical) model
___ 5. Pareto optimal policies
___ 6. public choice model
___ 7. rational
___ 8. sin tax

a. Approach in which one assigns a cost and benefit to alternatives, and draws a conclusion on the basis of those costs and benefits.

b. Policies that benefit some people and hurt no one.

c. A model that focuses on equitable distribution of power, rights, and income among social classes.

d. Tax that discourages activities society believes are harmful.

e. A model that focuses on the self-interest of politicians.

f. What individuals do is in their own best interest.

g. Achieving a goal at the lowest possible cost.

h. Even though the market is functioning properly, it is not achieving society's goals.

PROBLEMS AND APPLICATIONS

1. For the following situations, which of the following regulations would you recommend government implement?

    a. A regulation requiring airline mechanics to check whether all bolts are tightened. This decreases the probability of having an accident by .001. The cost of the average crash is estimated at $200 million for the plane and $400 million in lives. The cost of implementing the program is $16 million.

    b. A regulation requiring that all cars have driver-side airbags. This adds $500 to the cost of a car. Having an airbag in a car reduces the chance of dying in a car crash by 1/720. The average individual values his/her life at $500,000.

    c. A regulation stiffening government rules for workplace safety. The cost per worker is $5,000 and the regulations are expected to reduce workplace fatalities by .002. Workers value their lives at an average of $2 million.

    d. What are the problems with using the cost/benefit approach to decide parts *a*, *b*, and *c*?

2. Why does it often appear to the lay public that economists never agree on social policy?

3. Assume economists have undertaken cost/benefit analysis of a problem and are unanimously in favor of a particular policy proposal over all other proposals. Why might this policy recommendation not be enacted as policy?

MULTIPLE CHOICE

Circle the one best answer for each of the following questions:

1. One reason economists differ is that:
   a. they have different underlying value judgments.
   b. some base their view on models and not data.
   c. not all economists use cost/benefit analysis.
   d. models are not important to all economists.

2. Pareto optimal policies:
   a. are policies that benefit some people and hurt no one.
   b. cause failure of market outcomes.
   c. are practically and easily translated into viable economic policies.
   d. are based on observed data.

3. Which statement follows from economic theory alone?
   a. The minimum wage should be increased.
   b. The minimum wage should be decreased.
   c. There should be no minimum wage.
   d. No policy prescription follows from economic theory alone.

4. It is important to be familiar with many economic models because:
   a. the models are objective.
   b. the models are subjective.
   c. each model captures different aspects of reality.
   d. the models are Pareto optimal.

5. When an economist states that whether baby seals should be killed depends upon the costs and benefits, according to the text they are being:
   a. coldhearted.
   b. subjective.
   c. objective.
   d. conjective.

6. In an automobile crash, people were killed because an automobile company saved $10 by placing the gas tank in the rear of the car. An economist would:
   a. determine whether this made sense with cost/benefit analysis.
   b. see this as reasonable.
   c. see this as unreasonable.
   d. argue that no amount of money should be spared to save a life.

7. Suppose that filtering your water at home reduces your chances from dying of giardia (an intestinal parasite) by 1/45,000. The filter costs you $400 to install. You have chosen to install the filter. Which dollar value best reflects the minimum value you implicitly place on your life?
   a. $400.
   b. $45,000.
   c. $1,800,000.
   d. $18,000,000.

8. The government is considering requiring auto manufacturers to reinforce the roofs of SUV vehicles to reduce their collapse in roll-over accidents. The reinforcement adds $600 to the cost of an SUV. The probability of a fatality from a collapsed roof is 1/1,000. The average individual values his/her life at $1,000,000. Economists would be:
   a. in favor of the regulation because the marginal benefit of $1,000 exceeds the marginal cost.
   b. in favor of the regulation because the marginal cost of $600 exceeds the marginal benefit.
   c. against the regulation because the marginal cost of $1,000 exceeds the marginal benefit.
   d. against the regulation because the marginal benefits of $600 exceeds the marginal cost.

9. If the equilibrium wage is below the wage necessary for survival:
    a. there is no problem because the market is in equilibrium.
    b. there is a market failure due to informational problems.
    c. there is a market failure due to an externality.
    d. there is a failure of market outcome.

10. Maximizing total producer and consumer surplus in a market means that:
    a. the economy is as well off as it can be.
    b. total market output is as large as it can be in that market.
    c. income is unfairly distributed.
    d. income is fairly distributed.

11. Efficiency is:
    a. distributing income as fairly as possible.
    b. achieving a goal as cheaply as possible.
    c. taking the least time to achieve goals.
    d. generating as much income as possible.

12. As economists generally use the term, in a society it is *inefficient* to supply medicine to those who do not have the income to pay for it. This statement is:
    a. correct because economists use the term efficiency as a shorthand referring only to total output.
    b. wrong because medicine is necessary for life.
    c. correct because economists do not care about the poor.
    d. wrong because economics does not take distribution into account.

13. If a person buys more of a good, that person is:
    a. better off.
    b. worse off.
    c. most likely better off.
    d. most likely worse off.

14. If society establishes a law preventing people from selling themselves into slavery:
    a. consumer surplus will be lowered.
    b. consumer surplus will be increased.
    c. economic theory will find that law incorrect.
    d. economic theory will find that law correct.

15. Markets:
    a. distribute income fairly.
    b. ensure individuals behave rationally.
    c. take into account inalienable rights.
    d. require property rights to function.

16. An economist might *not favor* undertaking a policy to correct a failure of market outcome because economists:
    a. don't recognize failures in market outcomes.
    b. see the possibility of government failure.
    c. are trained to support the market no matter what.
    d. see the possibility of market failure offsetting the failure in market outcome.

● POTENTIAL ESSAY QUESTIONS

You may also see essay questions similar to the "Problems & Applications" exercises.

1. What is cost/benefit analysis? How is this related to why economists often find themselves united with one another but at odds with the general public?

2. How can the presence of the economic (market), social, and political forces in all real-world economies, and economists' use of benefit/cost analysis help explain the disagreement among economists concerning what is considered "appropriate" social policy? Even if economists all agreed upon what is "appropriate" policy, why might that policy never be enacted?

━━━━ ANSWERS ━━━━

SHORT-ANSWER QUESTIONS

1. The statement is true to the extent that economists sometimes differ in their views on social policy. Three reasons for their differing views are that (1) they have different underlying values, (2) they interpret empirical evidence differently, and (3) they use different underlying models. (506-508)

2. Liberal and conservative economists often agree in their views on social policy because they use the same models, which focus on incentives and individual choice. (508)

3. Cost/benefit analysis is an analysis in which one assigns a cost and benefit to alternatives and draws a conclusion on the basis of those costs and benefits. The optimal amount of any activity is the level at which marginal benefit equals marginal cost. (508-509)

4. The typical economist views many government regulations as the result of political expediency, and not a reflection of cost/benefit considerations. Most economists believe that decisions should be made on a cost/benefit basis instead of on the basis of political pressure placed on politicians by special interest groups. (508-513)

5. Three separate types of failures of market outcomes include (1) failures due to distributional issues, (2) failures due to rationality problems of individuals, and (3) failures due to violations of inalienable, or at least partially inalienable, rights of individuals. (513-518)

6. For the government to correct a problem it must (1) recognize the problem, (2) have the will to deal with it, and (3) have the ability to deal with it. Government can seldom do all three of these well. (518-519)

7. You tell your friend to remember the admonition in your textbook: "Teaching a parrot the phrase *supply and demand* does not make it an economist." Elaborating, you tell her that economics involves the thoughtful use of economic insights and empirical evidence. Real-world problems are complex and cannot be explained just with simple models. You are right in taking the time to learn the details. (520)

━━━━ ANSWERS ━━━━

MATCHING

1-a; 2-g; 3-h; 4-c; 5-b; 6-e; 7-f; 8-d.

━━━━ ANSWERS ━━━━

PROBLEMS AND APPLICATIONS

1. For each of these, you calculate the costs and benefits of the regulation. If the cost is higher than the benefit, you would recommend not implementing the program. If the cost is lower than the benefit, you would recommend implementing the program. For each you are assuming you are given all relevant information.

    a. The benefit is saving a plane worth $200 million and saving lives worth $400 million. The regulation reduces the probability of a crash by .001. The marginal benefit is .001 times $600 million = $600,000. The marginal cost is $16 million. Don't implement the program because marginal cost is more than marginal benefit. (508-511)

    b. The benefit is the value of a saved life of $500,000, times the increased probability of living, 1/720 = $694. This is greater than the marginal cost to consumers of $500. Implement the program. (508-511)

    c. The benefit is the value of a saved life of $2 million times the increased probability of not having a fatal accident, $2 million×.002 = $4,000. The marginal cost is $5,000 per worker, which is greater than the marginal benefit. Don't implement the program. (508-511)

    d. The above examples include only quantifiable costs and benefits and involve a huge amount of ambiguity and subjectivity in the calculations. Economists' subjective estimates of the benefit of lives and costs of the program can vary enormously, thus affecting the recommendation enormously. (511-513)

2. Economists often disagree on social policy because of their different underlying subjective value judgments, because of imprecise empirical evidence and because they focus on different aspects of a policy or problem (because their underlying models differ). (506-507)

3. The policy makers (e.g. politicians) may have weighed the non-quantifiable (qualitative) social and political costs and benefits of the policy recommendation differently than the economists have. Equally reasonable people disagree over non-quantifiable costs and benefits. Therefore, what makes sense from a purely economic perspective may not be deemed politically, or socially, acceptable. (508)

ANSWERS

MULTIPLE CHOICE

1. a   Economists differ because they have different underlying value judgments, empirical evidence is subject to different interpretations, and their underlying models differ. There is more agreement among economists than lay people realize because they all use cost/benefit analysis. See pages 506-508.

2. a   Pareto optimal policies are policies that benefit some while hurting no one. No known policies are Pareto optimal. See page 506.

3. d   Economic theory must be combined with subjective value judgments and empirical evidence to arrive at policy recommendations. See page 506.

4. c   Models are neither objective, subjective, nor Pareto optimal. They simply are a framework for looking at reality. See pages 506-507.

5. c   Economists are trained to look at every decision in reference to costs and benefits as a way of maintaining their objectivity and keeping their subjective views out of policy. Conjective is not a word. While that may seem coldhearted, the text emphasizes that it seems so only in the short run. See pages 508-509.

6. a   Economists approach all issues with cost/benefit analysis. See pages 508-511.

7. d   You implicitly value your life at $(45,000 \times \$400) = \$18,000,000$. See pages 509-511.

8. a   The marginal benefit is $1,000 ($1,000,000 $\times 1/1,000$). It exceeds the marginal cost of $600. Economists would favor the regulation. See pages 509-511.

9. d   The market is working as it is supposed to but almost all would agree that the result is undesirable; there is a failure of market outcome. See pages 513-518.

10. b   Consumer and producer surplus focus on total output regardless of how it is distributed. See pages 513-515.

11. b   Efficiency refers to achieving a goal as cheaply as possible. Since fairness, income, and timeframe are a matter of opinion they are not in and of themselves efficient unless they are the agreed-upon goals. See page 506.

12. a   The statement is correct given the shorthand that economists use when referring to efficiency. What is efficient may not be desirable. See pages 512-513.

13. c   While economists generally assume that people will do what is in their best interest, it is still possible that they will not do so. See page 515.

14. a   Since the law involves a restriction of trade, consumer surplus will be lowered. It still is a good law, however. Economic theory does not find laws correct or incorrect. See pages 516-518.

15. d   Markets require that the people making the trade own the goods that they are trading.

This happens only when there are property rights. Markets operate within a set of laws. Unless the legal system protects the inalienable right, there is no guarantee the market will not violate it. See pages 516-518.

16. b   Economists see government failure as important and sometimes government intervention can make a problem worse, not better. See pages 518-519.

ANSWERS

POTENTIAL ESSAY QUESTIONS

The following are annotated answers. They indicate the general idea behind the answer.

1. Cost/benefit analysis is analysis in which one assigns costs and benefits to alternatives, and draws a conclusion on the basis of those costs and benefits. Note that it is marginal costs and marginal benefits that are relevant. Economists try to quantify those costs and benefits—to use empirical evidence to help reach a conclusion. The general public often does not.

2. Economists do take into consideration the economic, social, and political consequences associated with a policy. However, not all the costs and benefits associated with a particular policy are quantifiable with respect to each of these three forces. This leaves some room for subjective value judgments with respect to what the benefits and costs of a policy are. Moreover, empirical evidence is not exact. There is also some room for focusing on different aspects of a problem. Finally, if the policy is undertaken in a political environment, as is usually the case, then political considerations by policymakers may take precedence over the social and economic considerations.

Pretest
Chapters 19 - 23

Take this test in test conditions, giving yourself a limited amount of time to complete the questions. Ideally, check with your professor to see how much time he or she allows for an average multiple choice question and multiply this by 25. This is the time limit you should set for yourself for this pretest. If you do not know how much time your teacher would allow, we suggest 1 minute per question, or about 25 minutes.

1. The utility gained from eating one slice of pizza is 30 and the utility gained from eating a second slice of pizza is 20. From this we know:
   a. the marginal utility of the second slice of pizza is 50.
   b. the total utility of the second slice of pizza is 50.
   c. the marginal utility of the second slice of pizza is 20.
   d. there is not enough information to compute the marginal utility.

2. The price of good A is $1; the price of good B is $2. The marginal utility you get from good A is 40; the marginal utility you get from good B is 60. Assuming you can make marginal changes, you should:
   a. consume more of good A and less of good B.
   b. consume more of good B and less of good A.
   c. keep consuming equal amounts of both goods.
   d. realize that you don't have enough information to answer the question.

3. The rational consumer will buy more of good X when:
   a. $MU_X/P_X < MU_Y/P_Y$.
   b. $MU_X/P_X > MU_Y/P_Y$.
   c. $MU_X/P_X = MU_Y/P_Y$.
   d. the price of good X increases.

4. The income effect generally:
   a. contributes to the law of demand.
   b. is based on the substitution effect.
   c. is based on the change in relative prices on quantity demanded.
   d. determines whether a good is a complement.

5. The ultimatum game suggests people:
   a. ultimately care only about income.
   b. choose based on their own self-interest no matter what.
   c. care about fairness as well as income.
   d. behave rationally when it comes to income.

6. Game theory is a tool:
   a. used only by economists to study strategic interaction where individuals' decisions are independent.
   b. used by economists and other social scientists to study strategic interaction where individuals' decisions are independent.
   c. used only by economists to study strategic interaction where individuals' decisions are interdependent.
   d. used by economists and other social scientists to study strategic interaction where individuals' decisions are interdependent.

7. The Nash equilibrium solution for the following payoff matrix is:

	A	A
B	A: 1, B: 100	A: 0, B: 1
B	A: 2, B: 0	A: 5, B: 2

   a. 1, 100.
   b. 2, 0.
   c. 0, 1.
   d. There is more than one equilibrium solution.

8. If individuals can cooperate and share the gains, which payoff is the most likely?

	A	A
B	A: 1, B: 100	A: 0, B: 1
B	A: 2, B: 0	A: 5, B: 2

   a. 1, 100.
   b. 2, 0.
   c. 0, 1.
   d. 5, 2.

9. In the "trust game" a player is given money, which he can either keep, or give to someone else. If he gives the money to someone else, that money is tripled, and the second person can return some portion to the first player. The Nash equilibrium in this game is:
   a. for the first player to keep the entire sum.
   b. for the first player to keep half the money and give the other half to the second player.
   c. for the first player to give the entire sum to the other player.
   d. There is no Nash equilibrium for this game.

10. If most people don't conform to the assumptions of the standard model:
    a. the outcome of the model could not be true.
    b. the outcome of the model could still be true.
    c. society will have to better educate its people.
    d. the assumptions have to be revised.

11. Behavioral economists assume:
    a. complete rationality and enlightened self-interest.
    b. complete rationality and self-interest.
    c. purposeful behavior and self-interest.
    d. purposeful behavior and enlightened self-interest.

12. What type of economist is most likely to rely primarily on deductive reasoning?
    a. Behavioral economists.
    b. Modern economists.
    c. Traditional economists.
    d. Modern traditional economists.

13. Which types of economists rely on empirical work?
    a. Traditional economists.
    b. Behavioral economists.
    c. Modern traditional economists.
    d. All modern economists.

14. The supply/demand model is an example of:
    a. an empirical model.
    b. a regression model.
    c. a formal model.
    d. a heuristic model.

15. With regard to policy, traditional economists generally are more likely than behavioral economists to suggest that:
    a. the market is likely to be the best way to deal with a problem.
    b. there are limitations of the market.
    c. because there are multiple frameworks within which a problem can be thought about, there is fundamental ambiguity about the appropriate policy.
    d. there is a potential role for government interventions and public policy in the economy even when there are no externalities.

16. With regard to policy, behavioral economists are more likely than traditional economists to suggest that:
    a. free market policy guarantees both liberty and prosperity.
    b. there is an important role for government intervention and public policy even when there are no externalities.
    c. the market is likely to be the best way to deal with a problem.
    d. there is no ambiguity about what policy should be.

17. Who would agree with the statement, "Even assuming no externalities, voluntary trade might not necessarily make people better off."
    a. Traditional economists.
    b. Behavioral economists.
    c. Both.
    d. Neither.

18. Nudges:
    a. always make consumers better off.
    b. are often suggested by traditional economists as a way to guide individuals to make better choices than they would on their own.
    c. aren't controversial because they meet the libertarian paternalistic criterion.
    d. are sometimes used by firms to guide their customers to make choices that benefit the firm.

19. Structuring a health care program with a default option of automatic enrollment, is an example of:
   a. using choice architecture to influence people's choices.
   b. a policy that is neither libertarian nor paternalistic.
   c. a policy that will lead most people to not choose a health care plan.
   d. a policy that would likely be supported by traditional economists more than behavioral economists.

20. When the government uses a regulatory or tax policy to get firms or individuals to use "appropriate" nudges, it is called a:
   a. nudge policy.
   b. traditional economic policy.
   c. push policy.
   d. default option policy.

21. Which of the following is *not* a misgiving expressed by traditional economists about behavioral economic policies?
   a. The only nudges that help society are those by private firms.
   b. Very few policies meet the criterion of libertarian paternalism.
   c. It isn't clear that government knows better than individuals in most cases.
   d. Government policies may make the situation worse, rather than better.

22. Which statement follows from economic theory alone?
   a. The minimum wage should be increased.
   b. The minimum wage should be decreased.
   c. There should be no minimum wage.
   d. No policy prescription follows from economic theory alone.

23. In an automobile crash, people were killed because an automobile company saved $10 by placing the gas tank in the rear of the car. An economist would:
   a. determine whether this made sense with cost/benefit analysis.
   b. see this as reasonable.
   c. see this as unreasonable.
   d. argue that no amount of money should be spared to save a life.

25. Suppose that filtering your water at home reduces your chances from dying of giardia (an intestinal parasite) by 1/45,000. The filter costs you $400 to install. You have chosen to install the filter. Which dollar value best reflects the minimum value you implicitly place on your life?
   a. $400.
   b. $45,000.
   c. $1,800,000.
   d. $18,000,000.

25. If society establishes a law preventing people from selling themselves into slavery:
   a. consumer surplus will be lowered.
   b. consumer surplus will be increased.
   c. economic theory will find that law incorrect.
   d. economic theory will find that law correct.

═══ **ANSWERS** ═══

1.	c	(19:2)	**14.**	c	(21:16)
2.	a	(19:7)	**15.**	a	(21:18)
3.	b	(19:12)	**16.**	b	(21:19)
4.	a	(19:14)	**17.**	b	(22:4)
5.	c	(19:20)	**18.**	d	(22:5)
6.	d	(20:2)	**19.**	a	(22:6)
7.	d	(20:5)	**20.**	c	(22:9)
8.	a	(20:6)	**21.**	a	(22:11)
9.	a	(20:18)	**22.**	d	(23:3)
10.	b	(20:20)	**23.**	a	(23:6)
11.	d	(21:4)	**24.**	d	(23:7)
12.	c	(21:8)	**25.**	a	(23:14)
13.	d	(21:13)			

Key: The figures in parentheses refer to multiple choice question and chapter numbers. For example (1:2) is multiple choice question 2 from chapter 1.